Education and the
Structure of Knowledge

SYMPOSIUM PARTICIPANTS

CHAIRMAN. *B. Othanel Smith, Professor of Philosophy of Education, University of Illinois.*

PRESENTATION OF PAPERS. *Joseph J. Schwab, Professor of Education, Graduate School of Education, University of Chicago; Philip H. Phenix, Professor of Philosophy and Education, Teachers College, Columbia University; Harry S. Broudy, Professor of Philosophy of Education, University of Illinois; J. T. Tykociner, Research Professor of Engineering, Emeritus, University of Illinois; Norwood Russell Hanson, Professor of Philosophy, Yale University; Wm. Oliver Martin, Chairman, Department of Philosophy, University of Rhode Island; David P. Ausubel, Professor of Educational Psychology, University of Illinois.*

DISCUSSANTS (IN ADDITION TO SPEAKERS AND CHAIRMAN). *Donald Arnstine, Assistant Professor of Educational Philosophy, University of Wisconsin; Carl E. Bereiter, Assistant Professor of Educational Psychology, University of Illinois; Egon G. Guba, Director, Bureau of Educational Research and Service, The Ohio State University; Francis A. J. Ianni, Director, Cooperative Research Branch, Office of Education, United States Department of Health, Education and Welfare; Mark M. Krug, Associate Professor of Education in History, University of Chicago. Philip G. Smith, Professor of Education, Indiana University; N. L. Gage, Professor of Educational Psychology, Stanford University.*

SPECIAL OBSERVER. *Arno Bellack, Professor of Education, Teachers College, Columbia University, observed the symposium and prepared a paper which appears at the end of this compilation.*

STANLEY ELAM, *who edited this volume, is the editor of* Phi Delta Kappan, *the Journal of the Phi Delta Kappa fraternity.*

EDUCATION
AND THE
STRUCTURE
OF
KNOWLEDGE

Fifth Annual Phi Delta Kappa
Symposium on Educational Research

Sponsored by
Phi Delta Kappa
Pi Campus Chapter of Phi Delta Kappa
College of Education, University of Illinois

Rand McNally & Company   Chicago

RAND MᶜNALLY EDUCATION SERIES

B. OTHANEL SMITH, *Advisory Editor*

Broudy, Smith, and Burnett, *Democracy and Excellence in American Secondary Education*
Farwell and Peters, eds., *Guidance Readings for Counselors*
Ford and Pugno, eds., *The Structure of Knowledge and the Curriculum*
Foshay, ed., *Rand MᶜNally Handbook of Education*
Haines, *Guiding the Student Teaching Process in Elementary Education*
Kimbrough, *Political Power and Educational Decision-Making*
Lewenstein, *Teaching Social Studies in Junior and Senior High Schools*
Norris, Zeran, and Hatch, *The Information Service in Guidance: Occupational, Educational, Social*
Peters and Farwell, *Guidance: A Developmental Approach*
Phi Delta Kappa, *Education and the Structure of Knowledge*
Rollins and Unruh, *Introduction to Secondary Education*
Smith and Ennis, eds., *Language and Concepts in Education*
Trump and Baynham, *Focus on Change*
Zeran and Riccio, *Organization and Administration of Guidance Services*

Also published by Rand MᶜNally
Gage, ed., *Handbook of Research on Teaching*—A Project of the American Educational Research Association

TABLE OF CONTENTS

INTRODUCTION

Phi Delta Kappa symposiums on educational research are held for the purpose of exploring certain aspects of the frontier of educational thought. The first one was held at the University of Virginia and dealt with the status of educational research, its rationale, and its relation to the behavioral sciences. The second symposium was held a year later at the University of Minnesota and the subject was research design and analysis. The third symposium was at the University of Oregon and the subject was research dissemination and implementation. The papers presented at these three symposiums, together with discussions of them, have been published by Phi Delta Kappa. The fourth symposium was on simulation in operations research and was held at Indiana University in 1962. A book based on it will be published by Phi Delta Kappa this year. This book is based on a symposium held in 1963 at the University of Illinois. Its subject is knowledge structure in relation to education as a number of knowledgeable educators see those relationships.

Let me say a word about the importance of this symposium. In recent decades there have been two attempts to revitalize and rebuild the content of the educational program. The first of these began about fifty years ago and was aimed at making more practical that which the school taught. It consisted essentially of an effort to rid the curriculum of deadwood. The schools were teaching a mass of material that was considered to be useful to only a few students if any. For example, the spelling books were made up of hard words that were not used very often and the arithmetic books involved long problems of computation which people seldom dealt with. The same thing was true of the other materials that were taught in school. The dropout rate was also heavy and it was believed to be related to the lack of vitality of curriculum content. So, quite a movement developed to study the program and to define the content that would be useful to people in their ordinary daily activities. In consequence, the textbooks and the courses of study were largely rewritten to include materials that would have a place in the daily activities of people as adults.

In the twenties and thirties the leaders of educational thought became involved in efforts to redefine the categories of knowledge. They tried to rethink the educational program from the standpoint of how to repackage the material. They developed categories which were used in the building of child-centered programs, in core programs, and in other experimental programs of instruction.

After the Second World War a new interest in the curriculum emerged and focused on the development of a program that would be both theoretical and practical. It came to be seen, or at least believed, that if the instructional program placed greater emphasis upon theory, upon the basic elements of knowledge, and less upon the knowledge that would be used immediately in practical activities and technological operation, in the long run the learning thus acquired would prove to be more generally useful. According to this view, the educational program could be both more useful and more rigorous. So we have been witnessing in the last fifteen years the reconstruction of mathematics, science, history, English, and so forth along theoretical lines.

In the course of this development, the concept of knowledge structure has been at the forefront of a great deal of thinking. It is an expression that has been variously interpreted. Like the expression "whole child," it has come to mean a lot of things to a lot of people. One of the purposes of this symposium is to try to think through the meaning of the expression, to analyze the concept for which the expression stands, and to see what bearing, if any, the concept of knowledge structure has upon education and teaching.

There are four considerations, I think, that lead us to be interested in this particular notion. I shall simply list these and let them stand without discussion. One is that teaching will be more effective if it incorporates the ways the elements of knowledge are related logically. Second, what is learned will be retained longer if it is tied into a meaningful cognitive structure. Third, what is learned will be more readily transferable if it is tied into a system of knowledge. And fourth, the categories of the curriculum—what we ordinarily refer to in conventional terms as the subjects—are somehow related to the categories of knowledge and that knowledge can be categorized in ways more conducive to learning than is ordinarily done. I think that these are some of the main considerations that lead us now to look at knowledge structure and to analyze the concept in relation to certain educational problems.

Those of us who planned this symposium are greatly in debt to the men who prepared and delivered the papers reproduced here. We also wish to express our thanks to the discussants who spent two days with us and examined and corrected the transcripts later.

B. Othanel Smith

April 1, 1964
University of Illinois

CHAPTER I

PROBLEMS, TOPICS, AND ISSUES

Of the four topics of education—the learner, the teacher, the milieu, and the subject matter (that which is intended to be taught or learned)—none has been so thoroughly neglected in the past half century as the last. We have had more than enough scrutiny, discussion, and debate about the learning and teaching processes, thanks to the popularity of psychological investigations. Class, community, the political state, and school organization have similarly been defined and redefined, studied and re-examined. Only subject matter, among the four, has been relegated to the position of a good wife: taken as familiar, fixed, and at hand when wanted.

Introduction of the "new" mathematics by the School Mathematics Study Group was met with nothing less than incredulity. Teachers of mathematics were prepared for new "methods" of instruction, but most were wholly unprepared for a radical reorganization of content. They had, themselves, been taught their mathematics in such a way as to suppose that no other structuring of the field was possible. Curriculum-makers had so long been involved in the psychologically instigated habit of teaching mathematics as if mathematicals were indubitably abstractions from physical events that the introduction of the new mathematics left them first speechless, then resistant, and only recently prepared to do rational battle or collaborate.

My own efforts on behalf of the Biological Sciences Curriculum Study revision of high school biology were controlled by much the same set of conditions. Teachers, curriculum-makers, and administrators were prepared to believe that science might grow by accretion and that minor errors of past researches might be discerned and corrected. They were horrified by the suggestion that far more radical alterations of this body of knowledge had been made in the past twenty years. Yet the then-extant textbooks in biology reflected the state of the science some forty years earlier: concerned mainly with the macroscopic, largely taxonomic, and preoccupied with the discrimination and naming of parts of things. The new biology was concerned with the microscopic—microchemistry and microphysics. The merely taxonomic and analytical had long since given way to concern for dynamical investigations of evolutionary, community, population, organismic, and intracellular systems and processes. New conceptual schema had generated new problems; new problems had generated new bodies of data and knowledge whose very shape differed radically from the shape of the old. More than two years of intensive effort were required to persuade school men and women that such radical changes had occurred. The problem, indeed, was to persuade them that such radical changes were possible.

Humane studies have, I suspect, been accorded somewhat more realistic treatment. Nevertheless, even history, that most protean of the disciplines, is conceived by many to be a body of fixed and irrevocable fact and, on the whole, the diversities of view concerning the character of literature, music, and the fine arts have been given little attention and less scope as determining factors in planning the content and method of school curriculums.

It is in the interest, then, of refurbishing subject matter as a true commonplace or topic that the problems of the structures of the disciplines arise. (By "topics" or "commonplaces" I mean those foci of attention within an area of interest which fulfill two conditions: [a] They demand the attention of serious investigators; [b] their scrutiny generates diverse investigations and consequent diversities of definitions, doctrines, and emphases.)

The following treatment conforms to this line in two senses. First, it is educational rather than philosophical. That is, I make no attempt to provide an exhaustive conspectus of the problems, topics, and issues involved in the area called "structures of the disciplines." Second, I shall try to maintain, and, if possible, exacerbate the moot state of the matters discussed.

I have no doubt that many professional educators would dearly love a clear, uncomplicated, and definitive description of some univocal "structure" for each of the disciplines normally involved in the school curriculum. They wish, quite naturally, to be about their business of reconstructing the school curriculum and would like a firm foundation for doing so. Nothing, however, could be more unfortunate at this stage of the game than such an easy settlement. In the first place, American education has suffered too much in the past thirty years from the adoption of most recent doctrines about other commonplaces (e.g., learning theories). In the second place, problems about the structures of the disciplines have only recently been reraised. What is wanted, then, is enquiry, not dogma.

(I am obliged to modify the above stricture in view of the fact that some parts of what follows are adapted from a paper prepared, by invitation, for the Project on the Instructional Program of the Public Schools of the National Education Association. This paper was commissioned early in 1961, and I am indebted to the National Education Association for permission to reuse some of the materials contained in that paper.)

THREE BASIC PROBLEM AREAS

The Organization of the Disciplines

Is mathematical knowledge significantly different from knowledge obtained in physics and chemistry? That is, do mathematicals "exist" in a fashion radically different from the existence of the objects of physical enquiry? If so, how can we account for the extraordinary usefulness of mathematics to the physical sciences? If not, how can we account for the air of complete certainty which seems to distinguish mathematical knowledge from the knowledges obtained in the physical sciences through vexed and uncertain weighing of evidence?

Is practical knowledge merely the application of scientific knowledge? Or does science take hold of idealizations extrapolated from experience of things in such fashion that practical knowledge must supply an additional bridge for return from scientific ideals to the actual and practicable?

Are living organisms and nonliving organizations of matter so radically different from one another as to require different conceptual frames and different methods for their investigation? If so, what is the relation between biological and physical sciences? If not, how must we account for the largely independent development of these two sciences until recently?

Is "social science" a nomer or misnomer? That is, can there be reasonably certain and general knowledge about the collective behavior of men? Is the behavior of men in groups no more than an expression of their character as individuals? Or, conversely, is an individual personality no more than the outcome of membership in a social group? Or do individual behavior and the behavior of groups pose distinct problems? In short, are psychology and sociology parts of one science or separate sciences?

Such questions illustrate the problem of determining the membership and organization of the disciplines, of identifying the significantly different disciplines (for purposes of instruction), and of locating their relations to one another. I shall call this set of problems "problems of the *organization* of the disciplines."

The significance of this set of problems to education is obvious enough. To identify the disciplines which constitute contemporary knowledge is to identify the various materials which constitute the resources of education and its obligations. To locate the relation of these disciplines to one another is to locate one important factor which determines what may be joined together for purposes of instruction, what should be held apart, and in what sequence they may best be taught.

The Substantive Structures of Each Discipline

The classic experiments of Gregor Mendel on inheritance were dictated by a conception of unit genetic particles which behaved as do the terms in the expansion of a binomial. This conception dictated that the traits for original study should be "discontinuous traits" such as the presence or absence of wrinkles. The same conception required that the objects of enquiry be the offspring of "pure breeding" parents rather than the mixed populations studied earlier by Galton.

The Pavlovian study of animal behavior was regulated by a conception of the congeries of behavioral patterns as consisting of no more than combinations or modulations of a relatively small number of behavioral *elements*, the unlearned reflexes. Later studies of animal behavior were modified considerably by introducing the conception of "goal-direction."

Some historical study is regulated by the notion that human behavior tends to cluster around certain time points or epochs, each of which has its distinctive cast and flavor. Other historical studies proceed on the premise that human affairs run in cycles or mounting spirals. Still other historical studies seek only to determine who did what and when.

Harry Stack Sullivan initiated a new pattern of study of human personality by conceiving it as the relatively labile consequence of relationships established with others. Sullivan's predecessor, Freud, pursued much of his study of personality as if it were the outcome of the interplay of three interrelated psychic organs possessed by all men.

Much research in physiology was controlled by the Aristotelian notions of organ and function. In this view, the organism could be characterized by certain defining behavioral properties and consisted essentially of anatomically distinguishable parts. Each such part was to be understood in terms of the contribution it made to one or another of the behavioral properties characteristic of the organism. Physiological knowledge was enriched in the late nineteenth century by researches dictated by a quite different conception, one in which the central "wholeness" of the Aristotelian organism was displaced by a conception of a whole constituted of both organism and environment. Researches controlled by this conception sought knowledge of anatomical parts in terms of the role they play in regulating exchanges between organism and environment together with the role they play in maintaining the boundary between the two parts of this larger whole.

In general, then, enquiry has its origin in a conceptual structure. This structure determines what questions we shall ask in our enquiry; the questions determine what data we wish; our wishes in this respect determine what experiments we perform. Further, the data, once assembled, are given their meaning and interpretation in the light of the conception which initiated the enquiry. Thus we may discover and formulate some of our physiological knowledge in terms of organ and function, our knowledge of atomic structure in terms of particle and wave, our knowledge of personality in terms of the relative strengths and hierarchical relations among its organs.

The second problem of the structure of the disciplines is the problem of identifying these structures and of understanding their powers and limitations as *reflected in the knowledge they produce*. I shall call this set of problems "the problem of the *substantive* structures of each discipline."

There are at least two significant aspects of the problem of the substantive structures of the disciplines as far as education is concerned. In the first place, to know what structure underlies a given body of knowledge is to know what problem we may face in imparting that knowledge. The structure may be as simple as that of a classificatory scheme based on a single visible quality, and firmly embedded in the commonsense experience of the learning child. It may, on the other hand, be as complex as the wavelike particle of modern physics and alien (indeed, contrary to) commonsense experience. In this respect, the significance of substantive structures concerns curricular planning.

The second educational significance of substantive structures involves the desirability of including them as *constituents* of the curriculum, as part of the content to be understood by students. A given body of knowledge, arising under the aegis of a given substantive structure, contains only as much of the richness and complexity of the subject matter as the structure admits. Consequently, no body of knowledge is other than incomplete. Further, substantive structures succeed one another as the knowledge acquired through the use of one structure permits the conceiving and use of another which is presumably more nearly adequate˙ to the complexity of the subject matter. In some sciences, different substantive structures control different enquiries concurrently, resulting in the coexistence of two or more relatively independent bodies of knowledge about the same apparent subject matter. It follows then that it is desirable, if not necessary, that we so teach that students understand that the knowledge we impart may be incomplete, is relatively ephemeral, and is not mere literal, "factual" truth. This means that we need to clarify for students the role of substantive structures in making knowledge possible and limiting its validity and impart to students some idea of the particular structures which underlie the major bodies of present knowledge, together with the reasons for the appropriateness of these structures and some hint of their limitations.

The Syntactical Structures of the Disciplines

If different disciplines pursue knowledge of their respective subject fields by means of different substantive structures, it follows that there may be major differences between one discipline and another in the manner and the extent to which each can verify its knowledge. The warrant for asserting the desiderata which determined Franklin Roosevelt's decisions at Yalta would differ markedly in kind from the evidence required to assert with confidence where Roosevelt was on the last Monday of his life. More generally, the warranty for historically reliable statements would differ radically from the warranty of scientific statements. Further, the kind of evidence, and the degree to which it is evidential, required by different researches within the natural sciences differ markedly from field to field (biology as against physics, for example) and even between researches within a field. There is, then, the problem of determining for each discipline what it does by way of discovery and proof, what criteria it uses for measuring the quality of its data, how strictly it can apply its canons of evidence, and, in general, to determine the pathway by which the discipline moves from its raw data to its conclusion. This cluster of problems I shall call the problem of the *syntactical structure* of each discipline.

Again, certain obvious significances to education exist. Unless we intend to impart all knowledge as true dogma we shall need to impart to our students some idea of the degrees and kinds of validations which exist.

At this point, it seems to me that the history of our American educational practices dictates a *caveat*. So many textbooks and so many teachers of the sciences have reduced the question of the syntax of their discipline to such a vastly vague and general dictum about "method" that instruction in this respect has long been a farce. Let us try to avoid such extremes in the future.

THE PROBLEM OF THE ORGANIZATION OF THE DISCIPLINES

Enquiry into the organization of the disciplines is no more exempt from the need for guiding substantive structures than is any other enquiry. Further, since the disciplines are collectively complex and changing, the variety of structures devised for the investigation of their organization has been great. In the following paragraphs I shall review a few of the doctrines which have emerged. Let it be held in mind that the problem of the organization of the disciplines is a problem of classification primarily. The diversity and variety of available modes of classification is great. Consequently, nothing could be more foolish than to suppose that the problem posed to us by this variety of doctrines is the problem of determining which one is "right." With very few exceptions, each of them is, in its own way, "right." What is important about each one is not so much the list of disciplines and definitions which it may provide but rather: (a) the distinctions it uses to distinguish disciplines; and (b) the educational problems and issues which these distinctions raise to visibility.

Hierarchical Organizations of the Disciplines

THE HIERARCHY OF THE POSITIVE SCIENCES. Let us begin with a relatively modern hierarchical organization, that of Auguste Comte.[1] This scheme is based on the view that subject matter, and only subject matter, should provide the basis for classifying disciplines. (This subject matter emphasis, together with a syntactical structure consisting mainly of description, constitutes the "positiveness" of Comte's positivism.) The scheme (which should be read, for the moment, from the bottom up) runs as follows:

Sociology
Biology
Chemistry
Physics
Mathematics.

Ignoring mathematics for the moment, each of these disciplines concerns itself with a given "order" of phenomena, each order consisting of members of the next lower order organized into more complex structures. Thus, Comte locates physical things as the simplest of all. Chemicals come next as consisting of physicals organized in a new way. Then come biologicals as still higher organizations of chemicals. Finally come socials as organizations of biologicals. Note that though we might be tempted to insert psychology between biology and sociology, Comte would not, since psychicals would not be amenable to positive investigation.

The educational significance of this arrangement arises mainly from the increasing *dependency* which is alleged to hold as one reads the list upward. Sociology, it is supposed, cannot develop until biology is fully known. Biology, in turn, rests

[1] Auguste Comte, *Cours de Philosophie Positive* (4th ed., 1877. Paris. J. B. Bailliere et Fils).

upon chemistry, chemistry upon physics, and physics upon mathematics. A corrupted version of this dependency, uncritically accepted, underlies, I fear, a very high percentage of all the decisions about sequence and order of the curriculum at the high school and college level in this country. The biologist demands chemistry as a prerequisite for his science. The chemist requires physics and the physicist requires mathematics. There is some justice in this view, and Comte recognized it in his recommendations concerning a "dogmatic order" of instruction. Comte recognized, however, that other readings of the hierarchy were possible. One such is worth noting for its educational significance.

The principle of dependency enunciated by Comte asserts that each science in the hierarchy shall be well developed before the one above it can be developed well. Thus an adequate sociology must wait on a thoroughly adequate biology, and so on. This seems to suggest the ordering of prerequisites in the curriculum outlined above. However, if we look closely at the Comtian principles we realize that a complete positive knowledge of, say, physicals can be developed only if we have sought out and identified all the behaviors of which physicals are capable. At this point, a corollary can be seen which raises serious doubts about the soundness of the scheme which would put physics before chemistry in the curriculum. For, clearly, if chemicals are organizations of physicals, then chemicals constitute the one place in which some large array of physical potentialities become accessible to a positive investigation. It follows, then, that investigation of chemicals must precede any completion of physics. In the same way, a study of biology must precede any completion of chemistry and a study of sociology must precede any completion of biology. Organic chemistry has, indeed, developed only as we have studied the complex chemistry of the living organism; and the behavior of the human individual has become better understood as we studied human culture and society.

It is, then, just as plausible to read the Comtian hierarchy downward as upward, as far as basing curriculum practices are concerned. For example, we might argue that physics is well taught by examining the obvious behaviors of physical things up to the point where it becomes clear to student and teacher alike that further progress in physics requires mastery of certain mathematical conceptions or operations. Only at this point would we ask students to turn to mastery of the mathematics required. In the same way, only as we examine the macroscopic behavior of, say, muscle fibers and recognize the need for knowledge of their finer structure would we turn to the chemistry of the muscle cell.

Mathematics, of course, occupies a peculiar place in the Comtian scheme. When the list is read in the "objective" order (from the bottom up), mathematics takes on the character of "queen of the sciences," something prior to all the other sciences on which they depend. The ordering can, however, be read in such a way that mathematics takes on much more the character of Dewey's mathematics.[2,3] It becomes much more the hand-maiden than the queen of the other sciences. It becomes, partly, the discipline which abstracts and codifies the substantive structures which other sciences have invented *ad hoc* and have tested in their enquiries. It becomes, too, the discipline which accepts responsibility for the invention of new substantive structures for possible use in later enquiries by other sciences. This matter will assume curriculum importance later when we discuss the long-term syntax of the sciences.

In line with our decision to emphasize terms and distinctions rather than the doctrines generated by them, note the principles which are involved here. In the first place the organization rests exclusively on subject matter. The subject matters treated are restricted from the start to those capable of "positive" investigation, i.e., those capable of description based on sense experience. Within this limited range of subject matters, different orders of phenomena are recognized by reference to their constituents and their organization. Note the terms which are ignored or obscured.

---

[2] John Dewey, *Logic* (New York: Holt, 1938), chs. I, VI, XIX, XX.
[3] Joseph J. Schwab, "The 'Impossible' Role of the Teacher in Progressive Education," *The School Review*, LXVII (1959), 139–59.

There is no concern for a diversity of intellectual competencies, of different abilities required by different sciences. There is no diversity of aims among the several disciplines: All of them seek knowledge and all of them seek knowledge of the same kind. Finally, there are no differences of method except technical methods appropriate to subject matters of increasing complexity.

THE PLATONIC ORGANIZATION OF THE DISCIPLINES. The Platonic organization of the disciplines can be seen in the imagery of the Divided Line, with important supplements from the imagery of The Cave.[4] A summary diagram of this structure follows:

← Downward dialectic	← Upward dialectic	Pure reason	"Real" ideas	} The intellectual
		Understanding	Hypothetical ideas	
		Belief	Things	} The visible
		Conjecture	Images	

Where subject matter was the operative term in the case of Comte's construction, it plays no part at all in the Platonic. There are objects of enquiry (represented on the right-hand side of the diagram), but in three important senses these are not subject matters. In the first place, any sort of natural thing, such as one of Comte's orders of phenomena, will have its images. In turn, a diversity of such things will lead us to some smaller number of hypothetical ideas; these, in turn, will be representations of some still smaller number and more inclusive group of real ideas. Thus any and all subject matters in the Comtian sense will be represented by the four sorts of objects in the Platonic scheme. Chemistry could be learned as images, as in a vast number of elementary textbooks. It could also be studied in the laboratory at the

[4] John Davies and David Vaughan (trans.), Plato's *The Republic* (London: Macmillan, 1950), books VI, VII.

15

level of things with the aid of images. It could be studied more "understandingly" by moving through its images and things to its theories. Chemistry would not, itself, be studied at the level of real ideas, but a study of chemistry could lead to the grasp of such real ideas, and they could be turned downward to illuminate and correct chemical theories, our understanding of chemical things, and our understanding of other things as well. In the same way, any discriminated body of subject matter, such as living organisms, moving bodies, or human behavior, could be studied at the same three levels and be illuminated by the fourth.

Our use, earlier, of discriminated subject areas, such as physicals, chemicals, and biologicals, is forced upon us by modern habits and nomenclature. These discriminations have no real meaning in the Platonic scheme. Indeed, whatever the "thing" with which we begin the upward dialectic, we are quickly brought into touch with consideration of other and different things. At a low level of hypotheticals we may be concerned with hypotheses which embrace only biologicals or physicals or chemicals; higher on the third level we may be concerned with hypotheticals which take account of all three as one. In the Platonic view, such a move toward unity is a proper aim of the dialectic and reaches its limit at the top of the Divided Line, where it provides us with a single science of all things. It is this move toward unity which is the second sense in which the objects of the Platonic Divided Line are not subject matters in the Comtian sense.

The objects of Platonic enquiry are not subject matters in still a third sense—in that they are not mere patients (subjects) to be heard, seen, and remembered. Rather, they are object matters in the sense that confrontations by them can lead to some degree of opinion or knowledge only insofar as the objects do something to the "learner" which moves him to do something to or with them: compare them, contrast them with one another, oppose one opinion about them with another, seek exceptions to apparently general rules concerning them, and so on. This is the process called the upward dialectic. Its effective use at one or another level of the Divided Line leads to one or another of the states of mind given the names: conjecture, belief, understanding, and pure reason.

The dialectical process is in one sense the same, regardless of the level of the line at which it takes place; i.e., any of the objects can serve as goads and stimuli to the process. However, insofar as the dialectic is directed at different times to different kinds of objects, the process differs. The search for ambiguities and alternative meanings of words (images) is not the same as the search for different systems of similarities and differences among objects. The search for similarities and differences among objects is not the same as the effort to find new conceptions which will bind together two or more hypothetical ideas. Since the process does differ with different objects, we may suppose, with or without Plato, that different men will differ with respect to how far up the Divided Line they are capable of going. In this sense, then, we find that the Platonic construction adds an important term excluded by Comte: the learner, different kinds or degrees of competencies, individual differences with respect to the possession of these competencies. When this factor (learner, mental abilities, etc.) is coupled with the object side of the line, still a third factor emerges—the different resultant states of mind. In more modern terms, these states of mind could be equated, as Plato equates them, to "kinds" of knowledge, differing with respect to degree of clarity and embracingness.

The Platonic scheme and its modern analogues have educational significance in two major directions. On the one hand such schemes refer directly to such current interests as "problem-solving," "concept formation," and "teaching and learning through enquiry." On the other hand the scheme has bearing on all efforts at integration of the curriculum: unified science, unified social studies, integration courses generally, and so on.

With respect to "problem-solving," the scheme illuminates certain crucial problems which we must solve before supposing that we have in hand a mode of problem-solving which can be taught in lieu of varieties of solutions. Have we, for example, deluded ourselves into believing we have a universal method by the simple trick of forcing any and every sort of problem into a single pattern, a pattern which does not, in fact, apply as universally as its inventors suppose? Is the method sufficiently rich and flexible to permit adaptation to diversities of problems? Conversely, have we covertly or openly imported diverse classes of problems and a similar diversity of problem-solving methods? If so, have we provided an N + 1th method for relating solutions to one kind of problem to solutions to another kind?

With respect to concept formation, the Platonic construction tempts us, at first, to accept the notion that concepts are formed by working with and through things (i.e., the upward dialectic moves from things upward to ideas). Closer scrutiny reveals, however, the possibility that (a) images (culturally determined ways of looking) may be an important part of the process of seeing what we look at, and therefore an important part of concept formation. Closer scrutiny reveals that (b) the movement upward on the Divided Line is not smooth and unjointed. There is not only a radical break between the level of belief (things) and the level of understanding (hypothetical ideas); there is another between the level of understanding and the level of pure reason. The possibility suggested by the latter leap should remind us that in the order of enquiry many conceptions have arisen in which hypotheticals or things were only the occasions for thought and in no way the sources of the thought. That is, conceptions may arise not only from scrutiny of things and from the attempt to interrelate previously grasped conceptions but also "creatively," *de novo*, as genuine dialectical inventions. Certainly, some conceptions, though arising in connection with some restricted subject matter, have found meaning and application in a much wider area. It follows, then, that any act which consists of leading a youngster to form a concept via some restricted and chosen body of materials may be a mistake in either of two ways: it may corrupt the conception (as in those cases where numbers are taught as the outcome of counting things); it may artificially and undesirably circumscribe the youngster's understanding of the extension of the conception, the domain to which it may be applicable.

With respect to teaching and learning as enquiry, the Platonic construction should remind us that Plato may be wrong as well as right. There may be one mode of enquiry appropriate to all kinds of things and problems; it may be, however, that there are real diversities of problems and subject matters requiring a similar diversity of modes of enquiry.

In general, then, the Platonic construction throws light on and raises problems of unity and diversity with respect to all versions of "instrumental" learning, whether in the guise of the ancient liberal arts or more modern ones.

Problems of unity and diversity are similarly raised with respect to questions of the wisdom or unwisdom of unification in the curriculum of matters which are not yet unified by enquiry. Most of the sciences, including physics as well as biology, are today pretty much at the same level of the Divided Line as Plato saw them—the hypothetical. Enquiries in different sciences are pursued with the aid of different substantive structures and therefore yield bodies of knowledge which are distinctly plural —stated in different terms and often in terms so different that little connection of meaning may exist between one such set of terms and another. For example, we may be quite sure that economic, social, and psychological acts are closely interrelated, yet have little knowledge of them as one interconnected body of phenomena because workers in the field have yet to develop a substantive structure to embrace them. Given such a state of knowledge, curriculum efforts at integration inevitably yield a number of unfortunate outcomes. They may injudiciously and indefensibly assimilate one or more of the "integrated" sciences to another. They may protect the integrity of the several sciences by merely juxtaposing them, in which case one wonders why they should be said to be integrated. Or "integration" may be achieved by moving to such high levels of generality that the meaningfulness of the body of ideas when applied to things is lost.

A far more defensible integration could be achieved if we took from Plato his major lesson: that integration is achieved—by the scholar and investigator as well as the student—only as we master and use the overarching disciplines which stand apart from those peculiar to any bounded science or subject-matter, the intellectual-linguistic disciplines, arts, or skills by which distinctions and relations are made and their force and effect examined.

Finally, the fact that the modern sciences remain at the third level of the Divided Line reminds us once again of the extent to which their methods remain heuristic. That is, their enquiries move forward under the guidance of conceptions which are subject to change and improvement. Consequently the body of knowledge extant at any given time is subject not only to addition but to revision, sometimes radical revision. This should in turn remind us of the desirability of finding some way of imparting these bodies of knowledge while at the same time indicating their transient character.

The Aristotelian Organization of the Disciplines[5]

By means of the classic "four causes," Aristotle discriminates three classes of disciplines: the theoretical, the practical, and the productive. The theoretical disciplines are those whose aim is to know. They are concerned, consequently, with subject matters capable of being known, i.e., possessing the requisite stability. Commensurate with this aim and this sort of subject matter, the theoretical disciplines require certain specialized competencies in the investigator: the developed capacity to reason logically, the capacity to carry out an induction, the capacity to deal with matters of high abstraction. Aristotle identifies three such theoretical disciplines—metaphysics, mathematics, and the natural sciences. We would include the natural sciences, a substantial portion of most of the social sciences (excluding the normative portions), mathematics, and would probably have our doubts about metaphysics.

[5] See especially: Aristotle, *Metaphysics*, Book X, chs. 1, 2; Book E, ch. 1; Book K, ch. 7. Aristotle, *Ethics*, Book VI, chs. 3–8.

The Aristotelian practical disciplines include those concerned with deliberate choice, decision, and action. Because their aim is to do, to alter the course of events, the subject matter of the practical disciplines must be matter possessing precisely the contrary of the property required for the theoretical sciences. The subject matters of the practical sciences must not be inexorable in their behavior but capable of alteration, not fixed and stable but changeable. The most crucial of these changeables is, of course, human character—the leanings, the propensities toward action, and the competences of each individual person. (It is important to note, of course, that the deliberate actions with which the practical disciplines are concerned are those undertaken for their *own sakes*, the actions which in themselves constitute a good life.) The practical sciences were and are, therefore, ethics and politics together with the education carried out by the latter and yielding the former.

The productive disciplines are those concerned with making: the fine arts, the applied arts, engineering. Again, the appropriate subject matter must be malleable and, again, certain specialized competences are required of the practitioners.

The great educative significance of this organization of the disciplines for us derives from the extent to which our schools have tended to treat all disciplines as if they were theoretical. In the case of the practical disciplines, we manage this by ignoring them. No public school and few private schools expend any substantial part of their resources on character development. We pretend that the home and the church are still the appropriate institutions for this purpose; or we postpone efforts indefinitely on the pretense that a consensus about goods is a necessary prerequisite to character education; or we fail to find out how far the behavioral sciences are able to give us means and methods for character development in an institutional, urban setting.

In the case of the productive disciplines our failure is not as great but is great enough as far as the fine arts are concerned. Music appreciation is too often taught as if the purpose of the game were merely to remember identifying themes of symphonies, etc. Performing music is taught as if the aim were merely to follow the notes and obey the teacher's instructions about the score. Literature is taught as if drama and the novel were windows looking out on life or, worse, as if they were windows looking inward on the character, the life, or the times of the author. Art, similarly, is taught as if its aim were to provide a true, faithful photograph of life.

We will do well if we use the Aristotelian organization of the disciplines as a goad toward determining the desirability and feasibility of (a) character development and (b) development of abilities both to create and to enjoy created objects.

Efforts To Discriminate Unique Disciplines

Three disciplines have been perennially puzzling: mathematics, logic, and history. The reason in each case is obvious enough. Logic, because it allegedly gives canons to all other disciplines, raises a question as to what its own canons are. Mathematics, because of its apparently absolutely right or wrong character (as against the merely probable character of knowledge in other disciplines), raises the question of what its objects are and what sort of knowledge it is. History, because it is alleged to deal with the ultimate particular, raises questions as to what such knowledge is for or whether such knowledge is possible at all. And because history often lays claim to being the supreme integrative discipline, it raises questions about the legitimacy of such integrations.

The matter of logic assumes importance for us where it is proposed to reintroduce it into the curriculum on the bland assumption that it is the indubitable queen of the sciences. It is important, in such a case, to keep in mind that the question of the ultimate subject matter and character of logic remains unsettled. It may, indeed, be a codification of the laws governing movements of the mind or of language. It may, on the other hand, be only a handmaiden of the sciences, a codification of modes of enquiry developed and tested by other disciplines. (See, for example, Comte's conception of a "natural" logic and Dewey's theory of enquiry.)

Were it not for the efforts in recent years of the School Mathematics Study Group, the matter of mathematics would also be of considerable importance. It is still the case that much mathematics is taught as if number and figure were indubitably abstractions from experience of physical things. Such curriculum practice ignores the live possibility that mathematics derives from exploration of the furniture of the human intellect or from the invention of logical forms or from the exhaustion of a more or less arbitrarily chosen set of rules and starting points. Real differences accrue to the content of the curriculum and the understandings of mathematics from adoption of one or another of these views. They should, therefore, be kept in mind.

The issue concerning the nature of history is a live one, not because we have espoused a single doctrine in the schools but because we have, on the whole, left the whole matter alone. Should school history be a series of Platonic myths for regulating the attitudes of the young, or exposition of the ideas, controversies, decisions, and doctrines which have shaped our present, or what?

One other matter deserves attention here. Consider the series: inanimate, animate, human, ethical human. Are all of these equally and absolutely determinate? Almost every possible answer has been satisfactory to some one at some time. As late as 1880, it could be seriously asserted in a medical society meeting in London that the kind of generalizations appropriate to physics and chemistry were impossible in biology. Human affairs have perennially been supposed to enjoy a degree of freedom greater than that possessed by physicals or biologicals. The Kantian discrimination of nature and morals accorded freedom to the latter and fatedness to the former. Some positivists would assert the entirely fated character of all of them.

It is probably no longer viable to consider the possible drawing of the line between fate and freedom lower than that which discriminates ethical behavior from the rest. This discrimination, however, remains moot and important. The importance may be summarized thus: Shall we capitulate to a Skinnerian conception of character as wholly a matter of operant conditioning or shall we give some thought to the possibility that early character may be so shaped as, in fact, to confer on the individual some competence at controlling his own further character development? A similar question can be raised about the manner in which we should teach some parts of history and the social sciences.

Practical-Theoretical

In view of the many different social-political-economic services which the American school performs, the question of the nature of practical knowledge, of theoretical knowledge, and of the relations between them is of paramount importance. Yet no other issue is treated quite so cavalierly. Typically, the school administrator takes the position that practical and theoretical knowledge are noncommunicating species and that only the practical matters; "theoretical" becomes an epithet. Still other schoolmen uncritically assume that any and all items of scientific knowledge are immediately applicable to concrete and particular situations. These persons would be very much surprised to be told that the Newtonian equation, $F = MA$, will not predict the outcome of a child's push of a heavy automobile unless recourse is had to sophistries about friction or complications involving the kinetic molecular theory. It would be well, therefore, to examine a few of the different ways of treating the problem of the relation of theoretical and practical.

We can adapt the Aristotelian position to yield the following conception: Scientific investigation seeks to discover and formulate the *regularities* characteristic of a group of similar things. In so doing, it abstracts a general or ideal case from the variabilities exhibited by numerous particular instances. The resulting knowledge applies, therefore, only approximately to any given particular, whether it be one of the sample from which the knowledge was drawn or another. Medicine, for example, will have its classic description of typhoid fever. The description will be a description of a type, however, and no particular case of typhoid fever will correspond to the type. Yet it is the particular case of typhoid fever and the particular person who has it which constitute the problem of the "practical." It is this case of typhoid which must be cured and this patient who must be treated. Consequently, in this view, there is need for a special kind of practical competence which takes over where theoretical knowledge leaves off to permit reasonably sound judgment about the individual case. Aristotle called the developed competence to exercise this judgment *practical wisdom*. He (and we) considered it a competence which accrues from experience and which is more or less incapable of being formulated or taught. The view that practical wisdom cannot be taught is memorialized in our continued use of apprenticeship and internship, and, since both of these practices are extremely costly educational endeavors, it would be exceedingly helpful if someone were to challenge this Aristotelian view. However, let it be noted that, ironically, the challenge, to be meaningful, must be practical.

The Baconian variant of the Platonic Divided Line throws a different helpful light on the question of theory and practice.[6] Bacon erects a pyramid of theoretical sciences. Its broad base consist of "natural history," a catalogue and description of the variety of things to be seen in the world. The middle science, physic, is concerned with immediate physical causes and effects, e.g., that heat hardens eggs, that heat softens wax, what substances will bleach red colors, what other substances will render dyes fast. The apical science of this trio, metaphysic, seeks to discover the inner nature of those qualities (such as heat, hardness, gravity, motion) which, taken together, would be the constituent terms of all things. Metaphysical knowledge in this sense would correspond to the most encompassing and therefore economical theories of modern science.

[6] Francis Bacon, The Advancement of Learning, *British Philosophers of the 18th Century* (New York: Random House, 1939), Book VII, 1–5; Book VIII, 3.

It is Bacon's point that this, the most theoretical of theoretical knowledges, is at the same time of the greatest practical significance. As Bacon himself remarks,[7] "It doth enfranchise the power of man under the greatest liberty and possibility of works and effects. For physic carryeth man in narrow and restrained ways, give light to new inventions in *like* matter. But whosoever knoweth any form knoweth the utmost possibility of super-inducing that nature upon any variety of matter." We have only to remember the connection between the Einstein energy-mass equation and the atomic bomb as a case in point.

The Platonic original of this scheme would also affirm the notion that the most theoretical states are the most practical. That is, it is the man who has reached the top of the Divided Line, who has emerged from the cave and looks straight at the sun, who is most competent to return to the cave to teach and rule. However, the return to the cave, the descent of the Divided Line, the downward dialectic, poses its own difficulties. "Now consider what would happen if such a man were to descend again and seat himself on his old seat? Coming so suddenly out of the sun would he not find his eyes blinded with the gloom of the place."[8] Thus Plato takes note, as Bacon does not, of the need for a special adjustment to the problems of material instances presumably embraced by grand ideas.

In Bacon and Plato, then, the highest reaches of theoretical knowledge are the sources of most effective practice (with or without some added competence required to bring the theoretical knowledge to bear). In Aristotle the separate competences of practice and theory each reigns supreme in its own bailiwick. That is, politics, the major practical science, is called the architectonic science in the volume devoted to discussion of politics. In volumes devoted to the theoretical sciences, on the other hand (*Physics, Metaphysics*), we are told that one or another of these theoretical sciences is supreme. "Evidently, then, there are three kinds of theoretical sciences—physics, mathematics, theology. The

[7] *Ibid.*
[8] Davies and Vaughan, *op. cit.*, Book VII, 516.

class of theoretical sciences is the best, and of these themselves the last named is best; for it deals with the highest of existing things."[9]

If we emphasize the increasingly formal and metaphorical character of scientific knowledge as it grows more and more theoretically embracing, we are forced to still a third relation between theory and practice. Practice (prediction and control) becomes the only test of the goodness of the theoretical construction.

Finally, we should take note of the pragmatic-dialectical view in which practice and theory, though different from one another, interpenetrate and interact in such a way that they are interdependent. Thus it is the practical (felt, organismic needs) which instigates enquiries which may become theoretical. Conversely, the outcomes of theoretical investigations then lead to such modifications of both the organism and the environment as to enrich or otherwise modify organismic needs. That is, science arises as the codification and outgrowth of the accumulation of practical know-how. Science in turn gives birth to technology. Technology alters ourselves and the face of our world, thus creating new problems, calling for new know-how, and therefore leading to new theoretical enquiries and new bodies of science.[10, 11]

We have not exhausted the possible relations between theory and practice. There is still the radically empiricist view that scientific knowledge should be limited to the report of phenomena, in which case theoretical and practical knowledge become one. There is the positive view in which theoretical knowledge will be the sole source of guided practice but will require the development of special skills or rules for its application (engineering).

What all this boils down to, as far as the curricular preservation of practicality is concerned, is this: Different items of

[9] Aristotle, *op. cit.*, Book K, 7.
[10] John Dewey, *Experience and Education* (New York: Macmillan, 1944), Preface.
[11] John Dewey, *Logic* (New York: Holt, 1938), chs. IV, IX.

27

scientific knowledge, because of differences in the syntactical and substantive structures leading to their production differ with respect to their relation to practicality. Some bodies of knowledge (e.g., Freudian personality theory) are so highly metaphorical that it is only in practice (therapy) that they find their meaning and warrant. In the case of such items of knowledge, the important thing is to make sure that the learner knows how metaphorical they are; this means that teaching must not only interpret the results of practice in terms of the theory but reinterpret the theory in the light of disclosures through practice. Other items of scientific knowledge, such as disease taxonomy, have been developed at the expense of much of the richness of detail of the particulars involved. In such cases theoretical instruction must be supplemented by (practical) experience of the range and character of the individual variability involved, and of ways in which this variability may be taken into account in actual practice. In still other cases, the gulf between theoretical knowledge and practice is so great, as in the present primitive state of administration theory, that teaching must proceed mainly by doing. The theory must be seen as a first, tentative effort to encompass practice.

Meanwhile, as far as the preservation of the theoretical is concerned, we need only take note of the Baconian emphasis: theory contains the quintessence of practice.

THE SYNTACTICAL STRUCTURE OF THE DISCIPLINES

What a Syntax Is

As earlier indicated (p. 10), the syntactical structure of a discipline is not to be equated to "method," at least not to method as a highly schematized and abstract exposition. Rather, syntactical structure concerns itself with concrete descriptions of the *kinds* of evidences required by the discipline, how far the kinds of data required are actually obtainable, what sorts of second-best substitutes may be employed, what problems of interpretation are posed, and how these problems are overcome.

The syntax of Aristotelian structure-function physiology[12] as adapted by William Harvey[13] will serve as an example. Recall, if you please, that the substantive structure (the conception of organism) determining this syntax required that we terminate each enquiry by asserting with some warrant the function, the contribution, of each organ to the economy of the whole organism.

The first necessity in such an enquiry is an estimate of the character or nature of the whole organism involved, usually expressed in a catalogue of the capacities and activities characteristic of it. This estimate is obtained by means of a classical induction complete with all the doubts that accompany the inductive leap from the enumeration of instances with their individual variability to the terminal pronouncement concerning the nature of organism as such.

Given this estimate of the whole, the next step is the discrimination of "parts," e.g., organs. At this point in an adequate formulation of the syntax of such enquiries it is important to point out that the notion of "part" is flexible. In the case of the living organism, parts may be taken at one time as such gross parts as the entire circulatory system, digestive tract, and so on. At another point in the investigation, we may focus down, treating each such system as a "whole" and discriminating its parts, e.g., heart, arteries, veins, capillaries. Such organs, in turn, may be treated as wholes while we investigate their tissues or their cells.

Once parts have been discriminated and one part focused upon as the object of the present enquiry, the next step in the syntax is the attempt to determine the role or function of the part. Here, the task of an adequately formulated syntax of the enquiry, as distinct from an abstract schematism of method, consists in pointing out the concrete kinds of data which are taken

---

[12] Aristotle, *Generation of Animals*, Book I, 2; *Parts of Animals*, Book I, 1; *Posterior Analytics*, Book II, 19.
[13] Robert Willis (trans.), William Harvey's *An Anatomical Desquisition on the Motions of the Heart and Blood* (London, 1847).

as indicative of function and what principle warrants the use of such data and controls their interpretation. In the Aristotelian pattern, the principle, the crucial commitment, is this: The *structure* of each part, the *location* of each part, and observable *actions* of or in each part are appropriate to, fitted for, the role the part plays in the whole. This commitment permits a syntax through which the role may be inferred from knowledge of structure, locations, and actions. (Thus Harvey locates the chambers of the heart, the moveable flaps which guard entry into each chamber, the arrangement of the fibers which compose its walls. He identifies the fibers as muscular and traces the consequences of their contraction. He takes note of the consequences of the constriction of the heart's inner space which results and notes the impulsion of blood from heart to arteries. Harvey then turns to the question of the local relations of the heart vis-à-vis its neighbors and the visible actions seen among these neighboring parts following the action of the heart.)

An adequate formulation of the syntax of this pattern of enquiry would, of course, also include comment on its weaknesses and strengths. For example, it would point out that numerous "motions" (spatial, chemical, physical changes) may be seen in the neighborhood of a part, only some of which may be essential "actions." The syntax would remark on the fact that there is no infallible sign by which the important action may be distinguished from the nonevidential motions and that, in consequence, the inference of function from such evidence is always doubtful. The syntax would go on to point out the self-correcting feature of the pattern, that related organs are each treated in the same way and that error would be revealed by incoherencies among the conclusions reached about each such organ. The syntax would similarly point out the doubtfulness of the crucial commitment that locates the appropriate data of the enquiry ("fitness" of each part); it would indicate the extent to which heuristic adoption of the commitment permits test of the commitment itself. The syntax might end by pointing once again to the inherent doubtfulness of the original, inductive estimate of the character of the whole organism and show (again, a self-correcting feature) how inferences about organ-functions pursued under the aegis of this estimate could be used reflexively to test the estimate.

This example clarifies, I hope, the great difference between an abstract schematism of method and what is here conceived to be the syntax of a discipline. Of greatest importance, perhaps, in view of the present state of education in this regard, is that *syntax* effectively does away with the embarrassing divorce of "method" and "content." A syntax cannot be described except through reference to the concrete subject matter involved in concrete enquiries. It is equally clear, I hope, that adequate syntactical descriptions for purposes of instruction are almost wholly lacking in the available school literature. They are most wanting and most needed in history and in science.

Syntax of Discovery—Syntax of Proof

With respect to effective formulation of good syntaxes for the sciences, a special problem is created by the tyranny of the unbiquitous description of science as a series of steps by which hypotheses are "verified." Two matters cast grave doubt on the wisdom of this description of science. The logical factor involved is now familiar enough; experimental verification of the existence of the logical consequences of an hypothesis does not, by itself, constitute verification of the hypothesis. And failure to find these logical consequences does not constitute disverification. Only if it is possible to assert that the consequent in question is not only a consequence of the hypothesis under test, but also that it is *not* the consequence of any other conceivable hypothesis, does experimental verification of the existence of the consequent constitute verification of the hypothesis. Similarly, failure to discover consequents experimentally may mean that they do not exist but also may mean that we have looked in the wrong place or in the wrong way. Yet much science proceeds by precisely this "illogical" method.

The improbability of obtaining definitive proof or disproof

in science suggests that it might be wise, for purposes of instruction at least, to treat science not only as a process of proof or verification but as a process of discovery, a process of disclosing events in nature and of discovering ways of relating these events to one another in such fashion that our understanding is enhanced. It would be exceedingly helpful if our formulation of syntaxes emphasized science as a process of constructing bodies of tentative knowledge, of discovering different ways of making data coherent and "telling." In such formulations, the burden of "proof" would shift from the logical to the pragmatic. A body of tentative knowledge would be judged by its usefulness—its usefulness in practice, its usefulness in satisfying our demand for a coherent account, its usefulness in leading to further enquiry.

The recommendation gains force from another circumstance. In many short-term enquiries the verification of hypotheses via consequences is only dimly visible. Consider the investigator who wishes to determine whether secretion by the pancreas is stimulated by neural or humeral pathways. Nerves are anatomically discernible and any impulses they convey can be identified and traced. The possible hormone can be extracted, chemically analyzed, synthesized, injected at will. Such matters, if they are hypothetical at all, are "glass box" hypotheses, not "black box" hypotheses. Verification involves no painful application of the hypothetical syllogism. A "logical" consequence as the hinge of the investigation is only dimly present. Would not investigations of this kind be better described as efforts to "find out" than as efforts to "verify"—again, a matter of discovery rather than of proof?

The Long-Term Syntax of the Sciences

What was described and exemplified on p. 28 I have called the short-term syntax of the sciences or the syntax of stable enquiry. Such enquiries are stable in the sense that their authors think they know exactly what they are doing. There is no wavering about what questions to ask or what substantive structures to employ. If the current principles of physiology are organ and function, the stable researcher in physiology treats organ and function as brute facts: Organs obviously exist; equally obviously, each organ has a function. There is no asking whether the organism is well understood in terms of organ and function or better understood in some other way. The substantive structure guides the enquiry but is never itself the subject of an enquiry. I have called such enquiry short-term in the sense that separate problems can be pursued separately; each such problem, such as the function of the heart, can be settled in a relatively short time.

The syntax of fluid enquiry or the long-term syntax of the sciences arises when what the short-term enquirer assumes to be true is treated as a problem. The moving force back of fluid enquiry is the demand for increasing validity of substantive structures, i.e., that they shall reflect as much as possible of the richness and complexity of the subject matter to which they are applied.

The aims of fluid enquiry are four in number. They are, first, to detect among stable enquiries the incoherencies of data, the failures of subject matter to respond to the questions put under the aegis of the extant structures, the conflict of conclusions, which indicate inadequacies of the substantive structure used. The second problem of fluid enquiry is to obtain clues from current stable enquiries as to the specific weakness or inadequacy which characterizes the principle in question. The third problem of fluid enquiry is, of course, to devise a modification of the existing structure or a wholly new structure to replace it. The fourth problem of fluid enquiry is to test proposed new structures by submitting them to the community of the discipline for debate, defense, and attack.

I call such enquiries "fluid" for two reasons. They mark a period of fluidity in the science. Its underpinnings, its basic principles, are called into question. The enquiries are themselves fluid in the sense that there is practically no limit to the flexibility with which the fluid enquirer may work, or much chance of describing a fixed, generic pattern of fluid enquiry. The detection of inadequacies in current structures and the interpretation of diagnostic clues, as well as the invention of new or modified structures, are acts of creative "insight" and imagination. Nevertheless, a few guides for the formulation of fluid syntaxes can be suggested.

The existence of fluid enquiry, the replacement of one substantive structure by another as science enlarges its grasp of its subject matter, means that the existing body of knowledge is relatively ephemeral, subject to revision. It follows, then (as indicated on p. 8) that we convey to students: (a) the revisionary character of bodies of scientific knowledge; (b) the extent to which knowledge is yet knowledge, though provisional; (c) some idea of the enhancement of knowledge which accrues from the reflexive testing and replacement of principles. No such schematic presentation of these matters as is used here would be appropriate to the curriculum unless we are willing to commit, in the case of long-term syntax, the sin of grandiose abstractness characteristic of methodical talk about the short-term syntax. In short, I see no better way to convey viable understanding of the points numerated than by treatment of long-term syntaxes in the context of the enquiries which gave rise to them and profited from them.

Such a syntax would draw from selected stable enquiries the signs of weakness or exhaustion which they exhibited in their principles. It would relate the fluid enquirer's judgment about these weaknesses. It would quote, paraphrase, or summarize the replacements proposed. It would exhibit the arguments about the new principle with an eye to the exercise of four criteria as follows: their adequacy, their interconnectingness, their continuity, and their feasibility. The meanings of the four words are outlined briefly below. For a more complete description of them and their use in the scientific community, see reference 14.

ADEQUACY. The apparent capacity of the proposed new structure to establish such interconnections *within* the subject

---

[14] Joseph J. Schwab, "What Do Scientists Do?" *Behavioral Science*, V (1960), 1–27.

matter that the incoherencies and inconsistencies exhibited by the use of earlier principles will be repaired.

CONTINUITY. The extent to which the proposed new structure retains such connections of meanings with the old one that the work of reformulating existing bodies of knowledge and of maintaining communication between past and future researches is minimally onerous.

INTERCONNECTINGNESS. Principles vary in the extent and richness of connection which they promise to establish *between* subject matters formerly held separate (e.g., between terrestrial and celestial mechanics; between literary criticism and psychology; between psychology and economics).

FEASIBILITY. The ease, cost, precision, and reliability with which the data required by the proposed new principle can be collected and anlyzed.

THE SUBSTANTIVE STRUCTURES OF THE DISCIPLINES

Substantive structures underlie short-term enquiries and are the focus of long-term enquiries. Hence, much which needs to be said about substantive structures has already been said. On p. 8 we give the reference, role, and some instances of substantive structures. On p. 28 we supply in detail an example of the operation of a substantive structure as the ruling principle of a body of enquiries. On p. 32 we discuss the criteria which govern debate about substantive structures. There remains only the task of enlarging upon one or two matters and adding one new item— some idea of the variety of substantive structures used in the sciences.

Structure and Meaning

We remarked on p. 8 that a body of knowledge arising under the aegis of a given substantive structure contains only as much of the richness and complexity of the subject matter as the structure admits. We remarked further that different substantive structures succeed one another, leading to a distinctly revisionary character of scientific knowledge. We suggested that the revisionary character of scientific knowledge made it desirable if not necessary that a given body of scientific knowledge be taught in terms of the substantive structures and syntax which produce it. Only by such means can we convey to students the fact of revision of scientific knowledge, the significance of revision, and the real but limited validity of any given body of scientific knowledge. There remains the task of indicating another reason for the inclusion of substantive and syntactical structures in the teaching of a body of content.

The additional reason is simply this: The state of enquiry in most modern sciences is now such that there is hardly a single proposition from the corpus of one of these sciences whose meaning is clear when it stands alone. On the contrary, the body of knowledge which emerges from use of an effectively valid substantive structure is itself structured. The parts of this structure, like the organs of Aristotelian physiology, take their meaning and significance from one another and from the whole of which they are parts. Thus, it is virtually impossible to discuss energy in classical mechanics without discussing work. It is impossible to discuss work without discussing force; and force cannot be discussed without concern for momentum. Further, not one of these can be defined by mere pointing. Pushing, pulling, or lifting are ways of applying force but do not correspond to "force" as this conception appears in classical mechanics. In short, if scientific subject matter is not to be un-understood or misunderstood, it must be conveyed by a narrative of enquiry, thus rendering it visible to students as the structure it is, a structure whose cornerstones are the terms of the substantive structure which made the science possible.

It need hardly be added that if meaning is lost by the absence of the structure appropriate to a body of knowledge, that meaning is seriously distorted by replacing the appropriate structure by some other structure. Yet, in the past twenty years, we have warped and revised any number of subject matters in order to fit them to the bed of views about how and when and under what circumstances this or that is most readily learned. It would be well if, in future, we thought twice before we modified an item of knowledge in order to fit it to a psychological structure alien to it.

Reliability and Validity

Since substantive structures function to guide enquiry and organize the fruits of enquiry, they are significant to education, not as matters to be learned in their own right, but in the context of enquiry. They need to be understood, not in and of themselves, but in their effect and operation: how they shape problems for enquiry; how they point to the data required to solve these problems; how they require us to interpret our data and fit the interpretations into the structure of the science; how they emend and enlarge the scope of enquiries conducted under the guidance of earlier substantive structures.

In this regard, it is desirable that we note the two major (and often conflicting) qualities which acceptable substantive structures must possess in high degree. I have called them, respectively, reliability and validity. (See also pp. 32–35.) It will be seen that validity and reliability assimilate some of the notions referred to there.)

"Reliability" refers to the requirement that the guiding principle of an enquiry be free of vagueness and ambiguity, that the empirical referents of its terms have unequivocal location and limit, and that the measurements or manipulations of these referents be capable of being made precisely and of being repeated with uniform results.

The criterion of validity asks that the data we use shall be not only reliable but representative. It asks that the substantive structure which points to these data as the appropriate data of the enquiry shall reflect as much as possible of the complexity of the subject matter to which it is applied. Thus, the primitive notion of taxis or tropism (popular circa 1920), reflecting a naive view of the simple machine of nineteenth-century physics, excelled in reliability but was poverty-stricken as far as validity was concerned. It supposed that every movement through space of an animal was a response to some single, specific, stimulating factor in the environment. It further supposed that each such stimulated response could be one of only two possible kinds—a movement toward the stimulus or a movement away from it. Of course, this naive conception quickly became obsolete. It was soon noted that many organisms did not move indefinitely toward or away from a stimulus but came to rest at some place of "optimum" intensity of the stimulus. It was eventually noted that it was highly unlikely that any animal's behavior is likely to be a repertory of separate and independent events or that the numerous stimuli acting on it would each act independently of the others without some integrative and interactive processing by the organism.

The Forms of Substantive Structures in Enquiry

It need hardly be remarked that the number and variety of substantive structures used in the sciences are indefinitely large. Newton's "hard glassy particles," the *element* of nineteenth-century chemistry, the Pavlovian reflex, the goal-gradient of late behaviorism, Freud's psychic organs, Sullivan's interpersonal relations, Bernard's homeostatic mechanism, Aristotelian organ-function, the wave-particle of modern physics, the free market, and Hobbes's social organism are all cases in point.

In an earlier paper[15] I reported an effort to impose some order on this chaos. The ordering consists of a scheme of *forms* of structure consisting of five main kinds: reductive, rational, holistic, anti-principled, and primitive. Reductive, holistic, and anti-principled principles are each represented by subspecies. A brief sketch follows.

REDUCTIVE PRINCIPLES. Reductive principles instruct the enquirer to treat his subject matter as something which takes on its important properties from elements or parts of which it is constituted. Thus, the properties of the larger whole are accounted for by the summations, combinations, and interactions of the constitutive parts. The constituents in most such cases

[15] *Op. cit.*

go unexplained. They are treated as irreducible elements which simply "are."

The nineteenth-century chemical element is a typical instance. Chemical substances are reduced to the elements or simples and to the connections which exist between them (affinities or valences). Early atomic physics, with its irreducible electron and proton, is another case in point.

For obvious reasons, I have called this subspecies of reductive principles *atomic* reductions. There are also "molecular" reductives. A molecular reduction is the effort to find the irreducible minimum of the subject matter under investigation without denying to this molecule the existence of knowable parts, but insisting that further reduction to the irreducible knowable parts constitutes a movement *out* of the subject area under investigation into another. Thus we have the *family* of early political science, the cell of nineteenth-century physiology, the "dyadic group" of some recent sociology.

Molecular reductions are peculiar in that they are incomplete as principles of enquiry. Given, for example, the stimulus-response reflex, the enquirer must still decide what to observe or measure about the molecule and how to interpret his data. Hence he must add further principles.

HOLISTIC PRINCIPLES. Holistic principles are superficially the opposite of reductive ones. Where reductive principles instruct us to find our explanation of wholes in their constituent parts, holistic principles require us to treat the larger whole as itself simply "being" (i.e., describable but not explained) and demands an account of discernible parts in terms of the unexplained whole. The procedure dictated by such principles requires, first, that the whole of interest be identified, bounded, and described (via genus and differentia). Then various parts of this whole are discriminated and "explained" in terms of the contribution they make to the bounded whole.

Such principles are so numerous as to require no examples. They underlie all investigations which terminate in a classificatory scheme, such as that of biological taxonomy and geology. They give rise, also, to bodies of knowledge such as the Aristotelian physiology of organ and function.

Here, too, two subspecies can be identified. One of these, which I call formal-material, is almost precisely the original Aristotelian conception and is, by far, the most usual. This subspecies is characterized by hanging on to both formal properties and to material constituents as operative terms. In biology, for example, structure (anatomy) and the doing-undergoing relations among parts are treated as coordinate and complementary. The merely formal holistic principle is rarer. It treats the subject of interest as capable of embodiment in a *variety* of materials or sets of parts. The principle may use material parts as evidence of the character of the whole it deals with but the stable focus of enquiry is the pattern, the organization, or form exhibited via the material. It is a case of insisting that relations are of such efficacy that the relata are of little consequence. (Occasionally, indeed, the relata are made to take such a subordinate role that all their important characteristics are seen as determined by the relations. This is the case, for example, in exaggerated versions of interpersonal psychiatric theory.)

RATIONAL PRINCIPLES. Principles of this kind require that the subject of interest be seen as given its character by its place in some larger determinative whole or by some *ratio* imposed from without. Again, a psychiatric theory is a case in point, one in which the human organism is treated as mere prime matter on which society (taken as a formal pattern and not as people in their severalty) imposes some character.

It will be noted that rational principles appear to overlap the formal holistic. The difference lies in the fact that formal holistic principles seek explanations of parts in terms of the formal whole where both whole and part are conceived as the proper subjects under investigation (e.g., the human organism and its parts); the rational principle, on the other hand, attempts to account for what it treats as its legitimate subject matter in terms of a larger, pervasive formal pattern which is *not* its proper subject of study. Thus the psychiatric example cited earlier is concerned to account for individual, human personality and cites the determinative efficacy of the pervasive society without pretending to be competent to investigate this society.

Rational principles have a distinctly Platonic cast, which leads to the fact that many (but not all) bodies of knowledge generated by rational principles tend to be mathematical. The obvious example is the Relativity Field of Einstein, the Keplerian conic sections, and so on. A good example of a rational structure which cries for mathematical formulation but lacks it is the psychological field of Kurt Lewin.

ANTI-PRINCIPLED PRINCIPLES. Anti-principled principles embody the familiar view that science ought to avoid principles and stick to the "facts." There are two common forms of such anti-principles. On the one hand, the "facts" take the form of algebraic or verbal equations whose terms are supposed to be in one-to-one correspondence with objective, discrete, measurable quantities. This sort of anti-principle is commonest in physics.

Elsewhere, and especially in the biological sciences, the "facts" take the form of chains of Millsian antecedent-consequent relations. The antecedent and consequent events are treated as objectively given and no rash statements about "cause" are made. There is only the affirmation of invariant antecedent-consequent relation.

Some anti-principled investigations are carried on *on principle*. Their authors accept as prescriptive such positivistic notions as those of Mach and Karl Pearson. Such purposed anti-principled investigations, though numerous, are usually abortive. Most anti-principled investigations occur as preliminary skirmishes in a new field of enquiry and generate enough knowledge to permit their own retirement.

PRIMITIVE PRINCIPLES. Occasionally, a science may exhaust its current principles and find no effective replacements at hand. In such cases, enquiry may be refreshed temporarily by return to problems couched in common sense or practical terms. One conspicuous recent example is the large-scale search for a cure for cancer by discarding all available knowledge in favor of *ad hoc* empirical tests of an army of chemical materials chosen pretty much at random. Thus science, for the moment, becomes trial-and-error biological engineering, the search for a "cure." The strife and confusion of principles which currently characterize political science have also generated occasional returns to primitive principles. A few studies of political science return to such questions as who voted for whom and what economic, social, or ideological class the voters belong to. Some studies of the self-government of small groups proceed by asking what variations in self-government increase efficiency or loyalty to employer or task.

DISCUSSION OF DR. SCHWAB'S PAPER[1]

DR. PHENIX: May I ask you to explain just what you mean by concept formation *de novo*?

DR. SCHWAB: I am quite prepared to agree that only God can make something out of nothing at all—if that is what disturbs you about "*de novo*." However, what ideas are made of, psychologically, is another question. They arise in moments of enquiry which require them; they are designed to solve the problems posed by these moments; but I am convinced that they are often something "created" and not mere abstractions from the relevant facts. Men have ideas in much the same sense that women have babies—which is not to deny that in both cases there are raw materials, fathers and occasions.

[1] *Editor's Note*: Because of inadequacies in the transcription, subsequent discussion of Dr. Schwab's paper has been omitted. Discussion of the other symposium papers has been examined and clarified by the discussants themselves.

CHAPTER II

THE ARCHITECTONICS
OF KNOWLEDGE

PHILIP H. PHENIX

The architectonics of knowledge has to do with the principles of ordering knowledge into systematic categories. Such an endeavor proceeds on the presupposition that knowledge has discriminable patterns or structures and that these structures can be organized according to some intelligible master plan.

An architectonic is important for the educator because it provides a scheme for considering in orderly fashion the entire range of what can be known. By having a systematic view of the kinds of knowledge that can be acquired, he gains an essential resource for making intelligent decisions about the content of instruction. He can more easily evaluate existing or proposed curricula with respect to omissions and balance. In the architectonic categories he can also find suggestions concerning the organization of instruction and concerning possible productive relationships between studies in different categories.

However, it is not to be assumed that the architectonics of knowledge is necessarily the same as the architectonics of instruction. The relation between the two systematizations is a separate problem from the problem of organization either in knowledge or in instruction. More will be said below about this relation. The only assertion made thus far is that the categorization of knowledge is a valuable *resource* for curriculum-makers. How that re-source is used is another question.

The fundamental justification for categorizing anything is to render experience intelligible. A category is a class-concept by which distinct entities are related according to some formal identity. Without categories there could be no thought and no understanding. Experience would consist of a profusion of un-related impressions. A category marks a formal identity between different things. This capacity of discerning identity-in-difference is implicit in all intellectual activity.

Categorization has as its main function the simplifying of understanding. Intellectual effort is economized by treating large numbers of different things as though they were identical in respect to the aspects by which the categories are defined. In this fashion what applies to any member of a class, in respect to its class characteristics, applies also to every other member of the class.

In particular, the categories of knowledge are used to render the profusion of cognitive experiences intelligible. They are de-signed to economize intellectual effort in the understanding of what can be known. They define classes of knowledge or ways of knowing based on certain identities among different but related experiences of knowing.

Another way to speak of economy in learning through categorization is to use the psychological concept of *transfer*. Categories are patterns of identity that are the basis of transfer of learning from one situation to another of the same class. When learning occurs with respect to the defining characteristics of a class of things, by experience with one or more things belonging to the class, that learning holds good also for experiences with all other members of the class.

In particular, the categorizing of knowledge makes possible transfer of learning from one knowing situation to another of the same kind. From the classification of knowledge into char-acteristic ways of knowing, the educator should be able greatly to economize learning effort by making use of transfer from element to element within each way of knowing. He may thus concentrate on teaching the ways of knowing rather than multiplying particular elements in knowledge without reference to their membership in classes of similar elements.

In these considerations of economy lies the essential justification for linking the architectonics of knowledge with the architectonics of instruction. If the goal of instruction is to teach knowledge as efficiently as possible, then the curriculum should be organized to secure maximum benefit from the transfer of learning, and this requires the use of categories for systematizing knowledge according to characteristic ways of knowing.

Again, it should be noted that the organization of knowledge does not necessarily provide a complete basis for the organization of the curriculum. Other considerations—particularly developmental, cultural, and social factors—are also relevant. What is suggested here is that any pattern of instructional organization should be built upon a pattern of knowledge organization, the curriculum being constructed by using both the system of knowledge and the other pertinent factors.

Any consideration of architectonics must take account of the fact that for any subject matter an indefinite plurality of categorizing schemes is possible. There is no unique system of classification dictated by the matters studied. Any feature or features can be used as the basis for division into classes. For example, human beings can be classified according to place of residence, income, color of skin, level of education, or any number of other factors. Each system yields a different grouping, and each may be a reasonable way of organizing people. Category schemes are devised to serve certain purposes. The question as to whether or not any taxonomic system is a good one can only be answered by reference to the function it is designed to serve. Thus, income level is an excellent basis for classifying people for purposes of income tax assessment, but a poor basis for purposes of allocating educational opportunity.

The plurality of possible categorizations holds for knowledge as well as for anything else. For example, knowledge can be divided according to its object, as knowledge of persons, knowledge of natural things, knowledge of ideas, etc. It can be classified according to how it is acquired, such as by sense perception, by reasoning, by intuition, by revelation, etc. It can be organized according to degrees of particularity, moving from the one extreme of uniqueness to the other extreme of wide generality. It can be classified by date of discovery, by place of origin, or by any number of other such contingent factors.

In order to decide what system of classification to use for knowledge, we have to be clear on the function the classification is designed to serve. If one wants to allocate the credit for knowledge production to various nations, place of origin is an appropriate system of classification. If one has a scale of precedence for knowledge derived from senses, reason, intuition, and revelation, then judgments concerning what knowledge is of most worth and how study resources should be allocated require a taxonomy of knowledge based on these modes of acquisition.

For the educator, the functions to be served by classifying knowledge are two: *learning* and *use*. The teacher needs knowledge organized in such a fashion that the most progress in learning takes place in the least time. He also wants knowledge organized in such a way as to be as useful as possible to the learner in meeting the demands of life in nature and society. Furthermore, since education normally relates to communal living rather than to private and esoteric activity, the general classification of knowledge for learning and use should be defined by reference to society and culture rather than to individual interest, demands, or competences.

There are all degrees of learnability and usability of knowledge. We seek for visible evidences of maximally learnable and usable kinds of organization for knowledge. The answer to our search is found in the various specialized communities of men of knowledge that are customarily associated with the disciplines. A discipline arises from an association of specialized inquirers who follow certain common rules of procedure governing the scope and methods of inquiry. The accepted common rules define the special character of each discipline. Thus, the discipline of physics is defined by certain procedural canons and the discipline of history is defined by a different set of canons. Each discipline is characterized by its own principles. These are not always explicitly stated, nor are all inquirers in any particular discipline in agreement about what the defining canons are.

How, then, can we be sure that the concept of a discipline is definite and significant enough to serve as a basis for the organization of knowledge? The answer is empirical and pragmatic: disciplines prove themselves by their productiveness. They are the visible evidences of ways of thinking that have proven fruitful. They have arisen by the use of concepts and methods that have generative power. In understanding this organization of knowledge by disciplines the analogy of biological classification may be helpful. Organisms may be classified according to species, defined by the requirement that fruitful reproductive union can occur within the same species but not between members of different species. In the organization of knowledge, a discipline is like a species. It is a system of ideas capable of producing healthy and fertile epistemic offspring. It is a distinctive *kind* of knowledge with demonstrated generative possibilities. The ongoing traditions of knowledge and the communities of persons devoted to the preservation, criticism, enlargement, and improvement of these traditions are the outward consequences of the essential fecundity of the ideas that define the disciplines.

Disciplines arise because knowledge has certain inherent natural growth structures. These structures are not wholly natural in the sense that human decisions have no part to play in their formation. Knowing is a human activity, and human determinations enter into the formulation of knowledge. Nevertheless, the role of human determinations is limited. Only certain formulations prove productive. Most do not. Which ones lead to fruitful development is a matter to be discovered a posteriori, not to be decided a priori. Only a few methods of inquiry and a few conceptual schemes have growth potential.

Disciplines, then, manifest the discovered patterns of possible development in knowledge. Presumably many such patterns still await discovery. The history of thought makes it clear that new species of knowledge emerge from time to time as a result of structural mutations that prove viable. In recent times, with the rapid expansion of knowledge in all fields, many new disciplines have sprung up, and there is every reason to expect that these developments will continue at an accelerated pace.

Furthermore, just as species in the world of living things may run their evolutionary course and disappear through maladaptation, so it is possible that disciplines that have been fruitful may gradually exhaust their possibilities of development within the total context of human inquiry at a particular stage of intellectual evolution.

Hence the concept of disciplines as species of knowledge is to be understood dynamically. The disciplines are not an array of fixed traditional ways of knowing that have been ordained at some special creation. They are structures of inquiry and understanding that emerge out of the continuous process of epistemic development. This dynamic quality is important in considering the place of knowledge in the curriculum, since concern for the structure of knowledge can easily be misinterpreted as advocacy of return to a standard traditional subject matter curriculum. In reality, attention to structures identified as belonging to productive disciplines is the best basis for an ordered and fruitful progressivism.

We must now return to the argument that the disciplines are the answer to the educator's search for knowledge organized for optimal learning and use. The disciplines constitute the answer to the need for learnable knowledge because they are defined by the principles and standards that have in fact given rise to the communities of specialized men of knowledge generally recognized as having learned the most that is known in their respective domains of inquiry. The specialized men of knowledge are those who have identified and followed the ways of maximum learning in their disciplines.

Logically, of course, one cannot infer from the learning

occurring in the groups of experts representing the disciplines that maximum learning would take place by following the same paths in the substantially different social context of the usual school, the members of which do not for the most part intend to become specialists in the particular disciplines studied. Attention to the structures of knowledge in the disciplines is certainly not a sufficient condition for learning to occur. Aptitude, maturation, and motivation are other important factors in learning. Nevertheless, members of organized communities of specialists and students in school are alike in inhabiting a common world and in having the same basic human qualities. Hence it is reasonable to expect that the systematic learning experiences of the men of knowledge would provide useful standards for anyone who sought understanding in their disciplines. It does not seem too much to assert that while attention to the structure of the disciplines is surely not a sufficient condition for maximum learning, it is a necessary condition for such learning. It is difficult to imagine how any effective learning could take place without having regard for the inherent patterns of what is to be learned. In fact, to assert that knowing depends on concern for structure is virtually a tautology, for knowledge consists in the recognition of relationships or patterns. This tautology is like saying that one cannot really understand something unless he knows its nature. So, to learn anything means to become familiar with its intelligible patterns. Therefore the structures of thought in the disciplines must be relevant to the learning that takes place in schools. Insofar as learning occurs, it must occur according to the forms of the disciplines.

The second criterion for educational knowledge cited earlier was use. Some disciplines are primarily devoted to understanding apart from the service of practical needs. Others are concerned mainly with application. Physics is an example of the former and engineering of the latter. Economics is a purely cognitive discipline, while marketing and insurance are practical or applied disciplines. History comprises pure knowledge; law deals with practical matters. Knowledge in the applied disciplines has structures, just as in the case of the theoretical disciplines. The practitioners of the applied disciplines also form identifiable communities of specialists. Similarly, the practical disciplines owe their existence to the fact that productive ways of organizing knowledge have been discovered. In these cases, however, the productivity is measured by success in dealing with the problems of practice.

The fruitfulness of the applied disciplines is in proportion to their consonance with the structures of knowledge as revealed in the pure cognitive disciplines. Civil engineers are successful in the construction of buildings to the extent that their discipline embodies the principles of theoretical mechanics. Marketing is a productive field of inquiry to the degree that it is based on the realities of the world of economics. It follows that the applied disciplines are dependent on and derivative from the fundamental disciplines that have regard for cognition alone and not for the solution of practical problems. Hence use is really a corollary of learning. The only really useful knowledge is that which conforms to the structures revealed in the cognitive disciplines, where the growth of knowledge indicates that learning has effectively occurred.

The distinction between fundamental and applied disciplines can be pushed too far. Knowing in any discipline grows out of active inquiry and not merely from passive contemplation. Nevertheless, that the difference between the two kinds of disciplines still holds is demonstrated by the continual resort of the practical specialists to the purely cognitive disciplines for the interpretation and justification of their procedures.

Up to this point we have argued that the discipline is the basic unit in the architectonic scheme of knowledge and that each discipline is defined by the principle of generativity, the operation of which is evidenced by a community of specialists pursuing inquiries according to a common rule or methodology, which may be either implicit or explicit. Each discipline is a species of knowledge, the elements of which can enter into productive interaction, generating further elements of the same species. Within each species there may be many varieties of knowledge, represented by sections or departments within the discipline. Thus, in the discipline of mathematics there are such departments as number theory, algebra, geometry, and analysis. In the discipline of history there are such subdivisions as history of ideas, military history, and cultural history. The applied discipline of law may be divided into such specialities as contracts, criminal law, and constitutional law.

Each of the varieties within a given species of knowledge is characterized by a distinctive set of ideas and methods and is under the watchful care of a community of specialists operating according to the rules of their specialty. In each case, however, the rules are particular exemplifications of the more general principles defining the species-discipline, and fruitful interaction may occur among the varieties. Algebraists and geometers are mathematicians, and algebra and geometry may enter into fruitful union, as the development of analytic geometry demonstrates. Similarly, in the discipline of philosophy the two varieties, theory of knowledge and ethics, have distinctive characteristics, yet both belong to philosophy and are mutually relevant.

Sometimes what develop historically as distinct disciplines later prove to be varieties of one discipline. Physics and chemistry are a case in point. On the other hand, it is not so certain that the essential unity of physics and chemistry extends also to biology. While biophysics and biochemistry are productive fields of inquiry, it may be that they do not really constitute a union of biology with physics and chemistry, but that they are varieties of physics and chemistry specialized for the study of living matter. The physicalists, parading under the banner of the "Unity of Science," aim to bring all sciences ultimately within the province of physics. While this effort should surely be pressed to see how far it will carry, the indications are that relatively autonomous scientific disciplines will remain. It seems unlikely, for example, that the phenomena of mind and of society can be satisfactorily studied by using only the conceptual schemes of physics or even of biology. However, the matter can hardly be settled one way or the other on an a priori basis.

If we consider disciplines of radically different characters, the unlikelihood of productive unions becomes more certain. For example, music and physics are such different kinds of enterprises that one is at a loss to know how they could be combined. True, musical acoustics is a respectable variety of physics, and electronic music is one kind of music. But neither case is a real hybrid. One is simply an application of physical concepts to phenomena that occur in music, and the other is an application of musical ideas using materials derived from physics. In no sense does musical acoustics lead to an understanding of music as such, nor does electronic music lead to a knowledge of physics. In contrast, a person who learns physics today also learns chemistry, and vice versa.

The varieties into which the species of knowledge may be divided can in turn be subdivided and re-subdivided into more and more specialized domains of inquiry. A philosopher, for example, may not only decide to specialize in one variety of philosophy, such as logic, but to concentrate on one part of logic, such as the logic of mathematics. That subdivisions of this kind can be made is due to the fact that disciplines and varieties of studies within disciplines have discernible patterns. The various subdivisions into which any field of study may usefully be separated simply reflect the structure of the field. Thus, the subdivisions of history into periods is a direct consequence of the centrality of time in the pattern of historical knowledge. The subdivision of sociology into specialties on the family, the community, ethnic groups, and the like is similarly a consequence of the structure of the discipline of sociology as the study of organized social behavior.

Subdivisions that do not follow the structure of the disciplines tend to obscure understanding. For example, it would be of no help to mathematicians to specialize along the lines of the geographical or historical sources of mathematical ideas, nor would poets fare well if they divided their field into departments having to do respectively with light, heat, sound, motion, and electricity. These considerations bear directly on the problem of the organization of the curriculum. For the most efficient learning to occur, it would appear that units of instruction should be formed according to the structural patterns of the disciplines. Otherwise, interference of patterns takes place and the learner becomes confused. On this account, for instance, a curriculum organized around life-situations would be inadmissable for the study of almost any of the fields of knowledge, with the possible exception of practical ethics. Categorization along life-situation lines is largely irrelevant to the sustained and connected learning of what is generally regarded as knowledge, because it does not follow the structure of disciplines from which most knowledge comes. At best, studies organized in this way would serve a very limited educational function.

The next step in constructing an architectonic of knowledge is to show that the many species of knowledge represented by the disciplines can be organized into more inclusive classes on the basis of structural resemblance. In doing this we must relinquish the substantial guidance provided by the existence of identifiable communities of specialists, who by their visible organizations, publications, and educational provisions give body to the disciplines and their varieties. A generic classification of disciplines can, however, be made on logical grounds. The logic of structural similarly is of great importance for pedagogy, because it points to those common features of studies that can be transferred from one discipline to another, thus eliminating unnecessary duplication of learning and facilitating insight into relationships.

An analysis of the logical characteristics of what people claim to know reveals that there are nine generic classes of knowledge. This may be demonstrated as follows: Any epistemic meaning has two dimensions—extension and intension, or quantity and quality. That is to say, knowledge consists in a relation of the knowing subject to some range of known objects, and the import of the relation is of some kind. Extension has three degrees: singular, general, and comprehensive. That is, the knowledge is either of one thing, or of a selected plurality, or of a totality. Intensions in knowledge are also of three kinds: fact, form, and norm. In other words, the quality of the meaning is existential, formal, or valuational. Still another way to express the intensional types is to say that all epistemic meanings refer either to actualities, or to possibilities, or to obligations.

The nine generic classes of knowledge are obtained by pairing the three extensional degrees with the three intensional qualities. Each of these nine classes may now be briefly characterized and associated with the discipline or disciplines to which it applies.

SINGULAR FACT

The most elemental kind of knowing is the immediate awareness of another being (or of the self) in its concrete uniqueness. This is the kind of knowledge that Michael Polanyi calls "personal knowledge." It is what Martin Buber and other existentialist thinkers designate as the I-Thou relation—a relation they consider to be the ground of all meanings whatsoever. At this level of primordial relation, knowing and being are one. Henri Bergson intended the same kind of understanding in his concept of "intuition" as the means of coming into immediate sympathetic awareness of other beings in their singular wholeness.

The disciplines that are concerned with the knowledge of singular fact are existential philosophy, existential theology, existential psychology, and those elements in the literary enterprise (particularly in poetry, drama, and the novel) designed to portray unique personal encounters. Individual psychology and the various types of individual psychotherapy, counseling, and guidance also aim at an understanding of singular fact.

For want of a generally recognized term, the disciplines of singular fact may be designated by the term *synnoetics*, derived from the Greek syn- (together, with), noetic (insight, understanding), thus signifying direct relational knowledge.

SINGULAR FORM

Knowledge of singular forms constitutes the realm of *aesthetic* meanings. Aesthetic significance does not concern fact, or existence, but only ideality. The objects of aesthetic perception are unique and incomparable entities, enjoyed in and for themselves, without reference to any ulterior fact or consideration. What is perceived is an ideal abstraction, objectified in the object. But the meaning of the aesthetic experience is not in the facticity of the object; it is in the form of the ideated abstraction expressed by the object.

The various arts are the disciplines specifically devoted to the development of knowledge as singular form. The aesthetic disciplines differ according to the material used to objectify the expressive forms. Music uses sounds; painting and drawing use colors, contours, and light and shade; sculpture and architecture use masses, volumes, surfaces, and textures; the arts of movement use the positions, rhythms, and tensions of the human body; literature uses words. Whatever medium is employed, the aim of the arts is the production of unique compositions worthy of contemplation in their own right.

GENERAL FORM

In this class fall the disciplines that are concerned with forms in general, and not (as in the case of the arts) with forms in unique objects. Three main types of disciplines may be distinguished within this generic class. One type comprises the various ordinary languages, which are essentially conventional symbolic forms designed for purposes of communication. The forms of language are general in that the phonetic, morphological, and grammatical structures are standard patterns available for the expression of an indefinite variety of particular meanings.

Mathematics is the second type of discipline within the class of general forms. Formal logic also belongs in this class. Both disciplines deal with symbolic systems constructed on the basis of certain undefined terms and stipulated rules of formation and transformation. Here also the resulting formal structures are available for interpretation and application in an indefinite variety of particular cases.

The third type of general formal patterns may be designated by the term "nondiscursive symbolic conventions." These are not generally the basis for distinct disciplines in the way that the languages and mathematics are. They are usually regarded as parts of disciplines belonging primarily to other generic classes. Thus, the symbolisms of music and painting are developed in those arts. The symbolisms of myth and dreams are studied in connection with religion and psychoanalysis, respectively. The forms of gesture, ritual, ceremonial, and manners are generally not considered appropriate for disciplined inquiry, since they fall within the province of customary behavior and not of expert knowledge. Insofar as they are studied critically, they are most likely to be located in anthropology.

The entire class of general forms may be designated by the term *symbolics,* since all of the disciplines within this class have to do with systems of symbols, that is, with conventional formal patterns serving a general expressive function and pointing to meanings beyond themselves.

GENERAL FACT

When general forms become related to actuality, they express the kind of knowledge that is the special province of the sciences. This class may be designated by the term *empirics.* Knowledge in these disciplines relates to material truth and not (as in language, mathematics, and logic) to formal correctness. However, the goal in science is not the understanding of singular existents, as it is in the synnoetic realm, but the description and explanation of regularities. The empirical disciplines deal with generalizations that unite many particulars, with laws that describe certain invariant conjunctions of properties and certain probable sequences of events, and with general theories from which the laws can be deduced and that are productive of further hypotheses for inquiry.

The scientific disciplines form a hierarchy ordered according to the degree of generality of the abstractions used in the descriptions of phenomena. The physical sciences are the most general of all, being based on the metrical properties of all material things whatsoever. The life sciences are specialized to describe the properties of a relatively small part of the actual world, namely, of those things that are alive. Still more limited is the domain of minded things, studied in psychology. Most specific of all are the social sciences, in which the behavior of the organized human world is studied.

It should be added that the hierarchical order indicated above is not necessarily the one that will ultimately prevail. The organicists and panpsychists may eventually win out over the physicalists by demonstrating that the categories of life and mind are of even more general relevance than those of physical measurement.

SINGULAR NORM

This class comprises particular moral obligations. In the act of personal decision, within a given situation, one seeks for knowledge of what he really ought to do. The discipline of *morals* is concerned with the methods of making and justifying such decisions. The experts in this realm include the prophets and saints, who have served as exemplars of the human ideal.

GENERAL NORM

Generalizations concerning moral conduct and the development of moral principles are usually assigned to the discipline of *ethics*. Knowledge of singular norms and knowledge of general norms are commonly associated closely, since the latter is appealed to in justification of the former and the former is considered as the necessary source for the latter. Both singular and general norms are distinguished by the quality of obligation, setting them apart from both facts and formal conventions. While the ethical realm is not commonly divided into constituent disciplines, such a division is possible for theoretical analysis. For example, the methods and categories of social ethics differ from those of personal ethics, and each of these domains may be divided into ethical disciplines dealing with decisions in various aspects of life such as family, business, intellectual pursuits, technology, and political affairs.

COMPREHENSIVE FACT

The study of actuality from a comprehensive standpoint, including both the singularity of the unique event and the relationships of that event with other events, is the province of the discipline of *history*. It is the historian's task to tell what actually happened, in such a way as to take account of the existential decisions of those who lived in the past. In constructing his comprehensive account the historian has to employ knowledge in all the other classes. He is at once synnoetic, aesthetic, symbolic, empirical, and ethical, and these kinds of understanding are integrated by him into a *synoptic* perspective on what happened in the past.

COMPREHENSIVE FORM

A formal consideration of knowledge in all its kinds belongs to the discipline of *philosophy*. The philosopher's task is to interpret meanings in any realm or discipline by the use of concepts of wide generality, thus affording a synoptic view of all of the ways of knowing. If the philosopher is to be able to distinguish between aesthetic, scientific, moral, historical, and the other modes of understanding, he evidently requires a perspective that comprehends, or includes, them all.

COMPREHENSIVE NORM

When all kinds of knowledge are comprehended within a synoptic perspective controlled by the normative quality, the resulting discipline is *religion*. Religious knowledge is regarded as an apprehension of an Ultimate Good—a Harmony of the Whole, a Complete Truth—that is not contained in any of the more limited ways of knowing. Religious knowledge is usually thought to require an act of faith, by which a total personal commitment is made to what is regarded as ultimately worthy of devotion. In this essentially normative act all of the various classes of knowledge are synthesized: the elemental relations of singular fact, the general forms of word and symbol, the singular forms of aesthetic perception, the general facts of empirical science, the particular moral acts and the general ethical principles in which they participate, the integral understanding of the historical past, and the synoptic insight of philosophic interpretation.

The nine generic classes thus briefly characterized may be summarized in the following table:

The Generic Classes of Knowledge

Extension	Intension	Designation	Disciplines
Singular	Fact	Synnoetics	Philosophy, psychology, literature, and religion, in their existential aspects
Singular	Form	Aesthetics	Music, visual arts, the arts of movement, literature
General	Form	Symbolics	Ordinary language, mathematics, nondiscursive symbolic forms
General	Fact	Empirics	Physical sciences, life sciences, psychology, social sciences

Extension	Intension	Designation	Disciplines
Singular	Norm	Ethics	The various special areas of
General	Norm	Ethics	moral and ethical concern
Comprehensive	Fact	Synoptics	History
Comprehensive	Form	Synoptics	Philosophy
Comprehensive	Norm	Synoptics	Religion

The generic classes define the possible fundamental kinds of meaning. They provide the most inclusive categories of knowledge. They are important pedagogically because they describe the range of cognitive functions of which a person is capable and hence suggest the essential components of a curriculum for a complete person. Furthermore, a clear recognition of the logical features that define these fundamental patterns of meaning contributes signally to the effectiveness of instruction through transfer of learning, since the larger the scope of the congruence structures the greater the reduction in duplicated learning. It is of first importance that teachers and students understand what makes art art, language language, and science science—in short, what characterizes any class of knowledge as what it is and not some other class—so that the appropriate ways of knowing will be used with assurance, clarity, and skill.

The generic classes afford a logical basis for constructing the broad patterns of general education. They indicate the kinds of knowledge that are interchangeable for general curricular purposes and the kinds that are not. For example, a student may study either physics or anthropology in order to gain some sense of the empirical mode of understanding. He could not similarly interchange physics and mathematics or physics and history. Nor are existential psychology and experimental psychology interchangeable, since one is synnoetic and the other empirical. By studying all of the generic classes, the student is assured a complete and balanced education.

In the complete architectonics of knowledge the species-disciplines are arranged under the appropriate generic classes. The disciplines may further be subdivided into their several varieties, as described earlier. Each discipline or variety can be analyzed into a subordinate hierarchy of characteristic methods and concepts, ranging from the most general ones typifying the field of study as a whole (but less general than the logical features of the generic class) down to special subordinate features.

The architectonics of knowledge may thus be conceived as having three main components, each of which has distinctive pedagogical significance. The first component comprises the disciplines, the pedagogical significance of which is that they constitute the source for all curricular content—the basis for the civilized inheritance that educators should mediate. The second component comprises the characteristic methods and representative ideas defining the structure of the disciplines. These structural features provide the clue to the selection of instructional materials in such a way as to maximize the efficiency of teaching and learning. The third component comprises the basic patterns of meaning contained in the nine generic classes of knowledge. These classes provide a rationale of determining the scope of studies in general education and a basis for discriminating the most general structures that aid in transfer of learning.

The generic classes may also be used to define the possible logical modes of organizing instructional materials. Although the materials of instruction should all be drawn from the disciplines, they need not always be organized into distinct courses according to disciplines. The generic classes provide the possible general patterns of course organization. Each generic way of knowing is relevant both to the structure of what is taught and to the way in which whatever is taught may be organized. Thus the architectonics of knowledge provides a basis both for the selection and the ordering of the materials of instruction.

DISCUSSION OF DR. PHENIX'S PAPER

DR. BEREITER: I was struck by a similarity between the way you described disciplines and the way Professor Schwab described topics and commonplaces, both of them in terms of their ability to hold the interest of people over a certain period of time and generate new research. I was wondering whether you would accept grouping of these two together and, if so, I will add another part to my question. Are you not adding a good deal of surplus meaning when you treat these as disciplines and categories with the implication that they ought to fit into some formal logical structure, whereas if you treat them as topics they have a purely empirical status? They could be mutually exclusive or not. They could fit together into a hierarchy or not. You would never know until you tried.

DR. PHENIX: I am not sure that I know enough about Professor Schwab's "topics" and "commonplaces" to make this parallel. I am taking disciplines a lot more seriously than topics or commonplaces as normally understood. I do not, however, take the position that disciplines as I define them—by the historic communities that do generate productive inquiry—must fit into some neat hierarchial pattern. I want to leave room for all sorts of odd overlappings. One of the points I didn't get into the paper is the way the disciplines do as a matter of fact overlap in all sorts of ways. For instance, in the empirical disciplines symbolic and aesthetic ways of knowing are important elements. What this clearly indicates is that these classifications are not watertight; they are not pigeonholes into which one puts a discipline without any relation to any other discipline. You can't put disciplines into mutually exclusive categories. What I am doing is showing the dominant logical pattern in the respective disciplines.

DR. HANSON: Let me twist this another half turn. Early in Dr. Phenix's paper we read, "In fact, to assert that knowing depends on concern for structure is virtually a tautology, for knowledge consists in the recognition of relationships or patterns. So, to learn anything means to become familiar with its intelligible patterns." Again I would just like you to react to this: suppose a person says, "I know what salt tastes like," or "I know that John is next door." These seem to be relatively structureless. It's awfully difficult to see how they could be put into this total and intricate logical pattern that you are opting for here.

It says here that to know anything is to recognize it in terms of *patterns and relationships.* This is a very seductive position. Nonetheless it seems incompatible with the sorts of things that have been said in the history of thought about "simple ideas" and "simple knowledge." Thus my reference to knowing how salt tastes.

DR. PHENIX: It is also incompatible with what I appear to say about singular fact, namely, that there is no structure to the relationship. Structure is something that is abstracted from concrete relationships. I want only to emphasize the difference between the logic of singular confrontation—structure in that sense—and the logic of empirical generalization. This is really all I meant.

DR. BROUDY: I take it that you would distinguish the fact of "*A* knowing singular *X*" from the body of rules and principles (if any) by which one goes about getting *A* to know singular *X*. If you say that philosophy is the discipline which leads people to the knowledge of the singular, aren't you confusing philosophy with some branch of psychology or some form of clinical practice?

DR. PHENIX: I agree that knowledge of singulars belongs to certain practitioners in psychology—particularly the clinical psychologists.

DR. BROUDY: Would you let me ask it this way? Would you characterize this as character training?

DR. PHENIX: Character training has to do with the normative disciplines primarily, but it builds on the singular facts.

DR. BROUDY: This morning Professor Schwab called this character training. This is not getting knowledge.

DR. PHENIX: Character training belongs to what I call singular and general norms.

DR. BROUDY: In order to get it you would insist on the singular fact in addition to the norm.

DR. PHENIX: I maintain that singular fact comes first, that there isn't any norm that doesn't depend upon the singular existential facts.

DR. BROUDY: Yes, I am not arguing with that. I am thinking of it in terms of curriculum design or pattern. You would say that somewhere in the curriculum the student should be confronted with singular facts as well as categories and structures. Now who does this? Tell us who does this: is it the discipline or the norm of the character builder?

DR. PHENIX: Guidance counseling is the nearest thing to a professional discipline dealing with singular fact.

DR. BROUDY: And also the person who teaches literature.

DR. PHENIX: Yes.

DR. SCHWAB: It goes further than that, Phil. A very good teacher who can force a confrontation between a student and an immediate sensual experience—if only of a falling body—is providing the sort of immediate experience that will later constitute knowledge which is *general*.

DR. HANSON: The paradigm example of this, then, will be the laboratory supervisor, the man who shows you a typical titration or who rubs your nose into something obvious somewhere on the bench. Is this wrong?

DR. SCHWAB: Yes.

DR. HANSON: Why?

DR. PHENIX: Let me come back to Martin Buber, because he is my prime source here. He talks about the idea of relation, not only with respect to persons but to things. For example, Buber speaks of seeing trees and stars, not analytically, in categories, but personally; not in abstract realization, but with a sense of immediacy. I know it sounds romantic, but I simply don't see how one can leave this out.

DR. HANSON: Well, that's why one uses examples of titration. It's either red or green or orange; the kid has got to pick this up. If he's color-blind he can't do it; that seems to be the heart of all this.

DR. KRUG: My difficulty is in your classification of history. I have great difficulty in your definitions. You say, "History comprises pure knowledge." I don't think that history is pure nor comprises the knowledge of such. The difficulty is that there are no hard facts in history or reality in history beyond the investigator, and for that reason it is really subjective—the investigator's subjective appraisal of facts. I have very great difficulty as a historian in accepting your suggestion that the historian actually asks us to tell what happened. The great majority of historians have never accepted that we really know what actually happened. What actually happened for Beard in the New Deal is something entirely different from what happened for Hofstadter.

DR. PHENIX: I couldn't agree with you more completely. I didn't classify history under empirical fact; it is not general facts. I put it in *comprehensive* fact. The historian is concerned with knowledge of what happened. How does he know what happened? Here he must be comprehensive. He must use empirical facts and generalizations, but he must also tell a good story, and this involves the aesthetic element. Normative factors enter in deciding what is significant and what is not significant. The historian also has to decide about symbolic factors—the language forms appropriate to the story of the past. In this sense history is a comprehensive or synoptic discipline.

DR. SCHWAB: That really has nothing do with actuality or the study of actuality.

DR. HANSON: He can't tell lies can he?

DR. SCHWAB: He did his best.

DR. KRUG: Historians look at the same actuality and see it from entirely different points of view.

DR. PHENIX: True, but they are trying to assess the evidence. The point is that evidence counts. History is not a free construction. It is not an art. The historian uses artistic devices, but is supposed to say what happened. He recreates what must have happened, putting himself in the mind of the persons who made past decisions, taking account of ethical presuppositions and the cultural background. The relationships to other events and other persons are also included in the data from which the decisions were made. To refer to the constituents in the making of past decisions seems to me to be the way to defend assertions about what happened.

DR. HANSON: Consider the recent exchange (October, 1963) between Jack Plum and Will Durant in the Book Review Section of *The New York Times*. There were five points which served as Plum's indictment of Will Durant. One of them concerns, as Jack Plum put it, *a question of fact*, whether some particular of action took place in Coventry or in London. Now here's an issue on which Durant had to back down.

DR. KRUG: Dr. Hanson, did you read his answer really? He said that this fact really wasn't important.

DR. HANSON: Ah, yes, but he granted that he was wrong.

DR. KRUG: He said that it was absolutely unimportant. He would not even bother to correct the . . . .

DR. HANSON: But that is incompatible with Phenix. The *evaluation* is a different point.

DR. PHIL SMITH: I wonder if we could undercut this discussion by suggesting that your periodic table amounts to a kind of unpacking of what's involved in your original acceptance, as "given," of such primitives as fact, form, and norm? I wonder if you would address yourself briefly to why it is you see these as "given"? I mean, what is so "given" about them?

DR. PHENIX: You mean why these three intentions and not others that one might choose? I analyzed the logical structures of various disciplines to see if there were some common threads that would provide a basis of classification. The fact, form, norm triad seemed to encompass all the disciplines, as a very general logical basis of categorizing.

DR. PHIL SMITH: Are you suggesting then that these things have an empirical cast to them; that you discovered them; that they are actually "out there" rather than that they arose as your creation out of the impact of your looking at the data?

DR. PHENIX: Yes.

DR. BEREITER: I wonder if the distinction between fact and form doesn't break down at the singular level. I just can't see what is different in any sense in coming to know individual persons and coming to know an individual statue or musical composition. In one case you can separate the form out from the substance and in the other you can't. But this seems to be a trivial difference in the context of your exposition.

DR. PHENIX: It seems to me to be one of the errors of the modern age that we have aestheticized the inner personal relation. I am suggesting instead that it is not a matter of perception, but a matter of the reality of the relationship. The encounter with the individual person is unique, like an aesthetic perception, but it is not, like perception, the essentially subjective perception of a formal structure. One is concrete and the other is abstract. The singular form is an abstraction; the singular fact is a concretion.

DR. BURNETT: It seems to me that although you may have exhausted the categories given, the way of setting them up, one of the categories that you are talking about is really not needed. What you are talking about is having an experience, as it were, but at the same time you are trying to call it a discipline. There is a difference. I think that this category is superfluous, if we are talking about disciplines. To have the experience is not to have a discipline.

DR. PHENIX: One can have the experience in a disciplined fashion. Also one can have any of these experiences in an undisciplined fashion. One can have aesthetic experiences, but in an undisciplined way. One can have moral experiences, but in an undisciplined way. One can have historical knowledge of what happened in the past, but in an undisciplined way. I maintain also that it is possible to have what I call a synnoetic experience in an undisciplined way.

DR. BURNETT: Yes, but to have an experience in a disciplined way is still to have an experience, and when you start talking about the discipline you lose the quality of the experience in the structuring or analysis of the experience. A pig satisfied and Socrates satisfied, they are both having an experience. Now if we start ranking experiences—well, I join certain ones saying Socrates' experience is better. But Socrates is not analyzing—to have the experience is one thing and to analyze it another.

DR. PHENIX: Within any one of these ways of knowing there may be all levels of proficiency. A discipline is defined by a group of people who have become productively proficient in a particular way of knowing and who articulate and encourage understanding in that way.

DR. BURNETT: To articulate and to encourage goes beyond . . . .

DR. MARTIN: Excuse me. Would this be your point in answer to that question? Having the experience is not the discipline, but could not you say that discipline is defined in terms of the proposition sought, so that it is apparent you are seeking a fact of a general kind, and when you are seeking that kind of a proposition then that is kind of a defined position. Would that be correct?

DR. HANSON: No, I don't think that is what Phenix says. He claims a discipline to be a *group* of people. It sounds like a sociological term. Yet it could make perfectly good sense to speak of a discipline that no one is practicing at a given time. Experimental psychology was a *discipline* three hundred years ago before there were any experimental psychologists. A person could have referred to it as an area of inquiry, which might very well be explored some day. People could do that now.

DR. PHENIX: I am using the term discipline in a sociological as well as a logical sense. My test for a discipline is whether or not it has actually produced knowledge. I might also say that new disciplines can emerge and old disciplines may fall into disuse.

DR. SCHWAB: Now what does it produce, Phil? What does this first group produce? What kind of propositions have they produced?

Dr. Phenix: Singular fact?

Dr. Martin: Give us an example of the kind of fact that these people have produced, the singular.

Dr. Phenix: I mean instances of loving relationship and self-understanding.

Dr. Martin: Give us a case—now I can understand what you mean when you say the counselor aide produces an encounter, let's say, with reality. The student's thought was this, "Through these procedures I see that I am to blame," or something like that. Now the counselor can say, "On Monday morning I produced the singular fact that John Jones came to a realization of his predicament." The people who do this will then accumulate these facts and organize them, or will they just stop right then and there?

Dr. Phenix: They will develop a vocabulary to talk about the unique encounter, rather than about generalizations that apply to things that are not unique.

Dr. Schwab: When Aristotle writes a book called "Ethics" he defines ethics as a practical science, a practice which has to do with ultimate particulars. However, the book called "Ethics" is not a practical science in that sense. It is *talk* about the practical. This is to say that to assign immediate awareness to *one* discipline is to cheat all the rest of your disciplines of their basic raw materials.

Dr. Phenix: No. I am not saying that people whose expertise is in symbolics—e.g., mathematicians and linguists—can't give their formal structures to the sciences or use their linguistic structures for the arts or for literature. What I am saying is: the synnoetician is expert at recognizing and articulating unique experiences. He can call them by name and he can also serve other disciplines that depend on such experiences.

Dr. Ausubel: First I want to make a favorable comment about the nonimperialistic implications of the speaker's statement that "attention to the structure of knowledge in the disciplines is certainly not a sufficient condition for learning to occur." It would certainly be very easy to assert that the structure of knowledge is the *only* relevant variable with respect to learning a discipline.

Then I want to raise a question concerning your conceptualization about transfer to see whether or not I make an unwarranted inference about your meaning here. You say, "He may thus concentrate on teaching the ways of knowing rather than multiplying particular elements in knowledge without reference to their membership in classes of similar elements." The implication that I get from this is that the *only* basis for transfer in paying attention to the structure of knowledge is epistemological in nature. That is, what is transferred, once one knows the structure of knowledge, is *ways of knowing.* Do you preclude the possibility of transfer on the basis of the substantive aspects of knowledge? That is, can knowledge of particular subject matter content facilitate the learning of other subject matter content purely on a substantive basis.

DR. PHENIX: I did not mean ways of knowing as verbal statements about the kinds of knowledge. What I really meant was that the substantive materials used in teaching should be chosen in such a way as to be paradigmatic or representative of the ways of knowing. Transfer is a matter of homology between things to be learned whether that homology is expressed in abstractions or in concrete exemplifications. I would want to include both of those.

DR. ARNSTINE: There are a number of ways of coming to a decision as to whether or not we can live with this particular arrangement of human enterprises. It has already been suggested that this might be assessed as to whether or not your categories actually refer to anything in our experience. I would like to try another possible way of seeing whether or not we can live with this. Suppose we ask whether the categories that you offer have any utility in making decisions about the curriculum—what to include and what not to include. And I have a specific question respecting this way of approaching your categories. You indicate that your generic classes have "a logical basis for constructing the broad patterns of general education." Then you go on to say that these "indicate the kinds of knowledge that are interchangeable for general curricular purposes and the kinds that are not." Then you go on to suggest certain kinds of interchangeability. Each one of the categories represents several traditional disciplines in the category of general forms, for example, mathematics, languages, and some other things. Now I am sure you don't really mean that we can teach *either* math *or* language—that we take our pick. So if you are going to have a criterion for whether or not you are going to teach one or the other, neither or both, I should think you would have to go outside of your categories in order to make your choice. If you have to go outside the categories, then I would want to ask, of what use are the categories? Earlier, you say, "the goal of instruction is to teach knowledge as efficiently as possible." But that still doesn't tell us which knowledge to teach. Well, I am wondering where you are going to find a criterion for deciding what to teach even after you have all the disciplines lined up in all nine categories.

DR. PHENIX: I certainly would not want to say one could teach *either* mathematics or language. Both of them are essential in general education. If one takes my other example—physics and anthropology—I wouldn't like to be forced into choosing one of them for the curriculum. But I do say that either physics or anthropology can give some sense of fact, hypothesis, empirical evidence, theory, and explanation—all of which belong to any empirical discipline. But these things could not be learned in the study of music. What I am getting at in a very large sense is the vital elements in the intellectual or educational diet. There must be some things in everybody's learning without which he is seriously crippled. What I am asking is that no student should simply study music and painting and perhaps language and never have any sense about the meaning of science.

DR. ARNSTINE: This follows and it makes a lot of sense. But I wonder whether a person could arrive at that conclusion without your categories and, in fact, make better arguments for a certain sort of balance within the curriculum by using categories other than those you suggest. Your own example of music and physical sciences and anthropology really isn't derived from your categories but rather from another set.

DR. PHENIX: I think that unless you have some other name for what I call empirics, aesthetics, and so on you couldn't make those discriminations as confidently. To be sure, I began with notions of what the disciplines are and with an understanding that there is a homology of structure between physics and anthropology that does not prevail between physics and music. I don't care what you call it, but I think you are going to end up with certain very large realms or classes of meaning.

DR. ARNSTINE: I am wondering this: say I am setting up my curriculum in school and I want to make sure that each of the nine categories gets some representation, and I find that I am going to teach the arts in category No. 1, singular facts; No. 2, singular forms; No. 3, singular norms—and then someone says aesthetics also belongs in your category No. 5, which is, I guess, singular norms. I find my curriculum overbalanced with the arts because they keep popping up in different categories. Then I have to start making arbitrary cut-offs again, but on what criteria?

DR. PHENIX: My criteria are the functional criteria of whether you learn a particular kind of knowing. I am not concerned whether synnoetics, for example, is learned in existential psychology or as part of literature.

DR. HANSON: I am really confused with Phenix's term *discipline* because for him disciplines are collections of chaps. I would say that Maxwell's electrodynamics encompassed other subordinate disciplines such as Faraday's work on electricity and classical optics. I don't mean encompassing them in a way a building could encompass them, or as a fog might envelope them, but rather the encompassment that more general ideas and theories have over more restricted ones. Now you are quite right to take issue with the unfulfilled hypothetical character of my earlier examples; but one can always refer to "disciplines" such that *if* there were someone to articulate them they would form a sort of coherent doctrine. Think of space medicine in 1850. Let's consider also the disciplines that constitute anthropology as it is now. One is not really talking about the *fellows* who practice but rather about the things it consists of *in principle*. That was Martin's point about the proposition. That's the only viable way one can think of the interrelationship between disciplines.

DR. PHENIX: I buy this entirely. It's simply that I want to find out where to look for these materials, and so I have to look in journals, in professional societies, in university institutes, and in other places where the products and processes of disciplined inquiry may be seen.

DR. HANSON: Think of the Rosetta Stone. Suppose the Rosetta Stone had been a recapitulation of something in the last issue of the *Physical Review*. You wouldn't know anything about the chaps who did it. You might call all this a discipline because you can notice (after decoding) that it has logical interconnections with other subordinate disciplines.

DR. PHENIX: But I also want these logical interconnections to be such that they are productive. This is my basic idea. The discipline has to lead somewhere. And the only way it can lead somewhere is to see whether it does prove to be in a historical sense conducive to the generation of professional societies, journals, and the like.

DR. HANSON: But even that can be independent of the chaps!

ADJOURNMENT

CHAPTER III

THE STRUCTURE OF KNOWLEDGE IN THE ARTS

HARRY S. BROUDY

William Carlos Williams once wrote:
> It is difficult
> To get news from poems,
> Yet men die miserably every day
> For lack
> Of what is found there.[1]

That sums up the paradoxical situation with respect to the question of knowledge in the arts. Although by the customary interpretation of the customary criteria art appreciation cannot qualify as knowledge, the conviction persists that some works of art are "saying" something and often something important. The problem, both with respect to a particular work of art and art in general, has to do with what is being "said" and how the communication is being accomplished.

In education the problem of the structure of knowledge in the arts is important for several reasons:

a. If art does not add to the knowledge of the pupil in any important sense, then the justification and methods for teaching

---

[1] William Carlos Williams, *The Desert Music and Other Poems* (Random House, 1954).

it must be found in a change of attitude or behavior of which the work of art is presumably a cause.

b. The answer to question (a) determines what can be said *about* art in art education of one kind or another. At least some statements commonly made about art, namely, statements about what the work of art purports to say, would be ruled out if the work of art, in fact, says nothing.

c. If the school is to choose among works of art as more or less "good," there will have to be defensible criteria for making the choice. If works of art say nothing important about what is important, then this criterion, at least, is ruled out.

TYPES OF KNOWLEDGE IN ART

To begin with, when one speaks of knowledge in connection with a work of art the reference may be to:

a. The making of a work of art, as when a poem or a concerto is created. One can ask what an artist has to know in order to make a work of art. Plato, in Book X of the *Republic*, thought that with a good eye for superficial resemblances the artist could dispense with profound knowledge of the subjects he was "imitating." Some novelists, on the other hand, claim that they must acquire a first-hand knowledge of the people and events they write about. Shakespeare is credited with a profound knowledge of human nature. Cézanne is often credited with "knowing" that nature's forms are combinations of the cube, sphere, and cylinder.

There is, then, some difference of opinion as to the importance of the artist's knowledge about what he is presenting or representing in a work of art. Surely Plato was right in his contention that one can make an image of a bed without knowing how to make the bed itself but, on the other hand, the ability to make a bed or the knowledge of human nature does not guarantee the ability to make images of these objects. Where the work of art does not claim to represent or present anything outside the artist's feelings or impressions, the problem of his knowledge *about* the content of the work of art, if I am not mistaken, becomes irrelevant, if not meaningless.

b.   There is less controversy about the know-how of the artist. Some instances of modern poetry, painting, and drama to the contrary notwithstanding, artists *are* concerned with problems of technique. For one thing, their training, more often than not, has been involved with technique: of how to use the medium to achieve certain effects. Further, even with the greatest freedom in composition and painting, an artist develops his own way of being free, so that we do not readily mistake the painting of Marc Chagall for that of Jackson Pollock, the music of John Cage for that of Alban Berg, or the sculpture of Moore for that of Brancusi. To the student of art these differences are readily evident and quite frequently are expressed as differences in technique. As for Croce's contention that the materialization of the aesthetic intuition is aesthetically of little importance, this did not convince even his fellow idealist, Bosanquet.[2]

No great mystery therefore shrouds these two kinds of knowledge in the arts. Knowing about one's subject and knowing how to use a technique are not peculiar to painters, poets, and composers. The carpenter, the stone mason, and the teacher also utilize these kinds of knowledge in the practice of their respective crafts. It is of some significance to note that controversies about the proper training of craftsmen usually revolve around the proper proportions of each of these kinds of knowledge in the curriculum. Some want more knowledge about life and reality and less technique, some stress technique with a minimum of knowledge, and some who wish to elevate a craft into a profession want more of both.

In art education the problem is complicated by the role of technical competence, or at least knowledge about technique, in

---

[2] Benedetto Croce, *The Breviary of Aesthetic* (Houston, Texas: Rice Institute Pamphlets, 1915), II, 4, or Douglas Ainslie (trans.), *The Essence of Aesthetics* (London: W. Heinemann, 1921). Bernard Bosanquet, "Croce's Aesthetic," *Mind*, XXIX (1920), 212–215, and *Three Lectures on Aesthetic* (London: Macmillan, 1915), Ch. 2.

appreciation. Does painting pictures help one to appreciate pictures one did not paint? Does the writing of poems pave the way for the appreciation of the poems to be studied in school? Since the meaning of "appreciation" is far from clear, it is not easy to answer this question. If appreciation includes admiration for the dexterity of the artist, then trying to produce art helps us to admire those who can do well what we ourselves botch. If appreciation includes just and informed criticism, then knowing, for example, how tempera and fresco paintings are produced, will inhibit judgments not appropriate to these types of painting. Knowing something about how atonal music is written promotes patience with sounds that sometimes cause anguish. Perhaps know-how serves appreciation by making it easier for the appreciator to get into the proper posture for perceiving whatever it is the work of art presents.

c. Another kind of knowledge about the arts is so clearly knowledge in the conventional sense of the term that it will be sufficient at this point merely to make note of it. Historical knowledge about works of art comprises the history of artists, accounts of developments of the arts and of individual art objects.

I am distinguishing here historical knowledge *about* art from art criticism and philosophy of art, even though one can hardly carry on the latter without some knowledge of the former. Nevertheless, one can imagine some historian undertaking to trace the origins of a poem or a set of poems without having any particular interest in the nature of poetry or an appraisal of it. Indeed, such a historian could write an acceptable Ph.D. thesis as the result of such an enterprise. By recording and sorting all the things that had been said about his particular objects of inquiry he could, without holding a theory or an opinion of his own, become an authority of sorts.

In art, as in other fields, a sound knowledge of history is the best defense against narrowness and foolishness. For it is silly to praise an artist only to discover that he did not produce the works attributed to him or that they were produced by his apprentice. Judgments about style and influence should also be solidly rooted in fact so far as the facts can be ascertained. Further, historical adequacy empowers the critic and philosopher to make appropriate comparisons and contrasts with regard to styles and periods that, in turn, sharpen discrimination and judgment.

Accordingly, the history of art exhibits a knowledge structure no different from the history of anything else. Nor does it present any peculiar pedagogical difficulty. Like other historical materials it runs the risk of either being on the dull side so far as the ordinary pupil is concerned or inaccurately exciting. The pedagogical problem lies rather in the relation between historical knowledge about art and the aesthetic experience of art.

d. Knowledge about the content which the artist presents, knowing how to present it, and knowledge about artists and works of art are important and necessary for the production and appreciation of art. Nevertheless, if this were the whole story, we would not as philosophers or as educators be interested in it. Everything that has been said so far about art could be said about the making and appreciating of coins, or stamps, or rocking chairs. If fine art had remained solidly integrated with the handicrafts, as it probably once was, the problem of knowledge in the arts would not arise.

It does arise because in our culture a work of art is created or presumed to be created for a distinctive purpose, and once created it acquires a being of its own with a special value of its own. That special value may lie in the delight it affords, the interest it commands, and, possibly, in the price it can bring. In some cases, however, the value is attributed to a work of art because it allegedly "says" something or expresses something that has to do with life at its most important level. Consider for example the following statement:

Music "expresses in a concentrated way the shocks and instabilities, the conflicts and resolutions, that are the dramatic changes enacted upon the more enduring background of nature and human life. The tension and the struggle has its gathering of energy, its discharges, its attacks and defenses, its mighty war-rings and its peaceful meetings, its resistances and its resolutions, and out of these things music weaves its web."[3]

Or when Paul Tillich says that "All arts create symbols for a level of reality which cannot be reached in other ways."[4]

Such terms as "significant form," "expressiveness," and "com-munication" indicate that a work of art is making some cognitive claim; that not only is it an object in its own right, but that it also discloses, reveals, or illuminates something special. The nature of this something and the mode of its disclosure constitute an in-triguing theoretical question about art and the locus of the mys-tery is the aesthetic experience. Somewhere in the artistic trans-action the artist and the appreciator undergo an experience which is at the heart of both the making of a work of art and the ap-preciation of it. It is with the knowledge-structure of this aesthetic experience that one must sooner or later grapple.

COGNITION IN THE AESTHETIC EXPERIENCE

Insofar as the aesthetic experience is a mode of cognition it belongs primarily to perception. On philosophical grounds, Kant argued that unless the sensa are in some Gestalt or pattern they will not be perceived, and unless sensa clusters are interpreted by a categorial schema as being this kind of thing or that, or mean-ing this or that kind of object, the sensa will not be understood. In this sense the aesthetic experience is no different from any other perception. If it differs from other types of perception, it is in the way the sensory content, its relational schema, and its categorical structures are interpreted.

a. The sensory elements in scientific and practical percep-tion are used as clues to achieving knowledge and action, re-

___

[3] John Dewey, *Art as Experience* (New York: Minton, Balch & Co., 1934), p. 236. (See p. 195 for a lyric passage on art as revealing reality as unity of all things.)
[4] Paul Tillich, *Systematic Theology* (Chicago: Univ. of Chicago Press, 1951), I, 42.

spectively. The redness of a rose, for example, helps to identify the type of rose we are dealing with or to decide whether or not we shall choose it for the flower arrangement on the table. But only insofar as the redness is attended to for the sake of perceiving it as redness does redness figure in aesthetic perception. Thus it is that in some works of art the attention-compelling qualities of the sounds, textures, or colors are its most notable features. In perception whose goal is primarily knowledge or prosperous action, on the contrary, the particular quality of the sensory elements is not important in its own right. Black figures on a white dial and white figures on a black dial are equally good, if they give the same information with the same ease.

b. With regard to the relational elements by virtue of which the sensa are intuited as a pattern, one can say with Kant that space and time are forms of sensuous intuition in aesthetic perception as in other types. Certainly it is difficult to imagine images apart from spatial and temporal frameworks. The primary difference lies in the fact that formal properties are important in works of art not only as means to heightening perceptual effects, but also as perceptually interesting on their own account.

c. Scientific and practical perception interpret their sensa by use of categories that organize them for knowledge or for use. The chief goal of the interpretation is to relate the object or the cluster of sensa to other objects in some predictable fashion or as a means to some end. The interpretive phase of aesthetic perception, however, has ground rules of its own. First of all, whatever is perceived must be perceived as being located in the object. It cannot be perceived as located in one's memory or in some organ of sense within the body. Second, the interpretation always entails a displacement of modality. Sometimes this means that an auditory stimulus is interpreted as having visual or kinaesthetic qualities, as when a melody is described as jerky or bright. More often, however, the displacement is from secondary qualities of color, sound, and shape to tertiary ones such as are connoted by the adjectives cheerful, exciting, angry, sublime, sad, melancholy, etc. George Santayana regarded this form of displacement as distinctive of aesthetic perception, saying that it must always be a perception of value, never a mere noting of characteristics.[5]

Why certain patterns of sound and color have come to symbolize emotional states is a matter for anthropological and psychological inquiry. The fact is that they do even for untutored persons and that, therefore, they are expressive.

That the expression is not achieved by a proposition or set of propositions does not invalidate the claim of a work of art to be a source of information. The artist, says Dewey, has to think in terms of qualities. "To think effectively in terms of relations of qualities is as severe a demand upon thought as to think in terms of symbols, verbal and mathematical."[6]

The word ouch is not a sentence and, therefore, strictly speaking, not a statement, but that one can infer information about the utterer would not be denied.[7] How does a sound such as "ouch" become a source of information? By furnishing the hearer with a minor premise to the following syllogism:

All persons crying "ouch" are suffering pain;

This person is saying "ouch";

This person is suffering pain.

The major premise is a generalization from experience with pain in our culture.

Or a picture of a storm at sea becomes a source of information insofar as the picture resembles or purports to resemble

---

[5] George Santayana, *The Sense of Beauty* (New York: Scribner, 1896). For further and similar distinctions among modes of perception, see Iredell Jenkins, *Art and the Human Enterprise* (Cambridge, Mass.: Harvard Univ. Press, 1958), pp. 23–24, and Virgil C. Aldrich, "Chess Not Without the Queen," *Proceedings and Addresses of the American Philosophical Association,* 1957–1958.

[6] *Ibid.*, p. 46, 73, and David W. Ecker, "The Artistic Process as Qualitative Problem Solving," *The Journal of Aesthetics and Art Criticism,* XXI:3 (Spring, 1963), 283–290.

[7] That nondiscursive symbols can be cognitive is the burden of Susanne K. Langer's *Philosophy in a New Key* (Cambridge, Mass.: Harvard Univ. Press, 1942). This book has been especially influential with music educators, if frequency of quotation is any indication of influence.

storms in general or some storm in particular. Loud rolls on the drums are clues to thunderclaps in musical compositions because they resemble the sounds of thunder.

We can also glean information from expressions that by convention are clues or signals to the recipient. Thus the expression "How do you do?" in a greeting is not a genuine inquiry but rather a hint that the greeter is still a friend, or at least not in the advanced stages of hostility.

There is little doubt that works of art convey meanings by these uses of signs, but it is generally agreed that these instances are not what the controversy is about. The trouble is that in art the expressive elements or their totality must convey more than a literal resemblance and do more than trigger a random or conventional association. Further, the aesthetic response must not be the organic reflex to pain, but the apprehension of a logical expression of pain. The picture is asked to present a symbol that in color *looks* painful and in music *sounds* painful; it must locate pain where it cannot, in common sense, ever be found.

The work of art is expected to stimulate the perception of a meaning that, according to Iredell Jenkins, sharpens our insight into the actual character of things. If so, the actual character must be conveyed by the work of art and, since the thing is not in the work of art literally, it must be there as the form of the actual thing. And since this form is not the concept of the thing and not the literal imitation of it, it must be a metaphorical image, i.e., the representation of feelings, emotions, insights, and even ideas as sounds, colors, shapes, and motions.

How this can happen is still a matter of much theorizing. Virtually every aesthetic theory has some hypothesis as to why a poetic line, a colored shape, a gesture in a dance can symbolize in a way that is neither a literal reference, on the one hand, nor a more or less logically reconstructible association of ideas, on the other.

The fact that so many theories—that of Freud, Bergson, Reed, Jung, Cassirer, Langer, among many others—keep returning to myth, ritual, and legend as the source of the power of artistic symbolism leads one to conjecture that it is in the interpretive phase of perceptual experience that we shall probably find the significant difference from other modes of perception.

According to Kant, the interpretive phase of experience is structured by two systems of a priori operation. First, time and space as the forms of intuition organize sensa into some schematic design, and second, organization is affected by the categories of indentity, exclusion, causality, and the like. To qualify as experience at all, sensory stimuli must first pass these two gatekeepers and *put on* their perceptible and intelligible costumes, so to speak.[8]

Leaving aside the question of the a priorism of these interpretive operations, it seems as if in aesthetic experience the forms of sensuous intuition may apply as they do in ordinary perception, but instead of the intellectual categories by which the sensa are organized conceptually, we now use imaginative schemata, and these, according to the theories referred to above, are the root metaphors to be found in myth, rite, legend, and dreams. Presumably all members of the race, either by nature or nurture, have available archetypal images by virtue of which the artist can speak to them through the images he creates.

If it is asked why so archaic a mode of communication survives, the answer might be that there is no way even now of speaking precisely and conceptually about the subjective realm of life. This realm is incorrigibly teleological and can be understood only in dramatic terms—of agents and opponents, beginnings, climaxes, and resolutions. If this theory makes sense, then we can understand why in the aesthetic perception we cognize (interpret) not by recognizing a class to which our specimen belongs or by bringing into consciousness an idea associated in our previous experience with it. Rather, we cognize by recogniz-

[8] *Critique of Pure Reason*, Transcendental Analytic, First Division. Also see D. W. Gotshalk, *Art and the Social Order* (Chicago: Univ. of Chicago Press, 1947), 17–20.

ing in the image before us the very meaning that excited some racial ancestor to perceive it as something of unusual significance.

This hypothesis has some other consequences that it might be proper to mention without extensive discussion. One is that it helps to explain why response to art is, in one sense, universal and, in another, highly differential. Just being alive and living in a culture guarantee that the individual will be stirred by the metaphors of art. Fire will excite him, the moon mystify him, and the swelling of the tides fill him with awe. Art, using culture images of heroes and dragons, great adventures and escapes, will stir him even in childhood. Great rapes, battles with giants, struggles with angels, transformations of men into animals and trees need no sophisticated percipients in order to function in the aesthetic experience.

On the other hand, T. S. Eliot's *The Waste Land* or Dante's *Divine Comedy* are not for untutored readers. The great myths by being used in art become elaborated and refined, so that knowledge of these works is presupposed in many of their successors. For example, in line 408 of *The Waste Land* we read: "Or in memories draped by the beneficent spider."

As an image this stands on its own feet, yet in a note Eliot remarks anent this line: "Cf. Webster, *The White Devil*, V, vi: '. . . they'll remarry/ Ere the worm pierce your winding-sheet, ere the spider/ Make a thin curtain for your epitaphs.' " Here is a familiar case of an image being used again and again not only because spider webs suggest curtain making but also because poets read poetry.

Relevant to aesthetic education is the fact that when artists presuppose familiarity on the part of the percipient with certain root metaphors, their art is likely to become unsuitable for a generation that no longer has this familiarity. Thus poetry and other works of art that depend on the root imagery of Latin words, as in the case of Milton, or on familiarity with the Bible or Greek mythology are robbed of much of their impact if this background is missing. Hence the copious footnotes and glosses needed to teach Shakespeare, Milton, and perhaps even the literature of the last century as well.[9]

To summarize: the ground rules for qualifying as a genuine aesthetic experience are that it be predominantly an instance of perception rather than discursive reasoning or memory, that whatever is expressed be expressed in a symbol that embodies or presents the meaning rather than merely refers to it, and that the satisfaction or interest aroused by it shall be traceable to its sensory, formal, and expressive properties.

These requirements are reminiscent of the classical conditions for knowledge. Aristotle argued that certainty presupposed the *formal* identity of the object and the knower and explicated the psychological and epistemological apparatus that would account for such an identity. While modern theories of knowledge are chary of such demands and are willing to settle for far less than certainty in knowing, the ideal seems to linger on in theories of aesthetic experience. In the work of art par excellence reality is captured in an image and this form being identical with, or at least analogically identical with, certain life forms unites the perceiver imaginatively with the aesthetic object conveyed by the work of art. It may be profitable to explore this parallel a little further.

The meaning of knowledge, it seems to me, still entails some direct grasping of the object either in perception or by means of concepts or both. All other modes of knowing are approximations to the ideal situation in which the mind and the object are one. It is certainty that makes probability probable.

From the first, however, it has been clear that there is no certain way of knowing that the mind has achieved this unity except when it confined itself to juggling concepts it had itself

[9] On the role of myth, metaphor, rite, and language in art, cf., Langer, *op. cit.*, chs. 6, 7, 9. Also S. K. Langer (trans.), Ernst Cassirer, *Language and Myth* (New York: Harper, 1946). For a good sampling of selections from Freud, Jung, Bergson, Christopher Caudwell, and Nietzche, see Melvin Rader, *A Modern Book of Esthetics* (3rd ed.; New York: Holt, Rinehart and Winston, 1960).

constructed and defined. In matters of fact, however, the fallibility of sensory processes, while it did not rule out the possibility of certainty, cast a shadow on claims to certainty that no theory has ever dispelled.

To get around the difficulties imposed by the fallibility of sense, a superior faculty of intellectual intuition was proposed that would directly apprehend the essences of things and their relations. Not infrequently, as in Plato and Descartes, the condition for the illumination of the mind and the real was a state of purified receptivity. For Plato this meant a long period of training and discipline in the lesser forms of knowing and in the control of the passions. In Descartes systematic doubting until all possible subjective distortions are peeled away prepares for the moment of certainty. Bacon sought to exorcise idols of various kinds including those imposed by the peculiarities of one's culture. In all of these theories the moment of truth or illumination is not only a kind of knowing, but also a state of being that is supposed to provide a criterion by which to judge the claims of all subsequent "revelations." To the confirmed skeptic, however, "self-evidence" has always meant "no evidence."

The subjective determinants in cognition were regarded as inimical to knowledge not because they were in the person, but rather because they were peculiar to the person and therefore a threat to the claim of true statements to be universal. Subjective factors interpose themselves between the mind and the object and distort it. The skeptical, albeit optimistic, conclusion has therefore been drawn (a) that no freedom from distortion can be complete or (b) that distortions are all that we can have and (c) that truth can safely be defined as the distortions destined to be agreed upon by all competent observers. Whether the competent observer is one who finally gets rid of the distortions or the one with the right set of distortions is left open or dismissed as a fruitless question.

Nevertheless, the removal of distortions remains important in the cognitive and educative enterprise. Scientific method is one way of standardizing distortion or discounting it, and something of the same sort but on a different plane is suggested as a condition for creativity by Abraham Maslow. In his study of peak experiences, Maslow notes that they exhibit such characteristics as giving up the past and future, loss of ego, loss of self-consciousness, lessening of defenses and inhibitions, acceptance, strong aesthetic perception instead of abstraction, and trust *versus* trying and controlling.[10] These conditions of creativity resemble the conditions for achieving nondiscursive knowledge in that they mark the removal of the distorting conditions of self and culture.

There are then similarities between the creative attitude, the ground rules for the aethetic experience, and an ideal of knowledge in which formal identity between the knower and the known is achieved. In all three, there is an emphasis on getting the slate ready to receive the message from the object, on letting the real have its way with the mind. This does not prove that the aesthetic experience is cognitive, but rather suggests that the descriptions given of the aesthetic experience, both in appreciation and creation, have a structural affinity with the classical paradigm for knowing. If this argues for anything, it is for tolerance of the belief that at the heart of the deepest kind of knowing is revelation or a display of the real.

PERCEPTION FOR THE SAKE OF PERCEPTION

What has already been said about aesthetic perception indicates that it differs from perception controlled by the needs of action and that which is controlled by the need for knowledge. It is now a familiar story that our perception is selective, especially when guided by some active interest. The tailor perceives a person in terms of his clothing, and a football coach perceives people in terms of strenuous feats on the gridiron. Action and interests based on action suck from the object those

---

[10] "The Creative Attitude," *The Structurist*, III (1963), 4–10.

clues that are most relevant to action. The estimative sense, in the words of Aristotle, makes a judgment of this kind, and Henri Bergson, among others, argued that perception was eminently a practical faculty, suited primarily as a cognitive guide for action rather than metaphysical truth.

Perception for the sake of science, on the other hand, seeks clues in the object that will betray its inner properties, that is, those properties by virtue of which it can be classified and related to other objects and activities. The practical user of salt, for example, is interested in its appearance and taste; the scientist, in those properties that relate salt to other substances, a function for which taste and appearance are not of major significance.

The scientific function of perception has diminished in importance as the properties of objects most useful for understanding their behavior ceased to be accessible to ordinary perception. In scientific knowing, perception is still indispensable but it functions more as a check on the presence or absence of marks on dials and scopes than as a direct access to the structure of the object itself. Discursive reflection, that is, the whole complex of hypothetico-deductive reasoning with observation as a check, is the accepted pattern of reliable knowing rather than the unity of the mind and the object.

As differentiated from these two modes of perception, aesthetic experience has as its primary purpose the clarification and intensification of perception, rather than prosperous action or scientific knowledge. Aesthetic perception is complete rather than selective; reflexive rather than transitive. Gotshalk defined the work of art as an object of intrinsic interest to perception.[11] Whatever other goals it may and often does serve, a work of art must be interesting to perceive, although not necessarily delightful to perceive. This definition has the virtue of including objects or aspects of objects that on extra-aesthetic grounds are gruesome and revolting, and which can be found in many great works of art.

[11] *Op. cit., passim.*

Before proceeding to the further analysis of the aesthetic object and the factors that make it interesting to perception, it may be in order to ask why pure perception or perception as such should be a goal of human endeavor. Why should we be interested in perceiving objects just for the sake of perceiving them?

One possible answer is that pure perception is an acquired taste. On this view, the original interest of man was action, and the perceptual awareness of objects served a survival function. After appearance was no longer useful to guide action it could be regarded simply as an appearance. Hence, on this view, children are absorbed in the sheer appearances of objects because as yet they do not know how to exploit perceptual clues practically. Later, as action becomes the dominant concern, the aesthetic interest lapses and has to be recovered by effort and training.

Some doubt on this hypothesis as a complete explanation is thrown by (a) the universal impulse to adorn useful objects and (b) the inveterate tendency of peoples in all cultures to stylize life into musical, pictorial, and linguistic sketches. These activities are indulged in even when no use or improvement of use can be found to explain them.

It seems more plausible to conjecture that first of all, clear perception, like clear thinking and like efficient movement, is enjoyed for its own sake. When the vision is blurred or hearing impaired, recovery of clear vision and hearing gives a pleasure that is as indubitable as it is indescribable. That sense organs constantly adjust themselves for clearer perception, and our unceasing search for instruments to extend perception, are ample witness to an inherent, perhaps innate, tendency.[12] In the second place, the interest and satisfaction attendant upon perceiving a field are augmented when the field is structured so as to engage the activities of the perceiver more extensively and more intensively. It there-

[12] Cf. Emil W. Menzel, Jr., and Richard K. Davenport, Jr., "Preference for Clear vs. Distorted Viewing in the Chimpanzee," *Science*, CXXXIV:3489, 1531, and R. S. Woodworth, *Dynamics of Behavior* (New York: Holt, 1958), p. 192.

fore makes sense to contrive this enhancement of interest and satisfaction.

As an example of the foregoing thesis, suppose we begin with the activities of walking, running, and movements of the hands and torso as observed in ordinary life. Suppose we observe our neighbor walking briskly down the street of a weekday morning. The walk has a certain rhythm and pace, but our perception of it is likely to be no more than a registration of clues for inferences about what our neighbor is up to. We surmise that he is on his way to the office or the bus. Suppose now that our neighbor suddenly breaks into a little hop, skip, and jump routine. Our interest perks up immediately, forcing strange hypotheses into our minds as to what might be the cause of this unusual behavior. The walking has become expressive of something: joy, excitement, or nervousness. In any event, we now watch the scene more intently. As we do, suppose our neighbor wheels about to face us and begins a fairly simple tap dance. At this juncture we either call the police, or we become absorbed in the dance itself. The practical and intellectual attitudes will then have begun to turn into the aesthetic attitude. Our interest is in perceiving the field and the motions within it.

If, however, the neighbor continues the tapping indefinitely, our interest flags. The field has been explored; there is no further surprise to be anticipated, no further excitement. But suppose he varies the routine; suppose the rhythms become more complicated; suppose out of nowhere music sounds with a rhythm synchronized to the dancing; suppose a female dancer appears and joins our neighbor in his act. Suppose now instead of the drab ordinary street clothing, the dancers acquire brilliant costumes and that the simple music swells to a multi-instrumented orchestra. By this time our practical concerns with our neighbor will probably have been completely submerged in our aesthetic interest. Instead of one sense many of our senses are functioning at a high rate of intensity; instead of monotony there is variation of a pattern, there is contrast of pace, male and female, light and heavy, tension and release, a building up of climax and resolution.

Before our eyes, so to speak, an ordinary piece of pedestrianism has been turned into a work of art, that is, into a field designed for perceiving and for not much of anything else.

Why do two dancers in synchronization interest us more than one? Why does the matching of the dancing gesture with a musical equivalent interest us more than either separately? Why do costume, setting intensify the interest? For one thing, each complication engages more of us; in other words, we are more *"inter esse"* within the field, not physically but imaginatively. The field becomes vivid, highlighted, red-lettered, and we too feel more alive, freer from the restrictions and distortions of ordinary life, freer to be ourselves because we have lost ourselves in the object and have, in a special sense, become one with it. However, there seems to be still another dimension of involvement. How interesting an object for perception will be depends on which nerve of life it touches. The little tap dance stirs a life rhythm, but no matter how it is complicated, varied, and dressed up, it still remains a delightfully refreshing but not a profound experience. Should the rhythm become more violent, our interest will increase, but delight gives way to a disturbed excitement. If on the stage Salome waves her grisly props, our perception acquires a depth of life involvement in comparison with which the tap dance is trivial and shallow.

If the dance is a caricature (a sketch) of war, of death, of love, of tragedy, of triumph, our perceiving becomes serious in the sense that we are beholding an expression that is also trying to be a statement about something so important, so close to the big issues in human life, perhaps so dangerous, so revolting that we have not yet formulated language to state it clearly. Perhaps as Jung, Freud, and others have conjectured, these works of art portray impulses and instincts that man would just as soon forget he had.

I have not taken the trouble, as one could, to argue that free activity of any kind is a source of delight. Perceiving and imagining as sheer activities disporting themselves for their own sake and freed from the stresses of need and duty are genuine values that need no justification, although indirectly the amount of such freedom a civilization permits is a good measure of its worth. This is so because this freedom for an adult population is a luxury that only substantial control over nature can make possible. As for duty, there is no little truth in Santayana's observation that morality is concerned primarily with preventing suffering and evil rather than with positive values.[13] If this is so, the more control a society has over natural and social evil, the less need is there to rely upon duty and conscience to prevent them.

But to return to our problem: is this knowledge? Is it verifiable knowledge? We must answer that in this sense it is not knowledge. The dance is not a set of propositions but a set of percepts organized into a total individual perceptual field. The components—however one decides to divide the field—do not have univocal meanings with interchangeable synonyms. The referents, if any, are themselves so vague, so amorphous, so indeterminate that some have never been named, much less defined.

If we are to call the deliverances of a work of art knowledge, it must be on a quite different conception of knowledge. It is no good to insist that a work of art refers to itself, for that is precisely what we do not mean by knowledge. It must refer to that which it displays and which is not completely identical with it. I have tried to indicate what this referent might be, namely, the import of reality for life on a scale running from the trivial to the profound. Since such an import is not a physical object there can be no question of public verification.

Nevertheless, the claim is often made that works of art display universals in a particular percept. The serenity of the ideal Greek character is supposed to be displayed in classic Greek sculpture and the grandeur of the creative powers of man and God in Beethoven's Ninth Symphony. This claim is not so mysterious as it sometimes sounds. Abstract qualities such as kindness, cruelty, and excitement can be symbolized pictorially much as a good caricaturist can in a few lines capture the essen-

[13] *Loc. cit.*

tials of a building, a fact, or even a mood. The rhythms and motions of nature and of life can likewise be captured in images, and there is then a truth expressed about them that is verified as all caricatures are, viz., by recognizing a structural resemblance. Thus twenty-five different caricatures of Winston Churchill could be "true" of Churchill. In this sense a caricature of Sir Winston could be said to capture *his* essence. And if his essence is to be blunt, aggressive, and lofty the artist may capture these qualities also and, if so, convey information not only about Churchill but about the bluntness, aggressiveness, and loftiness of the human spirit as well.

ART THEORY AND ART CRITICISM

The problem of the structure of knowledge in the arts involves not only the cognitive status of (a) what the work of art itself says or is supposed to say but also (b) what critics and theorists say about art. In one sense (a) collapses into (b) because works of art say nothing about themselves; only critics and theorists talk about what the work of art says. On the other hand, (b) the truth of what the critics and theorists say the work of art says depends on the truth of their theory about cognitive deliverances of works of art. If, for example, the work of art says nothing, then the critic who purports to interpret what it says is either a dupe or a fraud. In either case one would be wise to protect children from them and perhaps art as well.

On the other hand, even if an art work says nothing or nothing that can be stated intelligibly, it still may be possible for critics and theorists to say many things about art that are intelligible and which may help the individual to enhance the aesthetic experience.

Art criticism involves explication of the work of art and appraisal of it. Neither activity would be possible if some analysis of the work were not possible; if it were not possible for the critic to point to certain identifiable features of the work of art. Rational appraisal would be impossible if there could be no statement of rules and principles that works of art exemplified, or failed to exemplify, or exemplified in varying degrees. In addition, critical discourse is useless if it is so private and esoteric that others cannot understand it. Although some works of criticism themselves approach the status of works of art, most of them are discourses about works of art. These discourses are composed of (a) statements descriptive of the contents and structure of the work, (b) statements asserting the conformity of the work to a rule or principle, or (c) statements indicating possibilities that the artist might have realized but did not.

The content of critical discourse will be more apparent if the kinds of description and appraisal that can be made are sorted out. This analysis also indicates the way in which knowledge about works of art can be organized for instruction, because to learn to appreciate art is to learn to perceive and appraise it as a cultivated critic does.

Any work of art in any medium can be examined and evaluated with respect to the following factors: (a) the sensuous materials, (b) the manipulation (technique), (c) the formal design, (d) the expressiveness or significance, (e) the general function of being interesting to perception, and (f) the extra-aesthetic functions that it is designed or happens to serve.

For example, the colors in a painting may be brilliant or subdued, the sonorities in a piece of music can be pleasant or unpleasant. Different colors, sounds, textures, gestures are more or less attention-compelling, more or less pleasant, more or less interesting. Different media employ different materials and knowing how to handle these materials is part of the technical equipment of the artist. These sensuous materials are never found without some rudimentary form and therefore they carry some expressiveness. Even the syllables "zig" and "zag" do.

The important point, however, is that discriminations among the sensory qualities can be made and assertions about them can within reasonable limits be verified. Educationally, moreover, such discriminations can be learned and improved by learning; even pigs have been trained to distinguish among different pitches.

95

The case with regard to techniques needs even less argument. For centuries men have learned "how" from masters, and there is no great difficulty in ascertaining how well they have learned.

The problem in formal design is more complicated but in principle no different. The principles of form, for example, harmony, balance, centrality, and development can be specified by such devices as recurrence, similarity, gradation, variation, modulation, symmetry, contrast, opposition, equilibrium, rhythm, measure, dominance, climax, hierarchy, and progression.[14] These refer to qualities in the work of art that can be identified. Certain patterns of formal arrangement become conventional and traditional, e.g., the sonnet form, rondo, terza rima, passacaglia, triangle, oval, etc. These properties of the work of art can be noted, discussed, and judged, and one can learn to do so under tuition and improve one's performance by experience and practice.

With expressiveness we enter upon less firm ground for the reasons already discussed in relation to the nature of the aesthetic experience. In addition, one must consider that not all works of art are conspicuously expressive. A decorative design for a wall paper may not be. Some works of art play down expressiveness except as it issues from the formal properties of the work, although romantic works are less restrained in this matter. Some expressions are of the trivial, and some are of the profound aspects of life. This difference has been used to differentiate excellence in art from greatness.[15] So although every work of art, indeed every component of such a work, has some expressiveness, just as every component has sensory content and form, the charm or power of a work of art to command interest for perception may lie in, primarily, the formal qualities, or the sensory ones, or even in technical brilliance rather than in the overtones and undertones of human import.

On the other hand, in a painting such as Grant Wood's

---

[14] Gotshalk, *op. cit.*, 114ff.
[15] Cf. Leonard B. Meyer, "Some Remarks on Value and Greatness in Music," *The Journal of Aesthetics and Art Criticism*, XVII:4 (June, 1959), 486–500.

American Gothic is it the expression of an idea that attracts and holds our attention and makes us want to explore it further with the eye of the head and of the mind. Its form and sensory quality contribute to the expressiveness but in themselves are not especially interesting.

Next, there is the judgment about the general effectiveness of the work of art in capturing and holding perceptual interest, whatever the means and devices employed in doing so. Does the work expand under close scrutiny? Can it withstand repeated scrutiny? While such judgments are, to a large extent, based on subjective impressions, and while the range of difference in judgments of this type is wide, nevertheless, that this kind of judgment is not simply a register of purely subjective preference is proved by the fact that with experience and study the critic can dissociate his own immediate preference from his estimate of the potentialities of the object for the preferences of others.

The judgments of these potentialities can also be based on systematic analysis of the sensory elements, the formal components, and expressiveness. By comparing a given work of art with others of its kind, a judgment of potentiality is founded. Long experience also reveals discrepancies between expectations and performance, or strokes of genius where none had been suspected. To repeat, these judgments can be explicated and defended in terms that others with comparable experience can understand.

Finally, an intelligible judgment is possible about whether or not, or to what extent, a work of art fulfills whatever extra-aesthetic functions it may claim. To what extent does a monument express the purpose for which it is erected? To what extent does the marching band arouse the spirit of the football fans? To what extent does the form of a ritual intensify the meaning of a wedding or a funeral? How does the architecture of a school building enhance the educational significance of the goings on within it? How does the shape of a boat affect its motion through the water? How well does a novel or an epic exhibit the value schema of an age so that it can be used educationally as a value

exemplar? Whenever an extra-aesthetic claim of this sort is made
for a work of art, the critic should be able to make some sort
of defensible judgment. However, the number of variables in this
kind of situation is large, and only rarely do works of art clearly
enhance or detract from their extra-aesthetic functions. But of
course we are speaking here of judgments made prior to the
judgments of history. Given time, the judgments converge because the doubtful cases tend to drop from the competition.

In review then, it would seem that if our analysis is plausible
it is possible to make the following intelligible and defensible
judgments about a work with respect to: (a) the sensory elements, (b) the formal elements, (c) the expressive elements, (d)
technical competence, (e) the general perceptual interest, and (f)
the extra-aesthetic functionality. In addition to these six judgments it is possible to examine and judge the way in which
items (a-d) contribute or are related to each other and to items
(e) and (f). This adds up to quite a number of possible critical
judgments about a work of art.[16]

Some of these judgments are instances of subsumption. "This
is a sonnet" may be concluded from the definition of a sonnet
plus an examination of a given poem to see whether it conforms
to the definition. There is no lack of definitions of periods, styles,
and techniques in the arts. The characteristics and generalizations
on which definitions of styles and periods are based present difficulties but are not essentially different in kind from those facing
other classificatory definitions. Some aestheticians are not optimistic of ever getting a set of necessary and sufficient characteristics that would define the nature of art itself,[17] but again art is not
the only complex human activity that is difficult to capture in a
set of precise concepts, especially if one is serious about finding
something like a real definition.

Nor does artistic criticism suffer from peculiar difficulties

[16] For a somewhat different calculus, see Gotshalk, *op. cit.*, 183ff.
[17] Morris Weitz, "The Role of Theory in Aesthetics," *The Journal of
Aesthetics and Art Criticism*, XV (1956), 27–35, and Paul Ziff, "The Task
of Defining a Work of Art," *Philosophical Review*, LXII (1953), 58–78.

when it comes to the formulation and application of rules. The rules for composing sonnets are based on the definition of a sonnet which, in turn, was taken from the characteristics of certain poems accepted as typical sonnets. Once the choice of the example was made, the rules of sonnet-making could be formulated. The same procedures resulted in rules for the proportions of various types of buildings or the canons for the proportions of the human body, as in Vitruvius. Given the ideal case, the logic of the rules and principles of art presents no peculiar difficulty.

The difficulties come not from doubts about procedures but rather in the choice of the typical or ideal examples. There is much to be said for the contention that in any period the feature that is used to characterize art represents something that critics or artists feel has been neglected.[18] In a period in which formal considerations have been ignored in favor of the expressive elements, the accent of the reformers is likely to be on form. The ideal objects to be used as exemplars for defining art tend to be chosen accordingly. Transitional works appear and finally the new trend becomes established. During this transitional period there is much talk of freedom from the rules. However, it is a truism that this is merely a struggle for a different set of rules. In any event, neither critics nor philosophers of art are forced into silence during these unstable periods.

Educationally, the important point is that there are definitions, rules, and procedures in art that can be identified, pointed to, and stated. This means that there can be systematic instruction in or, at least, about art, and that it need not be confined to apprentice training in art production.

SOME EDUCATIONAL ISSUES

The impact of this discussion on the problems of art education can be gauged by taking up briefly the following questions:

[18] Weitz, *op. cit.*

1. Can the modes of analysis developed by art critics and philosophers of art be translated into curricular contents and teaching procedures?

I believe it has been shown that within the total domain of art there are many sectors—history, classifications of all kinds, analyses of art objects in many schema and on many dimensions—that can be taught. They qualify as knowledge in the conventional senses of that word. The question is not so much whether this kind of material can be taught, but rather whether the teaching of it will promote or hinder the aesthetic development of the pupil. By the aesthetic development of the pupil is ordinarily meant (a) the improvement of taste, (b) the improvement of the standards by which taste is justified, and (c) the increase of the quantity and quality of subjective enjoyment or satisfaction with aesthetic objects.

Clearly, the word improvement implies choice among alternatives according to some value scale. About the only way to avoid this conclusion is to argue that quantity—or intensity—of subjective enjoyment is the only relevant criterion. Whatever the theoretical difficulties involved in such a forthright hedonistic standard of aesthetic value, there still remains the relevant question: if John enjoys hillbilly music as much or more than Paul enjoys chamber music, should something be taught to John so that he too will prefer chamber music?

If it could be shown that John could be no more happy with chamber music than with hillbilly ditties, or if it could be shown that he would be no more happy with any other music than he is with hillbilly songs, there would be no point to aesthetic education so far as John's musical training is concerned on the ground that one might increase his pleasure thereby. Short of this condition, however, there remains the possibility of using the kind of knowledge and analyses mentioned above to maximize the recipient's pleasure. Even if, conceivably, teaching the pupil to discriminate tonal and rhythm patterns more finely leads him to prefer hillbilly music to string quartets, on sheer hedonistic grounds, the teaching would be successful and justified.

This way of looking at art education is not to be dismissed as an academic gambit. Especially in a period when rules are ill-defined there is a strong tendency to throw up one's hands and reduce aesthetic education to the refinement of those discriminations that maximize vividness of perception, regardless of other critical considerations and norms.

2. On what grounds can a school justify shaping aesthetic preferences on standards other than psychological hedonism?

A case for changing taste in a given direction can be argued on the following grounds: (a) that it will increase the well-being or happiness (not merely the momentary pleasure) of the individual and/or (b) that it will increase the well-being of the social order on which the well-being and happiness of the individual are predicated or dependent.

The first claim has to be based upon testimony of individuals, and unless some observers are more qualified than others, the testimony will be inconclusive. In the counting of noses, a pig satisfied counts for as much as Socrates unsatisfied unless Socrates' qualifications make his judgments count for more than one. But what could give him this superiority? Knowledge, experience, and a set of standards for life that are, to some extent, independent of the object to be judged. These standards are grounded in a theory about the good, about reality, and about knowledge itself, i.e., by a complete philosophical system. In other words, if the quality of pleasure is to be taken into account, pleasure is no longer the crucial criterion. Once knowledge and experience are admitted as criteria for well-being or even pleasure itself, connoisseurship or expertise becomes the only practicable standard for the school.

I say practicable for two reasons. One is that theoretically there is no way of certifying experts and connoisseurs that will remove the disagreement among them. The other is that when we propose to operate our culture rationally, we mean that of two or more doubtful opinions, assertions, and hypotheses, that which is based on study and experience is to be preferred. As between judgments based on other grounds or no grounds at all, no rational choice is possible. The case in the arts is no different from that in any other department of instruction.

The justification of art education by the social welfare argument rests on whether art can serve an extra-aesthetic purpose and whether, if it can, it should do so. Part of the answer to the first query depends on the cognitive potential of works of art. If a work of art tells us something important about life, then insofar as this knowledge can be used apart from the aesthetic experience in which it was achieved, it acquires a social value. If works of art can develop certain aspects of personality needed for social justice or stability, not necessarily as sources of knowledge but simply as causes for the formation of attitudes or alterations of habits, then again art can be said to have extra-aesthetic social values.

The intimate relation of art to religion indicates in a more general way how and why art is used for extra-aesthetic purposes. A wedding, funeral, or birth acquires added significance if accented by rituals that employ music, costume, and stylized gestures. Artistic means can be used to capture attention and to rivet it to the event under scrutiny. In Dewey's terms, art converts the conglomerate of actions into *an* experience, framed and outlined, with a beginning, middle, and end. It makes the event vivid for perception and paves the way for intensified feeling and involvement. Much of what we call civilization consists of sublimating biological activities by imagining them as significant beyond their biological utility. Eating is transmuted by imagination which is then objectified by art into dining. Similarly, sex gratification is transmuted into more than coitus, fighting into more than mutual destruction, and human society into more than mutual aid.

There is little question that art has been used for extra-artistic purposes and that such purposes have often been the causes or occasions for the production of great works of art. The only methodological stricture seems to be that in making judgments about a work of art the aesthetic and extra-aesthetic criteria be kept separate and distinct.

The chief problem is a moral one. Should artists be used as instruments of social policy at all? Or should they be so used only if such use does not impair their aesthetic integrity? The schools face the same questions.

Let us somewhat arbitrarily answer the moral question by deciding that in principle artistic autonomy is more important socially than any specific nonartistic use that can be made of it. Without going into detail, an argument could be made that without such autonomy not only will art suffer, but also that its usefulness as a social instrument will deteriorate.

If we make this kind of decision, then the school would seem to be directed to promote that autonomy wherever possible and to give it priority in cases of conflict. This would mean that aesthetic education is not to be justified solely by its social consequences or other nonaesthetic consequences.

It would mean that literature would not be selected and taught *primarily* to inculcate democratic values or to develop character of one kind or another. On the other hand, given restrictions of time, the school may be wise to choose literature for the curriculum that is not only good art but also an aesthetic presentation of a value system important in the understanding and appreciation of our culture. Of course, if theory precludes the work of art from "saying" anything of this sort, this principle of selection would have no meaning.[19]

The other consideration that enters into the decision to foster aesthetic education for its extra-aesthetic consequences is that popular art is already being used to shape the values of the people. Because this kind of art can function with virtually no formal instruction in art, it can easily be used as an instrument of social control. Government, industry, and other power complexes can become the taste-makers by control of the mass media.

[19] One need not accept Leo Tolstoy's dictum that only art which communicates an affirmation of the ultimate values of an age is good art in order to justify the use of this criterion in the selection of items for the school's curriculum in aesthetic appreciation. However, if no art or no good art can in principle communicate such an affirmation, then the criterion is meaningless.

The serious artist makes a claim that insofar as his art does make pronouncements about value they are dictated by his aesthetic perception alone and not by parochial interests that have become vested within him. In this sense, he makes a claim to serve truth and can act as a corrective to art that is not so directed and motivated. I do not know how to evaluate this claim except that in any given era it might be shown that the serious artist has felt what events later confirmed; that dislocations between the individual and his society are often sensed by the artist without his even being consciously aware of what was disturbing him. I take it that this was what the quotation from William Carlos Williams meant to convey.

If at least some of the propositions in art theory and criticism have cognitive status, then art education could be the means for safeguarding the body politic from itself. Just as science is society's defense against distortions of intellect by prejudice and special interests, so high cultivation in art is society's defense against undisciplined feeling swayed by parochial interests and limited experience. If art does make some connection with reality, i.e., with the import of life, then art education at a high level is as essential to individual development and social health as is science or industry. The distortions and aberrations of subjective experience, i.e., the life of feeling, are as dangerous as aberrations in knowledge of physical reality, perhaps more so.

SUMMARY

It is now time to pull together the numerous threads that have been introduced to this discourse.

The structure of knowledge in the arts leads us to inquire, first of all, whether anything that qualifies as knowledge is to be found in the arts.

To answer this question it was necessary to distinguish between what the work of art itself had to say, what the artist and appreciator had to know in their respective activities, and what could intelligently be said about works of art. Does a work of art say anything? If so, can it claim to be knowledge? Are the competences needed to make or appreciate works of art classifiable as knowledge, and if so, of what kind? Are theories about what the work of art is supposed to accomplish classifiable as knowledge? Are judgments made by art critics classifiable or warrantable as knowledge?

I believe that aside from the question as to what the work of art itself says, the problems are not of special difficulty. I believe that one can identify and classify the types of knowledge involved in knowing about the content of a work of art, the know-how of technique, and the judgments about the work of art. Certainly, there is no insuperable difficulty in classifying the cognitive activity involved in making historical statements about art and artists, about periods, styles, and developments. Judgments about the sensuous materials of the work of art, its technique, its formal properties, and its extra-aesthetic function can be made in propositional form and reasons given for them that can be understood and, in some sense, checked by those who are competent to do so.

The sticky points all have to do with the expressive function of the work of art itself and the judgments that are based upon it. With regard to the work of art itself, there is, I take it, no serious argument that holds that a painting or a concerto makes explicitly conceptual, descriptive statements about reality. Works of art are not constructed out of concepts whose purpose is to symbolize referents outside of themselves in a nonambiguous way. There is no lexicon or syntax of the images that constitute art. In short, it is exceedingly hard to construe works of art as *statements* of meaning. But as objects of perception they can and often do express a meaning by making an image of some feeling or idea or some combination of them.

I have argued that such expressions, while not statements, and therefore not assertions, are, nevertheless, clues from which inferences that are assertions can be made. Thus, while Beethoven's Ninth Symphony is not a set of statements about the exaltation of creation, the sounds are images of that complex of mood, idea, feeling, and action. Hearing it, one could infer that this is what creation feels like and that it is all very impressive and important. From the clues in some works of art one can make immediate inferences about the nature of love, of death, of war, of ideals, of every divagation of human experience, actual and possible. In this sense the work of art can be full of information for lack of which, if we do not die, yet we are immeasurably poorer and more ignorant.

However, works of art can express little or much, the trivial as well as the profound, and in many instances what they express is secondary to the stimulation of rich and full perception that they afford. This intrinsic value of the aesthetic experience in one way simplifies the problem of justifying aesthetic education because none is needed, but in the order of social importance means are higher than ends. Unless art has extra-aesthetic values it will encounter hard going in the competition for financial and curricular support.

It has been suggested that art education can make a case for itself if (a) one can defend the theory that it makes connection with reality in some unique way and is revelatory of it, (b) if one can defend the theory that one work of art is better than another, i.e., if there are intelligible standards, (c) that serious or fine art provides experience that is better than popular art or no art at all, (d) that art education, including the various knowledge forms it contains, can make a difference in preferences, and (e) finally, that such education can be protected from abuse in the form of political manipulation or social engineering.

Perhaps the safest and most modest claim that one ought to make for art education is that it helps to develop the perceptual habits of the person in that peculiar mode we have called aesthetic. To paraphrase Jenkins, from this aesthetic perspective, we exploit things in terms of their particularity by transforming them into images, which by virtue of art sharpen our insight into the actual characters of things, rather than enlarge our conception of relations among things, or bind them to our purposes.[20]

[20] *Op. cit.*, pp. 37 ff.

DISCUSSION OF DR. BROUDY'S PAPER

DR. HANSON: I'd like to begin with some laudatory comments about Dr. Broudy's performance; there are a number of orthodox mistakes several of us would wish to pounce on—mistakes which you exposed beautifully—particularly this one: I get upset when one trots out a potted version of the history of philosophy, a version within which the so-called problem of meaning comes up. I am referring to the picture theory of meaning. This was an attempt to show that a statement has the meaning it does have in virtue of its pictorial (or quasi-pictorial) connection with some state of affairs. By turnabout, what is obtained in a work of art has a *propositional* impact like what one expects in a statement. You, Dr. Broudy, have driven a torpedo into this whole position. Perhaps all right-thinking professors of education do the same, but it *was* refreshing.

DR. SCHWAB: A knife must be very long when it is preceded by so much butter.

DR. HANSON: Crap! But really there is so much crap that comes out of the picture theory. When you started to talk I expected to hear that, after all, artists have things to say, too, you know, and they can *tell* us "the truth."

DR. BEREITER: I realize this is a philosophical discussion. I don't know whether I should raise psychological issues at the outset, but it seems to me that before philosophical analysis can proceed far on this particular topic there are some things that do have to be worked out. I am left right at the starting gate wondering whatever made people think there might be knowledge conveyed by art in the first place. Appreciating art may be received psychologically as consummatory behavior (in the sense that it is not instrumental in obtaining ulterior goals), and it may be viewed experimentally as sensuous in character. Now, people have been consuming alcohol for years, and it has been a full, rich, sensual experience, but nobody has seriously claimed that alcohol contains knowledge. It might stimulate you to seek knowledge and it might lubricate, in a way, but that there was knowledge in alcohol itself, why, I don't know that anybody has claimed this. Could I go ahead with a little conjecture on this point? I think one idea which is a very cynical one but one that we ought to consider is the possibility that all that art contains is the illusion of knowledge. It has the power to give you the illusion of knowledge and in this it is comparable not to alcohol but to hallucinatory drugs, and the parallel is very close. What lies behind the claims that people make when they say they have gained knowledge from taking a hallucinatory drug? Well, they may claim to have comprehended the infinite or to have found the solution to a mystery (though they can't specify what the mystery is), or they claim that things fit together (though they don't know what the pieces are nor what the outcome is), or more often they may feel that some knowledge they already had is now more certain or more profound than it was before. In the light of several psychological theories, which I won't bother to go into, you could explain quite plausibly that art objects produce the same illusion. This is not to discredit art, but it is to discredit the question of whether art conveys knowledge.

Now it may be a very desirable kind of illusion and one that would justify art in society. It gives people a deeply satisfying feeling that may have side benefits in making people more serious-minded and giving them respect for profound thought, etc.; but it is an illusion nonetheless.

DR. BROUDY: Well, I too started with the question, "Why do people think and say some things?" and I tried to indicate what certain theorists had put forward as reasons for thinking so, and a good many of these theories are to be found in the interpretation of ritual, legend, and myth-making. And presumably at one time they felt that aesthetic experience did have a cognitive value. The angry sea, for example, typified something that had to do with one's relations to the god of the sea. We still make judgments about what people are going to do to us from their appearance. We use aesthetic clues to judge what kind of people they are. We say, "There is a shifty fellow." Well, why? He has the kind of face that *looks* shifty.

Now you were asking me about origins. As far as origins go,

I think that this is a matter of conjecture. I think there is something to be said for the notion that even today we have not completely dispensed with aesthetic clues to cognition and to action. They aren't the most reliable clues, but usually the first ones. The doctor looks at a patient and says, "He looks toxic." Then he goes ahead and puts a thermometer in his mouth and does more precise things to confirm the toxic hypothesis. Now if you want a theory on origins and why people think that a work of art has some cognitive values, it may be that at one time it offered usable cognitive clues. I prefer to believe that the reasons people think that there is a cognitive relevance in a work of art is that it makes them *feel* differently. Without resorting to alcohol or drugs, the work of art does make them feel that there is something more significant in it than the literal meaning.

You are using the word illusion quite properly. It is a deliberate illusion. Everybody knows that it is an illusion, so it is an illusion that fools nobody. The work of art gives you the particularity of an individual thing in such a way that it gets the kind of significance that it doesn't get in its literal meaning. Now apparently people enjoy this, and having this kind of apprehension they think it is a logical experience. They call it cognitive because they think they have learned something. (Aristotle)

DR. HANSON: You spoke the truth so articulately that it is hard to realize that anyone could ever have taken the other line; there is really some explanation of it. When Wittgenstein keeps calling attention (in the *Tractatus*) to the ways in which ordinary written discourse, like hieroglyphics, was somehow meant to *represent*—he doesn't actually say this straight out—he is encouraging his readers to suppose that communicative efforts by authors and by artists are pretty much the same kind of understanding. It can be a persuasive line. It's just false, that's all.

DR. BROUDY: Well, it's false, as I say, only if one insists on applying to it criteria appropriate to the truth and falsity of empirical propositions. Now is a caricature of Sir Winston Churchill false? In a sense, yes, because obviously Sir Winston Churchill is more than four lines, and no two cartoonists portray Winston Churchill in the same way. I want to distinguish caricatures from portraits.

DR. HANSON: You are considering *successful* caricatures now. Suppose that a man is just a poor caricaturist; he renders Winston Churchill as underweight, with masses of hair, and an enormous handlebar mustache. Is he telling a lie or is he just not up to his task?

DR. BROUDY: He may not be telling the truth about Sir Winston's weight, hair, and facial adornments, because we have criteria by which we can pass judgment on the facts of the case. But if one can recognize the caricature as one of Sir Winston (without reading the caption, of course), then the caricaturist has said something significant and true about how Sir Winston looks. My point is that often a work of art gives us the impression that a set of lines or shapes "looks" angry or serene, but since anger and serenity do not exist *in abstracto* as such, and we can never test the truth of the impression, it is pointless to call it true or false, while it still makes sense to call it expressive.

DR. HANSON: Now to the point that we disagree on; it can't be false because it is of the wrong logical type to be true. This is what I *thought* that you were saying so beautifully. Let me draw

a little diagram here to make the point.  No one

is ever going to see anything like that; the horns of the moon point the wrong way.

DR. SCHWAB: And everybody knows that the moon is not going to spill its elixir.

DR. HANSON: The point is this: if a chap draws the sunset thus he might even put a star in between the horns, as in certain near-Eastern flags. If he did that, we couldn't argue that what he said is *false*. He's not saying anything. He has misrepresented something, but he hasn't made any claim.

DR. BROUDY: This is only if you think he is misrepresenting something. He may not be representing anything. He may be presenting the image of a feeling and therefore he is not representing anything.

DR. HANSON: Consequently, it wouldn't be right to say that he told a lie.

DR. BROUDY: That's right. On the other hand, suppose the recipient says to himself that this (the moon drawing) is how the feeling of being rejected by one's best girl "looks"; that the moon drawing "expresses" this feeling. He is making a kind of knowledge claim in that he is asserting a resemblance or equivalence between his feeling state and a visual display. But there is no way of checking this; certainly asking the painter whether he intended this meaning would not alter the fact that the percipient received this communication of meaning. That is why I have tried to stress the belief that art communicates not by describing states of affairs literally, but rather by describing experience in one modality by images from another modality. Art, in this sense, gives you information about what *literally* could not be true. Let me give one of my favorite examples of displaced modalities. Like all coffee lovers, I dream of coffee that will taste the way coffee smells when it is being ground. This happens once in a blue moon. We are here invoking synaesthesia, in which a taste phenomenon is conjoined and equated with an odor phenomenon. In painting and music, one is forever translating moods into "looks" and "sounds" which, literally, does not make sense. Now if this strikes the perceiver as apt—I am not going to say true but apt—there is something given to the perceiver not perceived before. It is a kind of immediate perception of a kind of individual fact that we were talking about this afternoon. [Phenix paper]

DR. SCHWAB: Harry, I want to make an accusation against you. It is clear from your paper that whether the knowledge apparently delivered by a work of art be an illusion or literally representative or an illumination by the work of art, it is important because it is an element in enjoyment. I think that is a fair statement of your doctrine and I have no disagreement—quite the contrary.

My accusation is that in asserting this you sold art out to the didactic almost as completely as did Tolstoy. You described aesthetic growth as consisting of improvement of taste, the improvement of standards of taste, and the quantity and quality of subjective enjoyment. It seems to me that the problem of improvement of taste, at least of voiced taste, and the ability to spout critical doctrines, which constitutes improved standards of taste, are relatively easily solved in teaching. The real problem comes in the Dorothy Parkerism that "You can lead a horticulture but you can't make her think." It consists of the urgent and real problem of somehow breaking through the shells of young people to the point where the quantity and quality of subjective enjoyment is advanced. That, I submit, is not a mere correlate of improved standards of taste. This is why I say that you have sold art down the river.

DR. BROUDY: Well, this is kind of a serious accusation. Let me try to explain why I think you are wrong, even though you might have some grounds for saying what you did. First of all, the problem of aesthetic education is somewhat different from aesthetics.

DR. HANSON: And it is Number 3.

DR. BROUDY: The ground rule for achieving an aesthetic experience in itself presents the biggest and gravest problems because aesthetic experience asks people to suspend the cognitive and practical attitudes which in our culture are so dominant. At this point we have a problem of how this can be done. Are there any ways in which one can get children of varying ages to do this? One of the ways is to go through the gambits we have mentioned: drawing attention to the formal properties of things, training in simple discrimination, and studying "about" works of art. Now these are prosaic matters, but I think it is true that people who do get training in this way become more receptive to the aesthetic quality of objects. They are willing to look and listen the way the artist wants them to look and listen. Now as far as improvement in being aesthetically receptive is concerned, I don't know what more you can do systematically.

Of course you can and should rely on the seductive quality

of the work of art itself. This can be assumed with popular art, and, therefore, the problem of aesthetic education does not really arise with respect to the enjoyment of the popular art. Professor Schwab would like, I take it, for people to respond as spontaneously and genuinely to serious art or some selections from it as they do to popular art, and in this he is right. That certainly must be the ·proper outcome of aesthetic education. Unfortunately, much serious art becomes seductive only after one has become ready to be seduced, and I know of no systematic way of accomplishing this save by selecting works of art that do have a high artistic rating by experts and then help the student go through the kind of motions that connoisseurs go through, and you have to trust that in the end it will give rise to spontaneous enjoyment as it does with the connoisseurs.

I have some evidence, that I can only ask you to take on trust, that aesthetic training does change taste. If you ask literature majors to rate samples of avant garde poetry, classical poetry, and popular (greeting card) poetry on a "most liked" basis, they will tend to prefer the avant garde poetry. But this may not be the case with music or art majors, although within their fields the same trend toward preference for the contemporary is fairly evident. Incidentally, we took our samples of popular poetry from greeting cards, because there is no popular poetry (in the sense of popular music) around today.

DR. SCHWAB: You have musical comedy.

DR. BROUDY: Yes, but you don't hear it until you have disentangled it from the tune.

DR. SCHWAB: I had two points in mind. One was simply the plea to you to raise this problem somewhere in an added paragraph to a point higher than that background. The other is to suggest that it isn't as easy as you suggest. What it amounts to is that you have taught them technicalities and analysis and judgment, and I have any number of colleagues in the humanities who are the most expert analysts of the lyric poem, the drama, the novel, yet do it for the sake of feeling superior to the dramatist, the novelist, and the lyric poet.

DR. BROUDY: I have no remedy for that.

DR. SCHWAB: That isn't my point. I mean to say that the evidence is so indirect as to be no evidence at all. We need some way of knowing whether we have, in fact, so taught that we have increased the capacity for being moved, for having and enjoying an aesthetic experience.

DR. BURNETT: Harry, you talked about good connoisseurship and later Phil talked about the role of the experts and aesthetics and synnoetics, and I wonder if we aren't somewhat involved in a problem of cultural relativism here when you begin defining or deciding upon what constitutes the disciplines by going to the experts, especially in these realms. Well, I wonder if we must have a connoisseur of connoisseurs and an expert of experts in order to solve this problem. To get us out of an arbitrary way of deciding what the discipline is and selecting the subject matter, a man of great taste determines for us what the discipline is and what is good art. Then taste will vary from culture to culture. It also varies within cultures, and it would bring up the old problem in another way—that the experts are not in agreement. I raise this because I think there is a cultural relativity and if that's all we have, okay, but . . . .

DR. BROUDY: That's why I said in the paper "practical." Theoretically, everything you say would count but practically I am saying the only criterion of goodness we have in selecting the curriculum or making this kind of judgment is the testimony of the people who have done the most study and have had the greatest systematic experience in the field. Good chemistry and good art and good everything else mean that as far as the curriculum is concerned. That the experts differ I grant, but what else do you have? That's why I say practical. On the other hand, the amount of disagreement is highly overrated. Actually when you ask two critics to judge a work of art, if you subdivide adequately what it is they are supposed to judge, there isn't so much disagreement. Where the disagreement comes is, however, at the most important point, unfortunately. What does the work of art say? What is the expressive element of the thing? Now at that level, I am quite willing to leave this an open question. I just don't know how—if the expressiveness of a work of art is what I think it is—I can insist that the experts agree on what a particular work of art "says" in order for there to be works of art and experts. If there can be agreements about sensory qualities, about formal properties, about technical competence, about what the artist might have done, indeed if there can be intelligible discourse about these matters, then we can have experts and we can ground aesthetic training in the judgments of these experts, even if they do not agree on the expressive content of the work of art or its metaphysical significance. Dr. Schwab insists that this kind of training will not insure that students will have genuine rather than conventional tastes, but as far as systematic education is concerned it's a choice between exposing the pupil to lots of art and hope that something desirable (whatever that may be) will happen, or using training devices that one hopes will result in a more refined aesthetic experience.

DR. BURNETT: I will just ask you what about the experience with aesthetics and synoptics in, say, Nazi Germany?

DR. BROUDY: Are you sure you are not bringing up an extra-aesthetic question? That is another matter.

DR. BURNETT: Well, it's extra-aesthetic if you shift your cultural perspective.

DR. BROUDY: Well, all right, if you are going to use art for extra-aesthetic purposes, then your objection becomes valid because you may not want art to do the kind of thing that it is doing.

DR. HANSON: Just as in National Socialist Germany.

DR. BROUDY: In education this is a real question. It isn't art for art's sake because this isn't the way you can justify a program of art education.

DR. BURNETT: Of course aesthetics is the more serious problem, and moral philosophy, I think . . . .

DR. BROUDY: That's right. That's why there is a difference.

UNIDENTIFIED PARTICIPANT: I should think that the very disagreement was a mark of the expert because the experts know what questions to deal with. They are the people who actually investigate the problem and the difference between the expert and the nonexpert is that one knows what the problems are.

DR. BROUDY: Yes, try to get into an argument between experts. They may disagree violently but if you try to get into it they will kick you out unless you are an expert too.

DR. BURNETT: That is the same point that I made a moment ago. In this case, when some of the experts left, this proved to the ones who stayed that those who left weren't really experts in the first place. Those who stayed became the experts. So you are again having a cultural perspective.

DR. SCHWAB: You don't have to talk that. You know darn well that what the Nazi expert approved was the art which he thought would lead to certain behaviors desired by a central government. These guys weren't making aesthetic judgments, they were making judgments of propaganda.

DR. ARNSTINE: I would like to refer to Dr. Schwab's point, because I think the conversation of the last few minutes hasn't anything to do with aesthetic experience at all. It has to do with another sort of discussion, and I want to return to Dr. Schwab's very crucial point. Dr. Broudy, let's consider the extent to which aesthetic education is to be used either for the transmission of knowledge on the one hand or as a means by which students learn to find—I hesitate to use the words—an enriching experience. I kind of feel that to talk about art in terms of knowledge is to put the aesthetic out of the question, and I want to make a suggestion to make this more clear. Putting aside all allegations of the actual character of things that Jenkins talked about, you ask the question: "Why is it that people want to perceive?" Do they perceive for the sake of perception? It seems to me that to answer the question this way is simply to reaffirm the observation that people just *do* perceive. But I don't think that people perceive for the sake of perceiving, because when some practical motive is absent, lots of people just go to sleep because there is nothing left for them to do. These people are not interested in perception, and I would suggest that perception for the sake of perception is in fact perception for the sake of *changing* perception—which, put another way, would be to say that people don't like to be bored. They like to see some change in environment. Works of art do this pretty well, but philosophical speculations may do this as effectively as works of art. If this is the case, that people perceive and attend to perception for the sake of the changes in it, then the psychological question *why* they want to do this is answered by noting that they do so for the sort of *affect* which is aroused when a perception is perceived as changed in some way. This can be done visually or through music or any other kind of sense modality. Well, if this is the case, it would seem that aesthetic education would do well to focus on the affect aroused either by works of art or other things (that have nothing to do with works of art). Not knowledge, but rather affect would be the focus of aesthetic education and talk about the transmission of knowledge or the relation between art and knowledge would be to make it unclear why we deal in aesthetic education.

DR. BROUDY: Well, in the first place I don't think that to say that one desires clear perception is simply to say that we perceive for the sake of perceiving. If you will permit my retreat to Aristotle, I will merely say that the perfect functioning of any function is accompanied by pleasure. So good perceiving is pleasurable in itself. But if all you want is a change in the perceptual field, we certainly don't have to go to all this ridiculous effort to make works of art. Therefore, it seems to me we look to the work of art for something in addition to simply a change. Now, Gotshalk has defined an aesthetic object as anything that's intrinsically interesting to perception, but notice that to perceive aesthetically means *complete* perception rather than perception of clues to knowledge or action. Now if you can help people get the enjoyment that comes from complete perception, then it seems to me this is all you can do, and nowhere have I said that the primary justification of aesthetic experience is the transmission of knowledge. I think I have tried to say that if knowledge is what you want, art is about the most inefficient way of getting it.

I do think there is something I didn't do enough with. I think there is something to be said for the thesis that Oscar Wilde waggishly proposed, namely, that nature imitates art. That is, we don't know how to feel until somebody shows us how to feel—until the artist tells us how to feel. Art may, therefore, be regarded socially as a cultural discipline of feeling. The distortion of feeling that comes from the lack of discipline that comes from art might be another justification, if one could show that modes of feeling are influenced by art forms, as Wilde claimed. The evidence is conflicting on this, but there is some.

When you are trying to get a strategy for persuading school boards to give you money and curriculum time for aesthetic education, I just don't think that you are ever going to get it merely on the basis of the aesthetic enjoyment you promise. They will want to know the extra-aesthetic side of the program, its effect on the person and on the society. It would help if we could honestly say that they were good effects. In a great work of art carefully chosen you can sometimes get the feeling of a period directly and immediately better than you could by a great many discursive studies. If we could pick such works for aesthetic study they would have great pedagogical value in the sense that they would do things that we don't seem to do very well now.

DR. ARNSTINE: Now if we give our attention to the possible argument of a school board based upon the social utility of arousing and discriminating personal feelings, I think perhaps I overstated my case; and in any case, I didn't mean to accuse you of seeing art merely as a transmission of knowledge. But if the arousal of affect and the refinement of feeling are related to the sorts of affect that students are presently getting, wouldn't this be relevant to the selection of art works for the curriculum, such that one ought not waste the Ninth Symphony on some kids, if they are enjoying rock-'n'-roll?

DR. BROUDY: That might very well be.

DR. ARNSTINE: I wonder now if there is a relation between this sort of selection process and the criteria of selection for *any* sort of learning experience in school? That is, is the nature of the disciplines the *only* basis for selecting learning experiences?

DR. BROUDY: Well, this is a large question, but I think a little different question. I am saying if one could get examples of value embodied in works of art which are very seductive and persuasive, this would be a great lever in the hands of the educator.

DR. BEREITER: I would just like to point out that people are talking about three different aspects of the whole aesthetic situation here and Dr. Arnstine has raised the third. In any psychological situation you can look at the stimulus, the organism, or the response. We can do that in trying to cope with the question of who is a connoisseur and who is a clod and how we can develop into connoisseurs rather than clods.

DR. SCHWAB: Your substantive structure is showing.

DR. BEREITER: Well, I will try to make the most of my structure. People try to look at the stimulus by asking whether we can rank art objects on some continuum that everybody will agree to, but this turns out to force us into a relativism that embarrasses everybody. You suggested looking at the organism, that is, the credentials of the man who does the rating. This, I think, is also not too satisfactory. But I see no one looking at the response end. This is much more difficult, but it seems to me to be the only one that can lead us anywhere. What are the responses of which a person is capable? This is the obvious way to distinguish Socrates from the pig. The pig has as good eyes as Socrates, but Socrates is capable of affective and cognitive responses which the pig can't have and similarly . . . .

DR. BROUDY: What makes you think they are any better than the pig's?

DR. BEREITER: They don't have to be any better. At least you can distinguish them, and then you can argue about whether certain cognitive and affective responses are worth attempting to develop in people. If you can develop them, it may not matter which art objects come to elicit them. It may well turn out, however, that rock-'n'-roll never elicits certain experiences in anybody. This gives you a substantial basis for arguing that rock-

'n'-roll is different from classical music in the responses it can elicit. Then you can start claiming: if we can develop the ability to have these experiences then we are developing connoisseurs rather than clods.

DR. BROUDY: Well, I wish I could take that way out, because, you see, you are trying to avoid an evaluation and I don't see how you can, because the responses that I am going to try to reinforce I cannot choose simply on the basis that they are different.

DR. BEREITER: No, but do you know what you are evaluating now? You are not evaluating the art objects. You are not evaluating the people who have the experiences. You are evaluating the responses.

DR. BROUDY: I am not even sure that I am evaluating the total response. I will go this far with you, Carl, that for the lack of norms that are really definitive in education we can proceed to let the expert help the student experience as big a variety in fine discrimination as possible. This I would regard as a good initial response. Not to be able to distinguish two rhythms that are fairly close together is not so good as to be able to distinguish them. But in the end, either you just expose the youngster to anything or everything and hope you see that something will come of it—and this is not impossible—or you make a selection. The minute you start making a selection you are involved in this problem of standards. Now all I have said, not for theoretical purposes but for practical purposes, is that I know of no other way of doing it than to select those people whose credentials I respect.

DR. HANSON: Pigs don't drink hemlock; *that's* a pretty good thing about pigs.

DR. BROUDY: In that instance are they wiser?

ADJOURNMENT

CHAPTER IV

ZETETICS AND AREAS
OF KNOWLEDGE*

JOSEPH T. TYKOCINER

INTRODUCTION

One of the characteristics of the contemporary historical period
is the increasing tendency toward specialization which is taking
place in all domains of human activity. One hears repeatedly the
sarcastic remark that scientists and engineers get to "know more
and more about less and less." We are thus confronted with the
phenomenon of division of interests which makes it difficult for
members of a group of scientists and engineers to understand one
another and to agree on decisions in matters beyond their own
narrow specialities. Such blocking develops in groups whose members represent various branches of the humanities and the social
sciences in conference with scientists and engineers. The greater
the variety of participating special fields, the more inhibited
communication becomes, because of the existing fractionalization
of knowledge.

On the other hand, the growing complexity of industrial and
social organization requires the cooperation of larger groups or

---

* This article was published for the first time in January, 1964, in the form
of a pamphlet issued by the Electrical Engineering Department of the University of Illinois. It was used by students in Professor Tykociner's credit
course, "Research as a Science."

teams composed of multifarious specialists, often organized on a national or even an international scale.

How can these two opposite tendencies—specialization and cooperation—be harmonized to produce culturally desirable results? How can the gulfs dividing artists, scientists, engineers, educators, and scholars be avoided? The estrangement so characteristic of the relations between members of the various specialized parts of the intellectual community is partly due to a lack of understanding of the aims and tasks of one another's activities.

The main difficulty in the present situation is that the arts, sciences, humanities, and engineering are now regarded as isolated from one another, separated like islands. It is the role of zetetics, the growing science of research and artistic creativity, to study human knowledge as a whole: its origin, growth, and transitions. Moreover, it seeks to build a "bridge" between any two such islands of specialized knowledge which seem to be separated, but actually are interconnected by as yet unknown links. Since the discovery of gaps in our knowledge is one of the aims of zetetics, it may serve to establish the lacking means of communication between the four isolated domains of culture as they exist at the present time—arts, sciences, humanities, and engineering.

ZETETICS AND RELATED DEFINITIONS

The subject-matter of zetetics includes a study of the origin of systematized knowledge, of the mental processes involved in research, of the interrelations between various fields of science, and of the social conditions facilitating the growth of knowledge. Further subject matters involve an analysis of the methods of selection, delineation, and solution of problems in general. One of the main objectives is also the ordering of recorded knowledge, so that it can be retrieved when needed for further creative endeavors toward finding and filling gaps in human knowledge.

The word knowledge has been used extensively in the above introductory charting of the field of research as a science. To avoid semantic misunderstanding, it is necessary at this stage to describe briefly this and other significant words in the sense I use them throughout this paper. They form a part of my glossary and have the following *restricted* meanings:

Knowledge is the totality of information preserved by culture.

Science is the sum total of recorded systematized knowledge thus far accumulated by the human race.

Discipline signifies a collection of parts of systematized knowledge arbitrarily selected and bound together in a manner suitable for learning, mental training, and preparation for more advanced study and research.

Research is a purposeful activity aiming at the extension of the field of knowledge and experience by

a. discovering new facts and phenomena,

b. formulating generalized relations,

c. inventing mental and material devices for complementing human abilities.

Artistic creation is an activity which consists in applying knowledge, experience, imagination, and skill for designing and producing new visual and auditory patterns of aesthetic significance.

Zetesis is a term designating the activity of both research and artistic creation. It is a word of Greek origin which means *seeking*.

Zetetics is the science of research and artistic creation, concerned with collecting and systematizing data on the theory and practice of zetesis, and aiming at the expansion and unification of knowledge into a consistent system.

Returning to the definition of knowledge as the totality of information preserved by culture, the question arises: what is information?

In the sense I use this word, it signifies a phase in the process of learning which involves three stages. We first accumulate the material which may become knowledge; we do so usually in a passive attitude. The next stage is to bring the acquired information into some logical order, and this makes it into science.

The final stage comes with a critical attitude, which leads to research and results in innovations.

Another question in connection with the definition of knowledge is: how is knowledge preserved? It is preserved in the form of records and specimens in our libraries, museums, and archives. These serve as the depositories of knowledge.

THE DYNAMICS OF KNOWLEDGE

The above definitions do not stand entirely separated from each other. They form a spectrum in which knowledge spreads toward wider and wider roles. The definitions gain in clarity and concreteness by associating them with the two sources of knowledge: the part accumulated by the creativity of countless past generations and the supplementary part made by contemporary contributions.

The dynamics of these two components is pictured in Figure 1. Our store of knowledge is shown diagrammatically by the upper circle, whose inner space is divided into twelve sectors representing areas of knowledge. The whole circle represents our libraries and museums, where recorded knowledge is stored, catalogued, and maintained in such a way as to be accessible to everyone who wishes to make use of it. The young generation becomes acquainted with this store of knowledge chiefly through their parents and social environment (left circle) and through their teachers in schools and elsewhere (right circle). This knowledge develops their *native abilities* (middle circle) and makes them fit for a large variety of activities, represented in the lower part of the diagram by two groups of smaller circles. The activities shown by the left group of circles bring about the production of consumer and capital goods necessary to provide for the needs of human individuals. The activities shown by the righthand group of circles are the services humans perform for social organizations.

In addition, there is another kind of activity for which humans develop certain skills and creative abilities, and that is

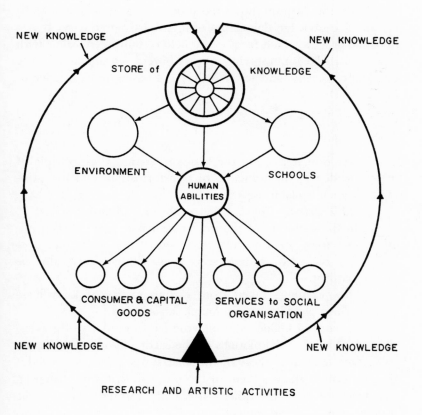

NEW KNOWLEDGE

NEW KNOWLEDGE

STORE of   KNOWLEDGE

ENVIRONMENT   SCHOOLS

HUMAN
ABILITIES

CONSUMER & CAPITAL
GOODS

SERVICES to SOCIAL
ORGANISATION

NEW KNOWLEDGE

NEW KNOWLEDGE

RESEARCH AND ARTISTIC ACTIVITIES

DYNAMICS OF KNOWLEDGE

Figure 1

zetesis, which includes research and artistic activities. The product of zetesis, symbolized by the shaded triangle, is the increment of knowledge which flows into the common store. In the store of knowledge we possess a treasure which is not depleted by use, but rather increased by it.

Thus, the diagram shows this process of growth and amplification of knowledge due to research and artistic activity. It is a dynamic process which feeds every field of human endeavor with new knowledge; multiplying our resources; enriching our life materially, socially, and aesthetically; and raising our existence to higher levels.

PRINCIPLES

Three principles form the basis of zetetics: the principle of interdependence, the principle of transformation, and the principle of a controllable future.

a. *The principle of interdependence* is as follows:

In the structure of the universe all parts are interdependent. Therefore, all the fractional knowledge collected, systematized, recorded, and preserved by culture must also be interdependent.

A few examples taken from various realms of knowledge may serve to elucidate this principle.

The work of Galileo and Newton led to the laws of gravitation which control the motions of the earth and of the bodies on its surface, as well as those of the solar system. So interrelated is the entire mechanical system of the universe that any change in any part affects all the other parts. Only the sensitivity of the measuring instruments limits the possibility of determining the intensity of the effects. So, for instance, the tides of the oceans and of the atmosphere, produced by the motion of the moon, affect the center of gravity of the earth and call forth frictions, displacement of the earth's center of gravity, and also variations in the angular velocity of the earth's rotation.

Any artificial satellite launched into space produces a reaction which gives rise to seismic waves, redistributes the mass of the earth, and changes the state of the entire solar system.

The slow periodic variation in the position of the earth's axis of rotation in relation to the ecliptic influences the formation

126

of glaciers in the arctic regions, changing the climate, the flora, the fauna, and human life on the surface of the earth.

The discovery of radioactivity not only influenced the development of physics, chemistry, and astrophysics, and revolutionized the economy of power production, but deeply affected the interrelations between nations.

Advances in the biological and medical sciences have extended the span of human life and thus moved to the fore the problems of excessive population growth.

The development of the arts has been influenced by the use of the third dimension, based on the laws of optics and the knowledge of projective geometry. It is sufficient to compare the twelfth-century painting with that produced during the Renaissance three hundred years later. A still greater influence on the arts was exerted by the invention of photography. It diminished interest in realism and accelerated the development of impressionism, cubism, and other nonobjective forms of art.

The principle of interdependence has been verified in so many fields that it may be safely applied in searching for interrelations between the arts and sciences. Thus, whenever interrelations are lacking in certain fields it signifies that there are gaps in our knowledge to be filled by persistent research.

b. *The principle of transformation* is as follows:

The universe presents itself as involved in a dynamic process of transformation. Everything, including human knowledge, is continuously evolving.

The concept of change has been stressed by many philosophers. Initiated by Heraclitus in the fifth century B.C., it has since then played an important role in human thinking. In modern times it was adopted by Henri Bergson as the only enduring principle and therefore the fundamental reality.

Our experience, as well as the study of various sciences, like cosmogeny, geology, anthropology, and history, supply evidence that the universe, as we know it, is subject to continuous change. This dynamic process, usually called evolution when connected

127

with biological phenomena, is being extended to cosmic development. However, the *process of transformation* may be a more appropriate term to characterize it.

The rates of transformation vary greatly, depending on the kind of phenomena. Some phenomena, as, for instance, the formation of the solar system with its planets and satellites, are estimated in billions of years. Others, e.g., geological stratification of the layers of the earth, proceed faster but still appear to be static, if time is measured by the scale of the human span of life.

On the other hand, many physical and chemical phenomena take place at a rate measurable by direct observation with the human senses; others require the use of more or less refined auxiliary instruments. We see changes accelerating at such a fast rate that the word explosive is applied to them. As an example may serve the birth of a star or of a nebula known in astronomy as nova or supernova.

A further example is the exceedingly short life of certain atoms and particles discovered by the modern powerful atom smashers and investigated by elaborate methods of measurement in atomic and nuclear physics.

Finally, viewing contemporary events, especially on the national and international scenes, we witness transformations going on at an astonishing rate. It would require a long list to enumerate just the striking scientific and technological developments which have transformed our lives and the relations between nations during the life-span of a twentieth-century individual. It is hardly an exaggeration to say that nowadays each generation lives in a world quite different from the preceding one's.

   c. *The principle of controllability of the future:*

Learning from experience and planning for the future makes it possible to utilize existing trends and thus partially to control their development in the interest of human survival.

Mankind's aspirations to influence the future, persisting throughout the ages, have had some successes. Growing knowledge of the universe is bringing us closer to realization of our efforts to shape future events by creative activity.

Systematized knowledge has brought to light many general-izations derived from a study of the world around us. They show that, in spite of the apparent randomness of phenomena, the changes and the resulting transformations are not entirely chaotic. They do not preclude a certain order in the universe. What has become the basis for evaluating the usefulness of theories is not only their consistency and agreement with observations, but also their predictive ability. The forecasting of weather conditions, of the exact time for sunrise and sunset, of eclipses of the sun and moon, of approaching storms, floods, and epidemics has demon-strated the practical value of such predictions.

Moreover, the qualities of inquisitiveness and creative im-agination which *Homo sapiens* has developed in adaptation to a world in continuous transition have made him capable of learn-ing from experience and planning for the future. This has led to bold attempts to influence coming events and consciously to control evolution in the interest of human survival, social welfare, and higher aspirations.

DESCRIPTION OF ZETETICS AS AN AREA OF KNOWLEDGE

Zetetics as an area may be briefly summarized as follows:

the totality of recorded, systematized knowledge related to such

methods of research and artistic production,
mental processes,
psychological factors,
environmental conditions

as

lead to new problems,
stimulate creative imagination,
enhance selective thinking, and
generate original, fruitful ideas.

Thus, it includes as its basic factual material all the available data concerning the origin of discoveries, inventions, works of art, and great systems of philosophy. It aims to improve methods of inquiry, especially by expanding scientific methods, finding interrelations between the arts and sciences, and formulating new problems. Consequently, zetetics will supply the *bases of education for research*. Finally, it will develop a discipline for disseminating new knowledge and skills helpful in zetesis.

From the original conception of zetetics as the science of research, it has grown in many directions and developed into an area of knowledge with eight main subdivisions:

a. Zetegeny studies the origin of sciences and of zetesis as an evolutionary process.

b. Taxilogy is concerned with the zetetic classification of the sciences, in particular with maintaining an inventory of sciences and with methods of discovering gaps in the system of sciences.

c. Problematology treats the selection and formulation of problems with the purpose of facilitating their solution.

d. Zetesis studies the abilities required for research, especially the psychology of creativity in the arts and sciences.

e. General methodology treats the methods of research common to all sciences and endeavors to provide a general terminology usable in all arts and sciences.

f. Education for zetesis.

g. The study of conditions and incentives which stimulate zetesis.

h. Research centers, their organization and development.

SPECIALIZATION AND THE WIDER GOALS OF ZETETICS

Specialization in research is necessary, and it is the prevailing tendency at the present time. This is due to the multiplicity and complexity of the phenomena encountered in every field and also to the great variety of techniques needed in research. However, inevitable and useful as specialization in research has proved to be, it has the following disadvantages and even dangers which should be avoided:

a. It limits the personal development of the researcher by

confining his horizons to details and makes it difficult for him to get out of a one-track way of thinking. His outlook becomes, thus, narrower and narrower.

b. It deprives him of the kind of beauty, enlightenment, and inspiration which only wide perspectives can give.

c. It reduces his chances of making discoveries which lie hidden on the outskirts of a particular branch of science, often within the area of two overlapping sciences.

d. It isolates him from understanding the work of his colleagues who are active in other fields of the arts and sciences and makes him thus unprepared for teamwork in the solution of problems which encompass wider fields of research beyond the reach of his special field.

Zetetics attempts to sustain a balance between the analytical and the synthetic approach and thus to increase the efficiency of the particular mental activity needed in research and artistic creativity.

In order to achieve such a balance, at least 10 per cent of scientists, engineers, scholars, and artists should take up a study of the synthesis of human knowledge as their life's work. The term zetetists seems appropriate to designate such devotees of the new profession.

As I mentioned before, the adaptation of a diverse society to new conditions changing at an increasing rate poses problems which cannot be properly studied within the compass of any particular science. In order to recognize the difficulties of such problems and chart the course toward their solution, we need first of all the means for an early orientation among the prevailing trends, so as to foresee coming dangers and counteract them.

Secondly, we need a rational way of selecting far-reaching research projects and establishing the order of their importance.

Thirdly, we need more systematized knowledge concerning the ways of research and of creative activities in general, so as to make them more productive and effective.

Finally, we must educate a new kind of imaginative explorer

capable of building structures of knowledge out of the materials supplied by various specialized researchers. The rapidly developing new world could use a great many such *architects of knowledge—zetetists*. They will have to learn how to combine knowledge derived from large groups of arts and sciences and to mold it into unified structures functionally suitable, aesthetically valuable, and ethically appropriate for a higher level of living.

TAXILOGY AND A SYSTEMATIZED INVENTORY OF ARTS AND SCIENCES

Of the eight subdivisions of zetetics, the one which treats knowledge as a system is *taxilogy*. Its objectives are:

a. To supply and maintain an inventory of all the arts and sciences.

b. To develop a zetetic classification of the arts and sciences for facilitating orientation in research and education.

c. To suggest to an inquiring mind new relations between areas of knowledge.

d. To search for possible new branches of science.

The term taxilogy was chosen as suitable to cover the above tasks. It is derived from the Greek words *taxis* (arrangement) and *logos* (science).

Every science, having reached a certain early stage of its development, requires as a condition of its further growth a systematic, exhaustive list of its ever-expanding subject matters. Within each particular science such a list constitutes an inventory to be studied and ordered. To obtain patterns of order in objects, phenomena, ideas, and generalizations—the very essence of zetesis—such inventories must be established and occasionally revised and supplemented.

Sciences which have reached maturity already possess such inventories. For instance, linguists have catalogues of words called dictionaries. Classicists have catalogues of manuscripts, and historians make use of chronological lists of events. Linnaeus, Buffon, and others created a system of classification with extensive catalogues of plants and animals which became the basis of systematic botany and zoology.

Mineralogists have catalogues of crystals and minerals. Physicists have their ever-growing tables of atomic elements and nuclear particles which are playing an outstanding role in furthering discoveries. Chemists keep up-to-date lists of inorganic and organic substances. A list of diseases and their symptoms, together with the famous *materia medica*, forms the foundation of medicine. Astronomers have produced catalogues of planets and stars.

Even mathematicians, who are so intent on claiming that their domain of knowledge is free from everything concrete, possess, besides lists of formulae, and of two-, three-, and many-dimensional curves, most interesting collections of very concrete models.

The time has come to systematize the sciences, their branches, and knowledge as a whole by making an inventory of ancient and modern sciences with their definitions and interrelations, so as to foresee their trends and envisage new developments. Indeed, it is one of the tasks of taxilogy as a branch of zetetics to supply such an inventory as a guide and tool for further investigations.

I have prepared a list of over 1,400 items enumerating the arts and sciences in alphabetical order. Each item is provided with a brief description. A supplementary list consists of the same items classified into groups according to their areas of knowledge.

AREAS OF KNOWLEDGE AND THEIR BASIC SCIENCES

Various classifications of the arts and sciences exist at the present time, but none has been designed from the point of view of serving as a *guide to find gaps* in systematized knowledge.

One of the objectives of zetetics is to obtain an over-all view of our continuously growing store of systematized knowledge. As a step in this direction, it is necessary to classify all the arts and sciences into a consistent scheme. The scheme used here consists in the division of knowledge into five zones and twelve

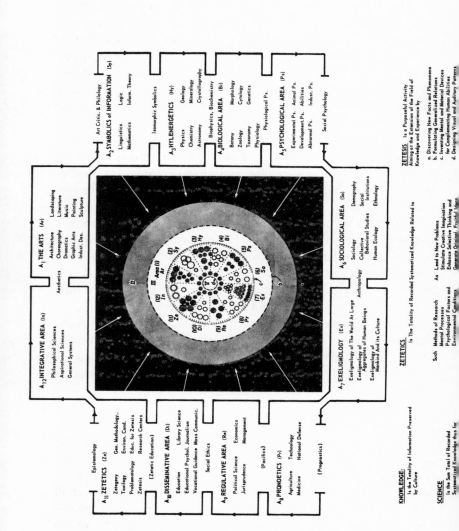

Zetetics and the Zetetic System of Knowledge

Figure 2

areas. Each area contains a number of sciences having a definite common function.

The chart in Figure 2 represents diagrammatically zetetics in a nutshell, with its definitions and its system of knowledge. The central portion shows the five zones and the twelve sectors of knowledge, surrounded by twelve rectangular spaces in which the particular sciences of each sector are enumerated. Below all this are definitions of knowledge, science, zetetics, and zetesis.

The purpose of the zetetic classification is to bring out inter-relations between the various areas of knowledge. It serves as a guide to the multifarious relations between the areas and the sciences. It facilitates orientation for goal-seekers just as a map does for travelers who are lost in the maze of roads and streets which cross a large metropolis in all directions. Every intercon-nected group of sciences, every subdivision of an art or science, and every particular branch of a science must find its place in the system.

The zetetic classification, as illustrated by the chart, consists of four concentric rings, a, b, c, and d, with twelve radii divid-ing the space between rings c and d into twelve sectors. Outside of the largest ring, a, extends the black region (I), the unknow-ables. This region is impenetrable by the human mind because of the limitations of both perceptual and conceptual abilities of *Homo sapiens*. In some distant future, parts of this region may become accessible, if evolutionary development favors the ex-tension of man's central nervous system. Between the large rings a and b lies the shaded region (II), the knowables which are not yet known; while the white region (III), between rings b and c, contains the as yet unsystematized knowledge.

Knowledge which becomes systematized occupies the region between the middle rings c and d. There it is fractionalized into twelve sector-like areas (*Ar* to *In*), each containing a cluster of small circles representing related sciences which tend toward unification. A single science is pictured as a starlike circle whose radius and circumference we can imagine as expanding with the growth of this particular science. The magnitude of the small circles indicates the relative amount of systematized information stored in each of the various sciences at a given time. The length and the number of the radial projections attached to the circles may suggest the extent to which the sciences are interconnected at the given stage of development.

These projections represent symbolically the origins of lines of mutual influence, not only between sciences within a particular sector, but also between the latter and sciences of other sectors. Drawing the complete lines was avoided so as not to complicate the picture. Similar projections are drawn on circle c to indicate the penetration of unsystematized knowledge from Region III into Region IV of systematized knowledge.

The overlapping of circles signifies a tendency toward unification. A nonshaded double circle within a sector indicates an interscience within an area, while double circles drawn directly on the radial border lines show sciences which tend to interconnect two areas. The more the areas become interrelated, the greater will be the number of double circles placed on the border lines. The more knowledge we gain concerning interrelations of the areas with each other, the closer they come to integration. For a complete integration of human knowledge, Region V is reserved.

In this diagram one such double circle has been placed on each of the twelve radial lines to indicate the particular science which at the present stage of development binds closely the adjacent areas of knowledge. For the sake of clear visualization, these sciences are collected close to ring d.

However, one of the radial lines shows two more double circles, which serve to indicate that more is known about the interrelations between areas Hy and Bi than about interrelations between other areas.

We may look on the three regions encompassed by ring d as an imaginative model representing the brain of mankind. Region V may thus become a coordinating center for all the recorded basic information which the human species has collected, systematized, and integrated during the historical period of its existence.

Let us review briefly the twelve areas of knowledge as represented in the diagram by sectors from *Ar* to *In* and indicate the principal links which bind these areas as a whole.

The Arts (Ar)

The arts occupy the first sector, *Ar*, of the diagram. They are the results of creative activity (zetesis) which, intensified by inspiration, produces unique objects of aesthetic quality. In their turn, objects of art evoke inspiration which sustains zetesis in all fields of knowledge. This area includes: architecture, choreography, dramatics, graphic arts, landscaping, music, painting, sculpture, literature, and industrial design.

Artists and writers are concerned with symbolic patterns of light, shade, colors, sounds, words, and sentences, all forming perceptual images which, besides evoking aesthetic emotions, enrich our experience and serve for *communication*.

Symbolics of Information (Sy)

The next sector, *Sy*, represents the result of a chain of developments which lead from primitive attempts of communication by sign language to articulated language and onward through systems of symbolic formalization to the as yet undeveloped stage of concept-formation. The *Sy* area includes linguistics, mathematics, logic, and information theory. Art criticism and philology (which is closely related to linguistics) may be regarded as connecting links between the area of the arts and the area of symbolics of information.

Mathematicians, logicians, and other scientists of area *Sy* are, like the artists, concerned with patterns. However, the patterns they form have a cognitive character which nonetheless evokes feelings of elegance and beauty. Their images consist of theorems, inferences, rules, and laws which are indispensable for the development of the sciences of other areas, and like the arts they serve for communication. Isomorphic symbolics—applied symbols of information—connects area *Sy* with the following one.

Sciences Dealing with Matter and Energy (Hy)

Next comes the group of sciences which we call hylenergetics, a combination of Greek words *hyle* (matter) and *energos* (active). This group is especially dependent on the previous one and is unified by the principle of equivalence of matter and energy. The basic sciences are: physics, chemistry, astronomy, geology, and mineralogy. The latter, mineralogy, contains a division of crystallography which manifests, if only partially, the first characteristic of living organisms, i.e., growth, and that binds this area with the following one, as shown by the lower double circle.

Biological Sciences (Bi)

The many aspects of the living world, as manifested in the processes of growth and reproduction, are studied by the sciences of group *Bi, unified by the principle of evolution.* Their subject matter ranges from the simplest units of life as they appear in single cells to complex organisms of the plant and animal kingdoms in an immense variety of forms and functions.

The basic sciences are botany, zoology, morphology, cytology, genetics, and physicology. They are related to the former area (*Hy*) by biophysics and biochemistry (shown by the two upper double circles) and are linked with the following area (*Ps*) by physiology, which is closely connected with physiological psychology.

Psychological Sciences (Ps)

Physiological psychology, first called psychophysics and then experimental psychology, started the modern development of the psychological sciences included in section *Ps*. Subsequently, experimental methods led to animal and comparative psychologies, group psychology, and social psychology, thus forming a chain which links them with sociology.

Sociological Sciences (So)

In the sector *So*, knowledge is being collected and systematized relative to the phenomena and conditions which produce, sustain, or change the many various forms of individual and group life. Sociology, originally called social physics and sometimes defined as the science of society, is the basic science in this area of knowledge.

The following main subdivisions of the sociological sciences, as represented by the circles in sector *So*, show the inherent interrelation of their subject matter with other areas of science:

a. Collective behavioral studies, by their relation to group and social psychology, represent the link with sector *Ps*.

b. Human ecology binds sector *So* with the biological sciences, *Bi*, by its connection with animal sociology and ecology.

c. Demography, the study of the vital processes, distribution, and composition of population aggregates, supplies the necessary data for the study of human ecology and social institutions.

d. Social institutions, their structure, statics, and dynamics, form the central part of the subject matter treated by sociology.

e. Ethnology is related to cultural anthropology.

f. Anthropology is closely related to the next sector (*Ex*), exeligmology.

Sciences Concerned with the Past (Ex)

Exeligmology is a word of Greek origin, meaning the science of unfolding. In zetetics, we use it as a collective name for the sciences of cosmogeny, evolution, and history.

Therefore, sector *Ex* of the diagram shows a cluster of circles divided into three groups. The group at the periphery consists of dark-shaded circles and represents branches of science concerned with cosmic evolution and the prehistory of *Homo sapiens*. The middle group consists of circles divided into a light and a dark part. These are concerned with biological and socio-historical aspects of man. Finally, the group closest to the center contains

139

clear circles which refer to the history of human culture. Please notice that there is a double circle on the borderline between the two sectors *Ex* and *Pr*, which signifies that it is based on the past but looking into the future. It is the budding science for which I think the name *prognostics* is the most suitable.

In the following table (Figure 3), branches of exeligmology are enumerated. It gives us a general picture of the development of the universe, including man and his culture.

Sciences Concerned with Providing for the Future (Pr)

Knowledge of the past stresses the need of providing for the future, and this takes us into sector *Pr*, called Pronoetics (a word of Greek origin meaning foresight). Its basic sciences are agriculture, medicine, technology (engineering), and national defense. All of these sciences aim to sustain life and provide for the needs of oneself, one's family, the community, the state, the country, and mankind as a whole. One of the branches of national defense which is becoming of paramount importance in our time is pacifics, the science of peace. It attempts to discover ways for nations to live together without recourse to warfare, thus filling a wide gap in our knowledge and relating group *Pr* to the next one, *Re*, the regulative sciences.

The Regulative Sciences (Social Cybernetics) (Re)

Life in large aggregates of human society requires a variety of systems for sustaining peaceful cooperation: jurisprudence, political science, economics, and management. These sciences reflect the basic knowledge which grew up in partial answer to the problems of individuals and groups living in families and societies of growing complexity. A tentative name for this group of sciences, namely, "social cybernetics," indicates their character of steering and maintaining balance in a process of gradual adjustment to ever-changing conditions.

The connecting link which binds this area of knowledge, *Re*, with the next, *Di*, the disseminative sciences, is a branch of social cybernetics which we call social ethics. It is concerned

FIGURE 3

I. Exeligmology of the world at large	1. Cosmogeny, a part of cosmology 2. Geogeny, a part of geology 3. Biogeny, a part of biology 4. Origin and development of species 5. Development and prehistory of *Homo sapiens*

II. Exeligmology of aggregates of human beings	1. a. Embryological development of members of a species
	   b. Biography of a particular individual
	2. a. Evolution of family, a part of sociology
	   b. History of a particular family, a generation, or a dynasty
	3. a. Evolution of a group (sociology and group psychology)
	   b. History of a particular group
	4. a. Evolution of urban, rural, and metropolitan populations
	   b. History of a particular population
	5. a. Evolution of ethnical groups, as part of anthropology
	   b. History of a particular ethnical group
	6. a. Evolution of communities, a part of sociology
	   b. History of a particular community
	7. a. Evolution of states, as part of political science
	   b. History of a particular state
	8. a. Evolution of empires, as part of political science
	   b. History of a particular empire
	9. a. Evolution toward a world community
	   b. History of a particular federation of nations

III. Exeligmology of mankind and his culture	1. History of the development of human culture 2. History of the development of sciences 3. History of the development of technologies 4. History of the development of art and literature 5. History of the development of systems of ideas (philosophy) 6. History of the development of aspirations

141

with setting up moral codes to orient social behavior for the harmonious functioning of human society.

The Disseminative Sciences (Di)

Knowledge accumulating from generation to generation could not be transmitted without a variety of public institutions —schools, colleges, libraries, museums, institutes of higher learning, and other means for disseminating the experience of earlier generations. Similarly important is the mass communication of current events and of all aspects of community, national, and international developments. The disseminative sciences of sector Di, like education, educational psychology, library science, and journalism, supply the knowledge available for this purpose.

A still wider objective of this area is to prepare the younger generation for creative activities by developing interest and skills necessary for the growth of the arts and the sciences. Zetetic education is the science which binds sector Di with the next one.

Zetetic Sciences (Ze)

For modern society, advancing in scope and population, it is not enough to record and disseminate the knowledge inherited from previous generations. New problems continually arise which require more knowledge than available at present. The sciences which study how knowledge can be increased in quality and quantity are included in sector Ze, to which the name zetetics has been given (derived from the Greek verb zeteo, to investigate). Its eight branches have already been discussed: (a) the origin of sciences, discoveries, and inventions; (b) the classification of knowledge; (c) the selection and formulation of problems; (d) the methodology of research; (e) the abilities required for research and all creative activities; (f) the environmental conditions and incentives which stimulate creative activities; (g) education for zetesis; and (h) organization and development of research centers.

The role of zetetics is to bring together and systematize

available information about zetesis. Thus, zetetics is the link which binds all the systematized areas of knowledge and tends toward their growth and unification. Epistemology and the philosophy of science are the links which bind this area with the next one.

The Integrative Sciences (In)

The last area, integrative sciences (*In*), can be described by the symbol

$$K_i = \int \text{cience}$$

where K_i stands for integrated knowledge and the word *science* is written with the elongated $\int$, representing the operation of integration. Accordingly, integration is:

an all-encompassing synthesis
leading to a consistent knowledge
of ways of life appropriate for
developing and sustaining a
creative human society.

In the area *In* are located the sciences which study the attempts so far made toward achieving integration. A circle is assigned to each of the following categories: general systems, various philosophies, theologies, and the many ideological patterns reflecting the highest human aspirations.

In our swift review of human knowledge, we have reached the borderline separating the area of integrative sciences, *In*, from the arts, *Ar*, which was our starting-point. We may now ask: is there any connection between these two adjoining areas? The answer is positive: a part of philosophy called aesthetics binds these two sectors together.

Synthesis of Systematized Knowledge

It remains to inquire about Region V, located at the center of the diagram. What are the contents of this region? Unfortunately, this region is as yet vacant, reserved, as was already mentioned, for the complete integration, that is, for a synthesis which would lead to a world view based not only on the totality of human knowledge, but also fusing the aspirational with the inspirational in human nature.

SUMMARY OF AREAS AND THEIR FUNCTIONS

By successive steps, aided by our sector diagram, we have succeeded in linking together the entire field of arts and sciences. We must keep in mind that the diagram represents symbolically the totality of our knowledge in a state of growth and transformation. Its dynamic quality suggests that a chain of reinforcing reactions is taking place throughout the twelve sectors of systematized knowledge in a continuous process of zetesis which tends to shape mankind's future as it evolves from the past.

We may summarize the twelve areas with the aid of a table (Figure 4) in which these areas are enumerated in five series, each distinguished by its particular function.

The first series contains two areas whose function is to facilitate communication by developing systems of symbolic representation of perceptual and cognitive activity.

The second series contains four areas of sciences which supply knowledge of facts and their basic relations to the world in which we live.

The third series, grounded on the second one, embraces four areas of sciences which extend our knowledge of the past and apply the results obtained by the second series, so as to provide and build for the future, while controlling the significant fluctuations *ever present* in a shift from past to future conditions.

The fourth series includes zetetic sciences, which are concerned with the growth of all the arts and sciences.

And, finally, the fifth series contains the area of integrative sciences which represent attempts toward an all-embracing synthesis.

And what is the deeper meaning of this system of knowledge? It gives a concise presentation of the totality of culture created by the human species: its accomplishments in the arts, its

FIGURE 4

FUNCTIONS OF AREAS OF KNOWLEDGE

Series	Areas of Knowledge	Function
I.	1. Arts 2. Symbolics of information	To develop systems of symbolic representation of perceptual and cognitive activity for purposes of communication
II.	3. Hylenergetics 4. Biological sciences 5. Psychological sciences 6. Sociological sciences	To systematize knowledge of basic facts and their relations
III.	7. Exeligmology 8. Pronoetics 9. Regulative sciences 10. Disseminative sciences	To systematize knowledge of the past, project future needs, and regulate activities
IV.	11. Zetetic sciences	To promote the growth of all the arts and sciences
V.	12. Integrative sciences	To create an all-embracing synthesis

accumulated knowledge, and its heritage of aspirations. Moreover, it brings out the close connections between the various areas of the arts and sciences and suggests the direction of their growth. This is the main function of zetetics.

The Links Between Areas

In our review of the five zones and the twelve areas of knowledge, we only casually mentioned the links which bind each area with the next one. It is helpful to imagine the lines of influence from each science breaking through the boundary of its area and linking this area with the other areas. Not in every case was the existence of links self-evident; some of them were found only by applying the zetetic principle of interdependence. Time limits permit the discussion of only one such link, i.e., zetetic education.

ZETETIC EDUCATION

As a link between the area of disseminative sciences and the area of zetetic sciences, zetetic education deals with the introduction of zetetic concepts into general education. Its aims are:

a. To familiarize students with the totality of the arts and sciences as a unified system.

b. To demonstrate the role of research and artistic creation in the growth of knowledge.

c. To make students aware of the treasures mankind possesses in the knowledge accumulated by the creative endeavors of past generations, and to awaken their interest in libraries, museums, and art galleries.

d. To help them project their personal role in society on the basis of their aspirations and abilities.

e. To facilitate the choice of goals and to coordinate them with their projected life's work.

f. To plan accordingly their further education.

Long-range planning is required to incorporate the above aims into the school curriculum and to develop new teaching aids for the entire course of primary and secondary education. This would have to be a major project for an extensive study by a team including numerous representatives from many fields of learning.

My suggestion is to start with experimental classes of integrated teaching based on the five interconnected series which I have shown you. This series corresponds to the five functions of the areas of systematized knowledge. Each of the five weekly school days could be devoted to one of the five functions. Instruction would thus sweep over the entire field of systematized human knowledge.

In the lower grades, an elementary approach would naturally be taken, which could be gradually expanded at the high school level.

FINAL REMARKS

The pertinent question now is: what is my conclusion in regard to educational research from the zetetic point of view?

At the present stage of development of zetetics, the answer can be given only in the form of a desideratum.

If our knowledge is to become a coherent, unified system, it should be disseminated by treating it as a whole. And that is the function of education.

Any division of instruction into separate cells, each containing a narrow range of subject matter, disconnected from the whole body of systematized knowledge, interferes with the acquisition of a broad perspective of the world in which we live and act.

It is, therefore, desirable to introduce as early as possible into the educational system of instruction a plan according to which the concept of unity is always kept in view.

Even on the level of professional education, the interconnection between all the arts and sciences should not be lost sight of. This applies to all domains of education, including the humanities, engineering, and adult education.

I believe that specialization should be postponed to an age when students have acquired a proper background for deciding what life work would give them the most satisfaction.

Meanwhile I wish all who are active in educational research great success in finding ways to solve one of the most *pressing problems of our time of rapid transitions*, namely, *to increase the scope and effectiveness of education.*

CHAPTER V

ON THE STRUCTURE OF
PHYSICAL KNOWLEDGE

NORWOOD RUSSELL HANSON

I

Under what circumstances would a person try to find some structural principles underlying all the physical sciences? Well, being *asked* to do so, for an occasion such as this, might be one such set of circumstances. But why should professional educators ask a mere philosopher of science to try? Presumably because if what I say is both true and new it might have constructive implications for the design of curricula in schools; let me at least hope that what I say will be true, even if not new. Whereas, if what I say is false, it may even then stimulate discussion which could, perhaps negatively, and certainly indirectly, affect the reflections of you pedagogical theorists; in that case I must hope that my views will be new, even if not true. With this much I am asking for it: "what Hanson says that is true, is not new—what is new is not true—and the rest is neither new nor true."

For reasons analogous to this "discussion-stimulating" function (of a structural analysis of physical knowledge) the chairman of a college's physics department might seek to order, classify, and systematize his own discipline—now in order to facilitate its consumption by undergraduates. The writer of a textbook in physics might be similarly motivated; here, too, what will constitute the best introduction to the subject will be determined by the author's conceptions of just what comprise the more elementary and fundamental problems; from these he will guide his readers to the advanced features of physical science.

But these all seem very practical reasons for undertaking such a study. One can imagine undertaking reflections on the conceptual structure of physical science *not* because of having been invited to so reflect, nor because of having to design a college science program, or a textbook's table of contents; one can imagine engaging in such an inquiry "for its own sake." Plato's discussions (in *The Republic*) of his Divided Line, Auguste Comte's "Classification of the Sciences" as well as those of J. A. Thomson and Hügo Munsterberg—these were studies of the conceptual interrelations of the physical sciences (amongst others), studies made for no reason beyond achieving clarity and understanding about how mathematics and the several physical sciences are related and hang together, and where they differ and should never be fused or confused. Knowing this much about the physical sciences is thus to understand each of them a little better —optics, particle dynamics, celestial mechanics, electro-dynamics, microphysics, etc.—just as being able to distinguish, in general, pure mathematics from mathematical physics is to have a more reliable comprehension of each. And, indeed, that is just where my analysis will begin today, for perceiving where to cleave the study of numbers from the study of matter-and-motion already invokes those principles operative in ordering the several physical sciences themselves.

II

A proposition of pure mathematics—one such as the Binomial Theorem—is often characterized as being "purely formal." Its validity is in no way contingent on observation or experiment, on measurement or microscopes. Indeed, the Binomial Theorem is something "merely unpacked" from the number-theoretic commitments one must make when playing the mathematics game at all. Follow the Rules Consistently—constitutes the *sine qua non* of pure mathematics. Of course, there can be endless discussions at the foundations; e.g., whether, for certain purposes, to accept Peano's Postulates, or Huntington's, or Zermelo's—Russell's or Hilbert's, Quine's or Kleene's, or Heyting's. But such inquiries turn on different considerations. Once one *has* decided to play the numbers game *à la* Hilbert, or *à la* Heyting, then the validity of all derivations generable therefrom is determined. Thus within either of these last-mentioned formulations the Binomial Theorem is quickly constructed.

Despite the indispensable role played by mathematical techniques in the articulation of physical statements, there must always remain a profound and indissoluble difference between, e.g., the "pure Binomial Theorem" and a description of physical phenomena in binomial form. In physics, following the rules is not enough. For the physicist's subject-matter is not exclusively determined for him by the postulates and principles of inference he accepts—as is the case in the formal disciplines like mathematics and logic. *Nature* has written the physicist's script—in invisible ink. The task is then subtly to devise techniques, theoretical and experimental, by which to render more and more of that script visible and intelligible. For in physics the inferential techniques are created in order to decipher the script, whereas in pure mathematics the inferential techniques *are* the script. Similarly, at war colleges generals play board games to sharpen their strategies and tactics for future campaigns. But those same games might be sold later to tired businessmen seeking diversion—sold under names like "Battleground," "Cavalry Tactics," or "Air War." Construed in this way the games are self-contained, closed, rule-governed, and impervious to questions of use—much as with the game now called "Monopoly." But for generals and physicists (as against tired businessmen and mathematicians) it is the degree to which such formal games can help them to "tell the truth" and "predict the future" which constitutes the rationale behind playing them at all.

This contrast demarcates the deep logical difference between physics and mathematics. Any well-made claim of mathematics, e.g., that $(x + y)^3 = x^3 + 3x^2y + 3xy^2 + y^3$, is such that its negation is not even false—it is self-contradictory. Similarly, to be playing chess and yet moving the rook diagonally is not simply to have made an error (as when one assigns the wrong melting point to phosphorous); it is to have broken the rules altogether! Game-like disciplines, chess and mathematics, are such that inferences, moves, and theorems permissible within them are *necessarily* permissible. Their negations don't even make sense—given the game's rules. Whereas in the physical sciences, despite their degree of mathematical sophistication, the observation-statements which form at the bottom of a page of calculation are not necessary, as are theorems of mathematics. The physicist may indeed reason that P will melt at 44°C. (ptc); but since this is not just a formal theorem, but an observation statement, it is not senseless to suppose that P might melt at some temperature other than 44°C.—at most it is false, not absurd. What temperature phosphorous does in fact melt at has been determined by nature, not by our rules. Well-made claims in mathematics, therefore, are either necessarily valid or necessarily inconsistent—depending on the local rules of the algorithm-game one is playing. Well-made claims within physics, however, are quite otherwise; that they are well-made may mean that they are legitimately inferred from initial conditions in accordance with certain laws and principles. But that they are *true*, or *false*, this cannot be ascertained simply from scrutiny of the physicist's inference. The best celestial mechanicians of the last century certified that, according to Newtonian theory, the perihelial point of Mercury's orbit should advance 528″ of celestial arc per century. But that observational conclusion is in fact false, however consistent with the theory. For Mercury's perihelion insists on advancing 528″ +38″ of arc each century (these are Leverrier's figures of 1859). This intractable fact forced physicists continually to amend Newtonian theory, and ultimately to abandon it altogether in determinations of near-solar perturbations. Is there anything comparable which, if it did occur in physical nature, would force our abandonment of chess, or of the number theories within which we generate the Binomial Theorem? No, nothing!

This logical ravine between the rule-governed sign-designs of higher mathematics and the mountains of observation statements articulated in physics is *the* major landmark in any charting of the structure of physical knowledge. On the one hand the stark simplicity of the distinction makes it fit for consumption by high school students, and even children in grammar school. Yet it is arresting to remark how late in the history of science this clear cleavage was effected. Galileo was not fully aware of the distinction, and many passages in Newton, Laplace, Lagrange, Maxwell, Whewell, and Thomson reflect considerable uncertainty over the matter. Even fairly recent works by physicists, like Kolin's *Physics* (New York, 1950) and Pieirl's *Laws of Nature* (London, 1955), decompose over this point. And it is easy to see why the glass darkens. Ask a student the following:

Q. Does $2 + 2 = 4$?

A. Of course!

Q. Does 2 quarts of mercury added to another 2 quarts equal 4 quarts of mercury?

A. Of course (really!).

Then, before his eyes you pour quarts of Hg into a precisely graduated beaker. The meniscus, of course, fails to reach up to the "4 quarts" line. Sometimes an astonished student will conclude that $2 + 2 = 4$ is not true! Sometimes the accuracy of the beaker is doubted. But more often, thankfully, the student will construe all this as marking something unusual about Hg itself. The moral? *No statement of pure mathematics can be presumed necessarily true when adapted to physical inquiry.*

A variation of this "philosophical quiz" consists in asking the student if substance A will be harder than substance C, given that A is harder than B and B is harder than C. Again the ready reply: "of course." Thence to the famous demonstration involving deformations—wherein three substances are chosen such that A deforms B (as, e.g., by scratching it) but not vice versa and B deforms C, yet A cannot deform C.

The point can be made to the student in an even more obvious way by asking him whether it is true that the sun rises in the east.

A. Of course!

Q. But what if, tomorrow, the sky lightens first in the direction of Monticello, and up comes the sun at 260° (instead of "where it belongs"— 90°, in the direction of Danville).

I have encountered two responses to this serio-comic query.

A_1. The sun would still be rising in "the east" since that is what we *call* the direction (*any* direction) in which the sun rises.

A_2. We would have to deny that the sun rises in the east, since that is a direction fixed by the North Star and the stellar constellations.

These two answers illuminate the distinction we have been delineating. For the student who answered as in A_1, "The sun rises in the east" is an *analytic* or a *necessary* claim—invulnerable just like the Binomial Theorem. It could not be false since all it does is to unpack what was built into his semantical rule box. For our A_2 student, however, "The sun rises in the east" is a *synthetic* or a *contingent* claim—vulnerable, just like saying that phosphorous melts at 44°C., a claim which *could* be false, but just happens not to be.

III

Some perplexing statements in physics have the same need for analysis, in the absence of which students often reach the Ph.D. level and remain unclear as to the essential differences between physics and mathematics. Consider these claims:

"No perpetual motion machine is constructible."

"An infinite amount of energy would be required to accelerate a body faster than *c*."

"Electrons must be described only in terms of partially defined states."

It is sometimes difficult to know whether such claims are only succinct restatements of the rules of an algorithm, or whether they are genuine empirical descriptions—whether they are like "No rook can move diagonally" or more like "Phosphorous melts at 44°C." Or sometimes they can be supposed to oscillate, as does "The sun rises in the east"—the real meaning of which is clear only in a careful description of the context of utterance. Professor Pieirls describes the Law of Universal Gravitation as being a mixture of empirical and mathematical elements (in his book *The Laws of Nature*). The valuable insight behind his remark is quite destroyed in his exposition, since (like oil and water) physics and mathematics don't mix, logically, however true it is that contemporary physics must be well lubricated mathematically at every turn.

In all the formidable jungles of pedagogy faced by physics teachers there seems to be no more troublesome pitfall than this one. And, as the mathematical sophistication expected of a physics student increases, the likelihood of perplexity on this issue likewise increases. Yet, the distinction is quite comprehensible even for youngsters. My eight-year-old son has understood the simple example I've tendered here. The trick is to keep the student alert to the distinction as he ascends higher into the more rarified structures of physical knowledge. Accomplishing this, however, will be inestimably easier when one's students have teethed on the contrast between the sign-design game of pure mathematics and the informative (hence vulnerable) claims at the bottom of every page of physical calculation.

IV

Once having located the edifice of physics on one side of this logical canyon, the local *intraphysical* geography becomes somewhat more tractable—although, again, intellectual wind currents caused by the canyon are continually felt at the upper levels of physical science. This is because our claims about the physical world *must* be embodied in the language of mathematical transformations and functions. This practical advantage constitutes a logical disadvantage and a pedgogic problem—one rarely known to biology teachers or to historians and philosophers of biology (e.g., Nordenskiöld, Woodger, Arber, Singer, Beckner, Gregg, Pirie, Fulton, Stannard, or Greene).

Very early in one's study of matter it becomes necessary to address the structure and properties of the subject matter, i.e., matter itself. The question "What is matter?" however, is too rarely faced *as such* in physics teaching; and, granted, it does seem a disconcertingly philosophical query—such as might trigger a symposium at Notre Dame. But in the context of physics teaching the question quickly transforms into a mosaic of constituent queries like "What is a body?" "What is inertia?" "What is mass?" "What is weight?" "What is a *c*. of *g*.?" "What is density?" "What is specific gravity?" Quite quickly the student learns a list of little rules by the use of which these properties of objects can be determined. Even here the exposition could be spiced up with puzzlers like "Could a physical object be intangible?" "Could a body be in two places at once?" or "Could two objects be in the same place at one time?" or "Could an event or an experiment be *exactly* duplicated at two different times?" and so on. Grappling with these would relieve the rigors of rote repetition somewhat; and let's face it, really rehearsing the formulae will always require some rote repetition. Furthermore, such examples would also test the strength of our earlier distinction, for more than one physicist has laid it down as "mathematically necessary" that bodies cannot be in two places at once—or more exactly, that distinct masses cannot be mathematically described by more than one set of coordinate values for any given value of t. (This must remind one of Phillip Frank's justifiable attack on a colleague who purported to "prove mathematically" that no body's velocity could surpass c [in *Philosophy of Science*].)

Talking about the static properties of physical objects—their equilibria, centers, stability, relative impenetrability, etc.—this comes seductively near to representing physics as "almost-pure" mathematics; indeed the history of analytical mechanics appears thus, and most of what one would master in that discipline figures within Part III of the *Mathematical Tripos*. For the extra-formal "physical" interpretations required at this level of natural science are minimal. It is as if we began with pure geometry, arithmetic, and algebra and added the fewest possible physical concepts (i.e., parameters pertaining to the properties of objects), their divisibility, their measurability, their ponderosity, their "balance," etc. Even here our earlier "mathematics *versus* physics" distinction obtains; but here it can appear that physics is simply geometry-plus-mass. Reflect for a moment on Galileo's references to the physical world as a book written entirely in geometrical figures, such that the nongeometer struck him as an utter illiterate amongst natural philosophers. Newton's use of the idea of punctiform masses—geometrical points which behaved on paper as do physical masses in our world; this is another example of the historical intimacy between physics and mathematics which obtained at the level of statics and the properties of bodies.

Once one brings in motions—in kinematics—the simplicity of a purely mathematical model for physics begins to get ornate. For it is not a *mathematical* truth that a body will either remain at rest or else move uniformly and rectilinearly to infinity (in the absence of impressed forces, the standard assumption in kinematics). Alternatives to this state of affairs can consistently be imagined. Our students should know that Aristotle and two millennia of Aristotelians would have denied such a kinematical claim. It was only three hundred years ago that this commitment was nailed to the top of the physicists' theoretical pages. As for the "Law" that the magnitude of a force is a function of the accelerations to which a mass is subjected—the status of this vis-à-vis our earlier distinction is markedly difficult to determine. Ernst Mach and C. D. Broad would cite this "Second Law of Motion" as an unqualifiedly empirical claim, a generalization of what we encounter when pushing pianos and catching medicine balls. But opponents of no less stature, e.g., Henri Poincaré and Victor Lenzen, would stress the conventional (or definitional) function of $F = ma$. They would argue that these symbols instruct us as to what we *mean* by "force," and that hence no mere empirical finding could upset it. For should an acorn kicked over smooth ice describe a "figure eight" we would not count the Second Law thus disconfirmed. Rather, we would hunt for the hidden forces, strings, air currents, or effluvia responsible for such a queer, noninertial, and force-bound motion. Indeed, we would be virtually certain a priori that *something* must have deflected the acorn into its lemniscoid path.

Again, here is an occasion for a student's speculative inquiry —inquiry of a type with the questions he will certainly encounter when he one day finds himself stranded and alone on the frontiers of quantum mechanics or astrophysics. Just as Florence Nightingale urged that hospitals should not spread disease, so also educators should insure that schools do not stifle inquiry. But how often all of us smother such searching questions in the interests of rehearsing the algebraic recipes needed right now to describe uniform motion in a straight line, or accelerated motion, or gravitationally induced motions, or rectorial analysis. It is sometimes too easy to carp on the cruel cutoffs we impose on students' conversations—in the business of "getting on with" the curricula. I've done it too often myself (cf. *Physics Today*, 1955). But when my own son asked me (just as I was starting the car), "Daddy, what *causes* gravity?" I felt the knife all teachers feel sometimes. Should I have missed my morning class and discussed the rudiments of general field theory with the boy? (He was also late for school!) We agreed to discuss the matter later. So I can well understand the teacher who opts for discussing the conceptual foundations of physics "later." A practical conscience makes intellectual cowards of us all. But in an ideal world of ideal schools composed of ideal students—we could there discuss the philosophical status of Newton's Laws of Motion to our hearts' content—without fear of falling behind the syllabus (or behind Canaveral's orders for more "slide-rule soldiers"). And our understanding of all the physics to follow would be broadened and deepened thereby.

Thus from statics (= the properties of bodies at rest), where we add but a physical minimum to our mathematical structures, to

kinematics (= the descriptive aspects of bodies in motion)—
where we add more. Thence to dynamics where we add much
more still. For here we do not simply describe the motions of bodies; it is the *causes* of those motions—the pushes, pulls, rubs,
attractions, and repulsions which set things off, keep them moving, or halt them—which hold us now. Classical particle dynamics is really a Pandora's box of philosophical perplexities, the box
out of which spilled some of the greatest glories of modern
science. For when Newton opened the lid he dimly perceived
the key for understanding *all* motions in our universe—from the
majestic circlings of planets, to the insignificant fall of a Lincoln-
shire apple. That key lay in $F \propto \gamma \, (Mm)/r^2$—The Principle of
Universal Gravitation. This mighty pronouncement at once fused
ballistics with kinematics, celestial mechanics with tidal theory,
hydrodynamics with particle theory. But, despite the dramatic
unification effected within physics by the Newtonian synthesis,
the box of Pandora dumped many further perplexities into the
Natural Philosopher's broad lap. For gravity was apparently a
universal *attraction* of all objects for all other objects, an attraction varying directly as the masses of the objects and inversely
as the distances between them. But what a remarkable *kind*
of attraction! The earth attracts the moon, and the moon
the earth—but no ordinary knife can cut the tie than binds
them. No leaden wall (laid Van Allen-wise) can affect gravitational attraction—as one might break up a comparable elec-
tromagnetic attraction with sheet copper reflections. No gen-
erator could increase such a gravitational attraction—only
increasing the masses of earth and moon or decreasing the distance between them will do that. No wonder my boy asked,
"What causes gravity?"

No wonder my best student ever urged rewriting the classical Law of Inertia to make it read "every two bodies in the universe are such that they move toward each other directly as their
masses and inversely as the distance between them." This is a
kinematical pronouncement *merely*, one which slices all the
specious causality right out of classical physics. That is, it lays

down $F \propto \gamma \, (Mm)/r^2$ as a descriptive fact about the motion of bodies, similar to the Law of Inertia as usually construed. So attraction need not serve as a ghostly explanation of, e.g., planetary motion, since this latter just *is* as $(Mm)/r^2$! Similarly, one doesn't explain the tangibility of physical objects, since that is what physical objects are.

v

Now, such an intellectual encounter *must* reveal elementary physics as an inviting path to contemporary natural philosophy, and not (as it so often is now) a rather boring, rote rehearsal of recipes preparatory to the "exciting, modern stuff." Once the student sees the *rationale* behind the controversy which rages over gravitational attraction, he can more fully understand other attempts to avoid animistic explanations in physics, explanations in terms of pushes and pulls. Thus a youngster *could* see the point of having planets move along geodesics within "space-time envelopes" whose geometrical properties are altered by the presence of large masses. General relatively, indeed, is the physical theory that treats planetary orbital motion not as a resultant deflection from "natural" inertial motion; rather Mercury's path is the most "natural" line (of least resistance) through spaces whose formal properties have been affected by the presence of other enormous bodies.

The relationship between classical optics and quantum field theory also reveals that a student's first questions are not about *elementary* physics, but about *fundamental* physics. For on reconsidering the vexatious debate over whether light was undulatory or corpuscular, the alert youngster *must* have questions concerning how such things as the findings of Young, Fresnel, Foucault, and Fizeau—while they *did* reveal light as wave-like —could also have proved that light lacked particularity. This latter was a massive inference made in nineteenth-century physics; all the more difficult then to move men's minds to where they could appreciate the findings of Hertz, Planck, Einstein, Compton, Raman, Thompson, Davisson and Germer, Stern and Gerlach —findings which established the "fine structure of light" as granular, in addition to its grosser undulatory manifestations.

In short, the departmental structures within physical science soon melt under the student's sizzling, searching questions—*if* he is encouraged to ask them. Quantum electrodynamics and classical optics emerge for him as two different attempts to comprehend the one subject matter, LIGHT. And General Relativity and Classical Celestial Mechanics also appear as different attempts to comprehend planetary perturbations. In this way physical science is a conceptual mosaic reflecting the natural phenomena of our world first this way, then that way—sometimes with quite different objectives. And *that's* the point: physics' objectives at different times may be quite distinct from what they are at other times. For a man building a radio telescope will not, and should not, get cramps over nuclear shell theory. And a man theorizing about theodolites need not wax neurotic about advances in the perihelion of Mercury. So specific tasks easily fall into compartments—but the content of physical science as a whole does not. In an engineering class on internal combustion engines the student who asks about solid state configurations of hot metal crystal lattices is just "changing the subject" and should be kept in line for the good of all. But physics is natural philosophy: the boy who asks "What causes gravity?" or "Why do planets move in conic sections?" or "Why does Mercury's perihelion show a secular advance?" is not changing the subject dealt with in "Physics I." Rather, he is deepening it for everyone around him. The student who *must* ask how physical laws came to be known at all *before* he can use them in churning out answers like a slot machine—such a student should be wreathed in gold stars, for he is showing his fellows, and his seniors, what kinds of questions will one day grip the man who fights to the frontiers of physics. Questions like "What is a measurement, really?" "What is an observation in physics?" "What should a theory do?" "How should a conservation principle be employed?" and "What is the relationship between a physical phenomenon and its mathematical description?"—these are the deep, exciting queries of contemporary physics, in response to which the slide-rule slickers fade in stature. "Getting the numbers right" and "Working the transformations well" are matters more for answer-giving machines, like the IBM 7090. But for those problems that make physics into natural philosophy, it will take a question-asking man every time.

VI

My thesis is now in danger of collapsing. Am I saying (the kind of thing sometimes said in pure analytic philosophy) that all questions are, ultimately, the same question—and that therefore the subject cannot be structured, save by second-rate textbook writers for second-rate students at second-rate colleges? No—that would be too much. Let me concede that there *is* such a thing as "changing the subject" in natural science—as when a discussion of semi-permeable membranes is halted by queries concerning interpretations of Quantum Mechanics. However, in physical science it is risky to draw any hard and fast lines. One should certainly not try to do so in the presence of students who cannot yet respond as the subject may later permit. The student who probes with "What is gravity?" or "What is space?" or "What is energy?"—he *may* be just a brat bent on battering the busy teacher. But he may also be tenacious enough to resist all pedagogic deflections and balm, in which case all around him may profit from seeing the paper walls set up in textbooks torn to shreds.

Let me conclude by saying again that physics, at its best, is natural philosophy. When any philosophy is too hastily restructured in "architectonic" terms the result can be dreary in its details and degenerate in its design. An architectonic of physical science, then, should never be more than loose guidelines for the guidance of syllabus drafters and textbook writers. But an architectonic ought never to crystallize into a set of *rigid* criteria for determining relevance or significance. Anyone who seeks to break down a wall rather than go through a door should be encouraged whenever possible. Physics today is a powerful instrument of mind and matter because of the irreverent wall-breakers of the seventeenth and twentieth centuries. A purported "Structure of Physical Knowledge" can never be more than a pedagogically heuristic blueprint. When conceived of as more—as an hierarchical series of disciplines, trials, and achievements—it must fail, even for the youngest students. For they will, after all, only ask the questions which a subject matter naturally presents to them. Their *genuinely* unsettling juvenile perversities are usually manifested in other ways.

DISCUSSION OF DR. HANSON'S PAPER

DR. SCHWAB: No one would deny that physics belongs on the side of the ravine that you put it on. However, I do want to raise a question as to whether you are quite right in your metaphor about mathematics and physics not mixing. To raise the question by noting a slip: at one point you said, "For it is not a mathematical truth that a body will either remain at rest or else move uniformly and rectilinearly to infinity in the absence of impressed . . ." what?

DR. HANSON: "Forces," I said quite clearly.

DR. SCHWAB: Yes, yes, I know, but is it not the case that at the moment you mention force you are no longer in kinematics but in dynamics?

DR. HANSON: Actually I want to do two things which are slightly inconsistent. I will grant that there is a real thrust to your question: in any discipline one must set up boundary conditions. One determines which set of unquestioned considerations is going to be fully operative in the discipline in question and then addresses an ideal case. The kind of kinematics we are discussing here resides strictly within analytical mechanics. There never has been a physical context free of impressed forces nor could there be. In other words, the physical discipline we have addressed is conditional, and unfilled; it is hypothetical all the way through. The theoretician here is simply telling us *what it would be like* to realize a physical state of affairs within which an ideal kinematics might be fully realized. What you are pointing out is that there is in fact no such state of affairs to be encountered, observationally or experimentally.

DR. SCHWAB: Yes.

DR. HANSON: And that much constitutes a dynamical statement. It's a statement of physics that there can be no such state of affairs as force-free motion. However, once one grants this the formal properties of a theory of motion which granted such a theoretical springboard might still be studied.

DR. SCHWAB: In a way this is more complex than I had hoped

to deal with. You have spoken to my point not as an answer to the question but as an agreement with a peculiarity which exists. I want to state it more simply.

DR. HANSON: I won't deny the peculiarity.

DR. SCHWAB: I know, but let me indicate the full range of what I think is peculiar and invite your response. You will recall that Karl Pearson, speaking in the voice of Clifford, says, roughly, "As for me, I would wish that the conception of force be barred eternally from physics and thus return dynamics to the pure science of kinematics." Now the fact that he could say this and that nobody listened indicates how far there is something about physics in which notions like force are so vexed that it is hard to know whether they are mathematical or physical.

At another point you did something which may have been tongue-in-cheek. You have a list of names, all of whom but one are physicists. That one is a logician, Whewell.

DR. HANSON: Sorry, Whewell was a *geophysicist*, and also the Master of Trinity College at Cambridge University. He was a professional scientist. He wrote an influential book called *Astronomy and General Physics*. The fact that his works on the philosophy of discovery and the history of science got more reputation for him than his works in science was for him a disappointment.

DR. SCHWAB: An interesting biography, which makes more interesting the fact that he expressed an idea developed by Einstein that the greatest mistake that we make about physics is to suppose that it is an "inductive" science. Einstein and Whewell suggest that physics, quite the contrary, is the imaginative invention of an essentially mathematical construction adequate to subsume the data which one is concerned to organize and account for. Now this in no way denies that physics is on the physical side of the physics-mathematics ravine, but it does suggest—and this is what I want to invite your attention to and your comments on— that the physics and the mathematics do mix in the sense that the set of what Einstein called primary propositions (from which one deduces propositions which are empirical) are *freely chosen*, and, therefore, have the quality of mathematics.

DR. HANSON: What you say is false.

DR. SCHWAB: Wait a minute. And consequently when the empirical test is made, as you are insisting that it must be made, it is made not of an isolated proposition alone but on the entire corpus.

DR. HANSON: That's all right.

DR. SCHWAB: That's all I am asking you to clarify.

DR. HANSON: Yes, that is true. But if I were to cast about for a mathematical paradigm within physics, Lagrange's analytical mechanics might serve well. There, from terse statements of abstract principles, even from "philosophical" principles, he's able to unpack a multiformity of observational claims, and to do so in a quite rigorous manner. The only test of the whole game is whether or not the stuff that comes out at the bottom of a page of calculation does truly square with the facts.

DR. SCHWAB: And all I am suggesting is that insofar as the whole big corpus of theory can be treated algorithmically then there is a funny way in which physics and mathematics do mix to such an extent that physics is, as you yourself were saying, peculiar among the sciences. Biologists don't have the problem.

DR. HANSON: That's what you are suggesting and that's what I am denying—that what comes out of the bottom of the page is invulnerable. The entire semantical structure of the rest of the system is affected in this because it is connected logically to the observation statements in the most intimate way. What this means, if I may just continue, is that even the most "transparent" principle, like the Principle of Conservation of Energy (which might well figure at the top of any page of calculation), looks like little more than a decision on the part of the theoretician to "balance" his equations in one way or another—even so, such as these remain empirically vulnerable claims. If one can make this point all the other jazz about the algorithmic similarities between doing pure mathematics and doing theoretical physics can be granted—because these are, after all, concerning one's self only with chains of inference and axiomatically designed systems. I can grant all that and still say nonetheless that, semantically, the pure physics and the pure mathematics are on opposite sides of the logical ravine; this goes for every single statement within the entire deductive unpacking.

DR. SCHWAB: We don't have any argument, so somehow or other you and I have not come to grips with the issue that I was trying to clarify. I will agree with every word you said . . . .

DR. HANSON: Say it again. I . . . .

DR. SCHWAB: Nobody in his right mind could argue against your thesis as to which side of the ravine physics is on.

DR. HANSON: Then I don't understand what *you* are arguing about.

DR. SCHWAB: I am not arguing. I am inviting clarification of the fact that as you do your algorithmic job down toward but not quite to the empirical level, the terms involved in the propositions are not terms that point to a physical, e.g., the conservation, law. The propositions are not talking about point-at-able things if one looks at them carefully. For example, you know very well that one of the particles that Pauli invented was invented precisely for the convenience of preserving one of the conservation laws as a convenient first gimmick at the top.

DR. HANSON: You are really answering my question for me, because it was the nature of that "invention" of the *neutrino* (in 1929 and 1930), an invention generated solely in order to save the conservation principle, which threw a shadow of dubiety on that particular discovery. It wasn't until the empirical work of Cowan and Reines in 1956 and 1957 (at Savannah River) that the neutrino became fully respectable; *there* was an observable effect that showed the physicist not only to be *inventing* entities to save a theory, but also to be discovering empirical evidence for this invention.

DR. SCHWAB: I agree.

DR. HANSON: This is what happened. I can give you scores of examples like this—Leverrier and Adams, for example. They were also concerned with a similar problem. They said, "Look here, the planet Uranus is not keeping time properly; the only way we can both acknowledge that fact and also save celestial mechanics is to suppose that there is another object, some 'dark body,' which has the following properties, a, b, c . . . etc." And they worked out the properties of this "in reverse," as it were. What would have to be the properties of a planet in order to perturb Uranus as it is perturbed?

DR. SCHWAB: And then you go and look and there it is.

DR. HANSON: Adams had entertained this hypothesis two years before Leverrier himself had. He argued that there might well be a body of this required sort—but he wasn't taken too seriously, for a number of reasons. This makes a long story, but certainly no one paid much attention to this early conjecture and it would have been a lot better for Adams if, in addition to generating the claim that would have saved celestial mechanics, he could also have located an observation then and there. Of course, there *was* material available in his manuscripts which, had observers then been more steadfast and careful, probably would have established Neptune's existence. But it wasn't until the insight which was precipitated by Leverrier's work, and the telescopic discovery by Galle in Berlin, that this actually became a vital hypothesis.

So you see, Joe, this is all still wide open vis-à-vis the question of what is the logical status of the claims. I want to argue that if there is an issue between Professor Schwab and myself, it is this: he's calling attention to the similarities between the inferential techniques that go into the doing of mathematics on the one hand, and those in physical theory on the other; this seems to be no more than the recognition that when you get a cluster of premises you unpack them by the logically most acceptable and direct techniques. Of course, it turns out that when the premises are expressed mathematically one unpacks them according to the techniques of *mathematical* unpacking. This, whether they be inferences in mathematics or in physics.

DR. SCHWAB: I thought I was adding one other thing: the

question of the purport of the terms in the premises. They do not refer directly to empiricals and consequently suggest something strangely mathematical about physics.

DR. HANSON: You are calling attention to something, but I think you are doing it in the wrong way. If you say that there is something strangely mathematical about physics this is like injecting the mistaken suggestion that after all when you are concerned with axioms as in physics the best people to have around are professors of mathematics.

DR. SCHWAB: No, no, I am not suggesting that.

DR. HANSON: Well, in any event let's *suppose* that you were. If you *had* suggested that, it would have been false. (It's sometimes difficult to know *what* you are suggesting!) I think you are calling attention to the fact that at the level of the highest order premises in advanced physical theory one can't always tie the constituent terms to observables. Take thermo-dynamics: you find a term like "$\sqrt{-1}$." What the hell does this tie up with?

DR. SCHWAB: Well, then, what the hell does force tie in within classical mechanics?

DR. HANSON: If there are problems about *force* and problems about $\sqrt{-1}$, what you have got to do at the top of the page is to make the machinery go well enough so that you can get observations at the bottom. Given this, one can tolerate some queer things topside.

DR. SCHWAB: That's what I am suggesting. And this queerness is very strangely mathematical.

DR. HANSON: No, the queerness is very strangely physical. This is what one must put up with in physics to get observation-statements at the bottom of the page.

DR. SCHWAB: Okay.

DR. HANSON: You don't have to do the same thing as that in mathematics at all.

DR. SCHWAB: Go back to the Mendel case that you were kind enough to refer to earlier. When Mendel invents his hypothetical expansion of the binomial it turns out, by the kind of empirical test you have emphasized, to take very good account of what kind of babies we have, depending on what kind of papas and mamas they have. The biologist nods and says, "how interesting," but always somebody has got to show me a gene under the microscope. Physicists don't do that.

DR. HANSON: Now, it depends. It depends on the physicist, you know . . . .

DR. SCHWAB: No, no, not about the terms at those high-level premises.

DR. HANSON: Well, I will make one reference to a remark made to me by the discoverer of the positron—by Carl D. Anderson. At the High Energy Conference in Rochester in 1957 we were discussing the evidence for the existence of the neutrino; the remark he made was significant for an experimental physicist. He said, "I don't believe there is any such thing. All they (Cowan and Reines) show are some numbers, and not all of the numbers. I can just barely believe there is a genuine effect." Now, of course, these doubts have been laid to rest; but what Anderson was saying then was this: "If you really want me to entertain the neutrino as a physical entity capable of all the explanatory tricks the theoreticians want, then show me something, in a cloud chamber or somewhere, something that is really going to make a difference. I want to see what the *difference* is that answers to the name 'neutrino.'" Now you are quite right to point out that, to theoreticians, this kind of complaint doesn't mean much—or not very much.

DR. SCHWAB: Well, this is all— I think I'll put it since you have gone back to those chaps that you wouldn't let Phenix have. For every ten Carl Andersons, there is also a physicist who postulates the existence of a particle which by definition was virtually detectable. You will agree that's why it took so long. . . .

DR. HANSON: Well, it was detectable but the whole occasion was just . . . .

DR. SCHWAB: You interrupted that time . . . .

DR. HANSON: Because I think you are going to make a mistake and I want to prevent that, for you, and for us; for the sake of the discussion, you know. Consider a radioactive source, a homogeneous source, and shield it against the beta and gamma rays. The alpha rays then emitted will trace out a star: spokes of a rimless wheel. Let us say then that all of these particles will be of roughly the same range; this we will call an "alpha star," it being quite compatible with the expected conservation of energy. But now change the shielding: shield the source against the alpha rays and the gamma rays. Then we get the beta *spectrum*, not a star. One little beta ray comes out there and another long one goes way over there, and every which way. It looks as if, since by the available theory all these particles had to be identical each to each, an energy loss is occurring. There is no way of setting out in the wave-equation appropriate to the beta particles any difference which could account for this. They are all supposed to have the same energy. What the heck is happening to the surplus energy? Now (here it seems to me) you can put it as you do. But it was necessary to *invent* a hypothetical particle which in each of these cases took up just what one needed in order to make an imaginary star out of neutrino-plus-beta-particle tracks; but you can't say there was no experimental occasion for this. The phenomenon is that the beta rays describe a spectrum of ranges, hence energies. They are all over the bloody map here.

DR. SCHWAB: There was an empirical *occasion* for the inquiry. One *can* say that if it weren't for the defect of the beta ray spectrum we would have no good evidence for the existence of the neutrino. This is the evidence—this is the way the neutrino shows its footprints and so there is nothing, as it were. However, there is another way to tell the story, namely, that the reason one invented the neutrino was to account for . . . .

DR. AGASSI: Perhaps what you are saying is this, that the physicist's problems are different from the mathematician's problem.

DR. HANSON: I am saying at least that, yes.

DR. SCHWAB: I do not suggest that physicists are lyric poets. Of course, there are empirical occasions for the invention of each of these things. I was only suggesting that contrary to the sorts of hypotheses constructed in biology for which verification is always defined as "show me," it is often the case in physics that high order concepts are considered verified when they take care of the problem.

DR. HANSON: Quite often indirect confirmation.

DR. BROUDY: Very indirect. They are blocked sometimes by definition. The finished article was ultimately possibly verifiable, but you must agree that the properties assigned to it were such that the quantity of mass to which they would have to move and the number of them which would have to move before you had a chance of getting assigned to their existence was exceedingly large.

DR. HANSON: Well, this was the first formulation of the hypothesis. It wasn't well made in 1929 and 1930. Now people know quite well what they are looking for in neutrino-work.

DR. SCHWAB: When you say not "well formulated" this is part of my earlier remark which you interrupted. I was going to say that for every ten Andersons there is one Fermi, who said it would be nice if neutrinos were verified in the way which neutrons, protrons, and electrons were, but I think it would be helpful to adopt it now.

DR. HANSON: Well, that is a nice statement about *you*, Joe. I am glad to know that you think that. All I am trying to call attention to is what you are obscuring (and in so doing you are being "nasty, brutish, and short"). If one stresses what you are stressing, namely, that in physics you . . . .

DR. SCHWAB: Well, you . . . .

DR. HANSON: If I may just finish, *please*. If one stresses what you have been stressing, that in mathematical physics one uses the techniques of mathematical deduction—hence many of the moves made by theoretical physicists and by pure mathematicians look like the same kind of thing—this naturally stresses the similarities, all of which are important to note. It is obvious that the best microphysicists are good mathematicians. No doubt about it; but if one is carried away with this, one fails to perceive the fundamental logical difference between every single proposition of physical theory and every single proposition in a purely mathematical algorithm. I say this despite the fact that many of the things that get set out at the top of a page in physical theory may indeed come from the back of some mathematician's head. It can hardly matter if, e.g., one looks at the Heisenberg (1956) "stuff" concerning "the propertyless wave equation for all matter." This certainly was designed as a pure form of physical science. The question is: what semantical and physical *content* does it pick up after actually having been exposed to the facts; when did it turn out that that particular suggestion was false, and *factually* false? There's a question one should never ask of any proposition at the top of the page in pure mathematics. So I agree that many of the inferential techniques are the same in physics and mathematics; and I want to agree that, genetically, many things in theoretical physics *get* to "the top of the page" much as they do in mathematics. But once one is in a position to say, "This theory is true and that high-order theoretical premise is acceptable," then one is playing the game on the vulnerable side of this dichotomy I am focusing upon. This makes a profound difference to our understanding of physical theory.

DR. SCHWAB: I shall withdraw here because we haven't really joined the issue and I don't think we can.

(RECESS)

CHAIRMAN CLARK: We have a lineup of people with comments and questions. We will begin with Professor Smith.

DR. PHIL SMITH: Professor Hanson, I would like to enlarge the context of the same point that was under discussion here, if I may. We, of course, recognize that the distinction between necessary and contingent statements is essential for understanding mathematics or physics. I wonder if it is not also essential for understanding a number of other things that we get concerned with in education. It seems to me that when you looked at the assertion, "The sun rises in the east," you correctly pointed out that only a careful description of the context of utterance enables one to determine what function such an assertion is performing. Is it acting as a necessary statement or is it acting as a contingent statement? At this point I am reminded of Quine, who said that if a person were obdurate enough, he could allow almost any assertion to perform this sort of analytic function. I invite your comments on this point.

Perhaps the problem, say in the case of students thinking in stereotypes, is that they are allowing empirical generalizations to function as if they were necessary statements in their lives—that is, in the way they are structuring their experiences. I submit that this point is crucial in a much larger context than you put it. I wonder if you would care to comment.

DR. HANSON: Well, only to agree. I believe that yours is a general recognition of what it takes to understand what another person means when he says anything at all. One must place the claim in a context of utterance. Let's imagine a bit of paper floats through the window and into this room. On it is written, "It is *close* in here." It's difficult to know what this could mean; but think of the impact of that message in a very smoky room. Or, its impact in a very small room, or in a closet. In a very large, airy room full of university provosts and vice-presidents the message would have quite a different force. Yet, to get the thrust of each of these claims is really to have placed it within a semantical interchange in a specified context. Now as to the other point you are making, namely, that students treat lawlike claims which have this unrestricted universal form in remarkable ways: I agree they use them almost as principles in inference; what it takes on the part of a teacher is a fairly sinewy attempt to show that every one of these claims looks as if *something* could count as evidence for, or against, them. They are not just definitions. Especially is this so if the claims have an empirical genesis and verification. But my point was that, concerning the claim "The sun rises in the east," although the context of utterance makes it clear *which* assertion a person is actually making, the two assertions are at opposite logical poles. You mentioned Quine and you also used the expression "obdurate." I think he *is* obdurate with respect to many of the things that "right-thinking" philosophers call attention to. (Smile!) He virtually plays on words in some of his writings. He would melt this "analytic-synthetic," or "necessary-contingent," distinction away on the grounds that it is awfully difficult in real life to find a genuinely invulnerable claim. Well, it may even be impossible, for all I care, but *that* doesn't obliterate the distinction. There *is* a distinction even though one may have to invent an almost ideal case as candidate for the title "invulnerable claim." If I say "All bachelors are male," that won't satisfy Quine as being invulnerable, and for a number of reasons. If I say "*A* equals *A*," that won't satisfy him either because he has problems about "equals." (He has problems.) That is what it comes to. But all these perplexities could be set to one side as a sort of professional skirmish. There is still a clear-cut contrast in principle between claims of the totally invulnerable kind and those which are quite vulnerable. Another way of getting "into" your comment is to point out that were the student apprised of this distinction earlier in life he might be much more receptive to your remark, namely, that many claims which are in unrestricted universal form—e.g., "All white, male, blue-eyed cats are deaf" (true so far as I know)—the student too often wants to treat these like the binomial theorem. I have seen this happen: if a pussycat walked into this room, white, male, blue-eyed and yet hearing perfectly well, will the student's whole concept of "cat" have changed? No! But if I let go of this pencil here in my hand and it levitates (and it's *genuine* levitation), then, in a way, our concepts of "physical object" and of "terrestrial space" are put in jeopardy. That's what makes the difference here.

To really generalize this for educational theory would be admirable. For, as soon as kids get into college and face their first philosophy course, if "the old man" up front knows what he is doing and makes this distinction well for them they'll keep using it back and forth, forever after. It's a very sophisticated thing to come up with Quine's doubts. It sometimes *is* difficult (as Quine perceived) to make this distinction *stick* all the way.

That's something that one could learn later on, though. If students could begin making this distinction in high school when doing physics—if they could sharply distinguish the mathematics within the ordinary dynamical computations from the strictly physical content—they would be a lot better off.

DR. PHIL SMITH: Well, one of the difficulties is that when an assertion performs this kind of analytic function then the teacher is, in some sense, being irrelevant if he tries to introduce ·a negative instance. I mean, if a first-grade child thinks that all policemen are mean, you don't destroy this stereotype by showing him a nice policeman.

DR. HANSON: No, because if he is nice he cannot be a policeman—not really.

DR. PHIL SMITH: I take it that some of the questions that you have given examples of later in the paper are related perhaps to the little circles of professors that straddle the dotted lines and those circles and your questions and especially your remarks at the end of your paper about paper walls that were set up in textbooks and possibly set up by administrators. All of these things have reference to this way of teaching the physical sciences that may either help or hinder learning in that field. I want to ask a question which isn't really on your paper because I don't know enough about it to disagree. It seems clear enough to me, so let me ask you a question not on your paper but which is suggested by your paper. Toward the end you mention structures of knowledge as being possible only in terms of a pedagogically heuristic blueprint. I would like to know whether or not you think that the current way of teaching the physical sciences, which presents areas within the sciences as separate and discrete, hinders or helps learning in the physical sciences.

DR. HANSON: There is first, if I may bifurcate that question, the issue of whether or not such departmentalization will help the student focus on particular problems without the encumbrances of other disciplines. And then, secondly, there is the auxiliary question of whether this will blind him to certain problems coming up again, intricacies within which make them important for newer disciplines like biophysics and biochemistry, etc. There can be little doubt but that teaching any of the natural sciences in this compartment-like way tends to make it difficult for researchers to branch out into these interim areas. The whole history of DNA lies in the middle of one of these interim areas; these turn out quite often to be the most exciting. One of the things that I am most interested in now is the history of theoretical aerodynamics. Chaps had an awful time getting off the ground on this "idea-side" of flight; they were too concerned with the tradition founded by Euler and Bernoulli in theoretical hydro-dynamics—a thoroughly classical discipline built upon the notion of an *ideal* fluid—inviscid and irrotational. For practical purposes, however, early aerodynamicists were concerned with the moving of a solid object through a thin, viscous medium, one not at all "ideal." *This* is the theoretical problem of flight and, of course, it all got confounded with the First World War and with stiff upperlips hurtling down the runway, hot-rods, parachutists, wing-walkers and "down he goes in flames"—all that sort of MGM rot. It was difficult during the first twenty years of aerodynamic theory to establish that all this was a genuine contribution to our understanding of physical phenomena. Even now, if I may harken toward a low-grade consideration, those great institutions in our country which are responsible for making grants in support of scholarly research projects, they also have difficulty in seeing that a history of aerodynamical theory could be anything but mere technology-plus-adventure-tales. They too are blinded by the high school myth that if one means to piddle about with aviation this means doing what bicycle engineers and hot-rod motor-cyclists did in the 1920's; but how could all that be a real contribution in the tradition of Euler and Bernoulli?

This is rather like what I am talking about in general. If and when you make it possible for a kid, when he raises a question which seems peripheral, if then you make it possible for him to feel encouraged, if he could be shown that although his query is slightly to one side of the central subject matter, the very determination of what *is* the central subject matter is itself undertaken largely for purposes of convenience, and administration, and for budgetary problems in teaching; *then* I think such a student might be heartened more to explore at the foundations and in the interim regions of the sciences.

Tomorrow's scientists may learn fewer long numbers via what I am advocating here, but their whole attitude might be inestimably improved nonetheless.

DR. PHIL SMITH: Do you think that the cultivation of an attitude in teaching the physical sciences is equally as important or more important than the cultivation of certain knowledges?

DR. HANSON: Far more important. Go to I.B.M. up in Binghamton, New York; you'll find slide-rule soldiers in abundance there; chaps who can trot out the factorial of any magnitude you please, quickly and efficiently. (One almost wonders who plugs them in each morning.) But ask them about something really fundamental like, "Are you satisfied with the current algebraic techniques in quantum field theory?" You'll get a sort of wide-eyed stare, and a "but I use it every day" retort. "I know you use it every day. You do lots of things every day, but isn't there something about renormalization techniques that *upsets* you? You *are* interested in the history of ideas?" The answer is usually that he is not, and that I.B.M. is not, interested in the history of ideas at all.

But this reminds me of a remark that Reynolds (of "Reynolds number" fame) made in 1903: freely rendered, the claim was, "Physics is all finished as intellectual discovery. It is just a question of graduate students running out more decimal numbers for the old prof's theories now. We have got a kind of periodic table for all physics set up." This in 1903; in 1905 we get the two Einstein papers on the Brownian motion and on the photo electric effect. Things began to rumble then, and we're still quaking.

What Reynolds was saying was a clear reflection of the compartmentalization standard late in the nineteenth century. It's also interesting to note that, in the *vive voce* part of his M.A. examination, Einstein had a difficult time because some of his responses didn't fit into his examiner's conception of what a well designed scientific discussion should be like.

The attitude is all important; this is what distinguishes the great men in history—not just that they got the numbers right. Some of Michelson's determinations were wrong, but he certainly had the right idea about how to learn of light's velocity. The conception, the overall attitude, the sorts of questions one asks; these are what I am getting at. That's the kind of interest we ought to cultivate more in high schools and colleges. That's what we can easily do. But when, as now, we turn scientific training into a kind of rehearsal of quantitative magnitudes, we lose an opportunity to encourage *thought*. It's necessary, a little bit—I did make that remark about *rote* repetition. We've all got to go through a little bit of it. If we make all scientific education a kind of navel contemplation, an adoption of *postures* toward problems in physics, then it gets too much like philosophy; this isn't altogether a bad thing, but it is a different subject. We must straddle these things a bit. But if *I* had to put the pedagogical center of gravity somewhere, it would definitely be on the student's attitude.

DR. GAGE: If I may follow up what you are saying, it means if I were a teacher, I would have trouble in telling the difference between a student who asks a profound question like, "What is gravity?" and one who is faking. A psychologist of reading I know about had a theory that reading deficiencies are caused by an absence of some juice in the brain—acetylcholine.

DR. HANSON: Carrot juice.

DR. GAGE: And what the psychologist hadn't done or what the bright eight-year-old or fourteen-year-old hadn't done who asks, "What is gravity?" or "What causes it?" was his homework. My reaction is they are not really entitled to be asking questions. The psychologist wasn't really a physiologist. He didn't know enough physiology. He hadn't done his homework, and he had no right to make up theories about reading deficiency as a result of this lack of acetylcholine in the brain. So I say to him, "Get out of this or go do your homework." And I'd say to the bright eight-year-old or the fourteen-year-old, "Don't ask these unsettling profound questions until you learn your twelfth-grade physics. Then you earn the right to ask proper questions. But you can't really get into the act—you haven't bought your ticket yet —until you have learned your ninth-grade algebra and other prerequisite subjects."

DR. HANSON: Well, Professor Gage, we are *really* in disagreement. It was the thrust of my exposition to counteract just what you have expressed. I'll never forget when I used to attend the quantum field theory seminars of Dirac at Cambridge—a very great physicist. Some highly paid help came to the seminar and a very valuable encounter it all was. But even there questions would come up like, "What *is* gravity really?" Or, "What indeed is one prepared to say a law in micro-physics consists in?" These were even then dismissed as merely philosophical questions.

DR. GAGE: Now those men had bought their tickets. They had done the homework.

DR. HANSON: No, there is no such thing. Nothing corresponds to "buying the ticket" here. There isn't some prerequisite course which terminates in *permitting* the student to ask a question like, "What is gravity?" The very rails are made out of such questions. Unless the point of these questions can be felt right from the very beginning all the other jazz about doing the calculations and working out the numbers will operate at quite a different level—the level of the calculational engineer rather than that of the problem-solving physicist. I am in a slightly compromised position here because I have to admit the point about rote repetition. To that extent we are agreed: if a kid systematically won't do his homework and doesn't give a tinker's damn about how $a = o$ when $F = ma$ and $\Sigma F = o$, then it is clearly difficult even to converse with him about *why* $F = ma$ and about the significance of the Fs in mechanics. But once he has done this bit, that he *has* done only a bit doesn't in itself serve as a measure of the perfunctoriness of his question. A man doesn't have to do much classical mechanics in order to be asking questions like, "What is the nature of this attraction in $F \propto \gamma \, Mm/r^2$?"

Berkeley did not know much—he was not I.B.M. material—but his questions constituted some of Newton's greatest challenges. It is the *beginning* stages of a theory that must be understood in order to grind out the numbers. Yet it is also those beginnings which are most difficult to comprehend.

"Who said that a body free of impressed forces would move in a straight line ad indefinitum uniformly?" *Let* the lad ask it! Can *you* give him *any* answer? What *is* the empirical evidence for this claim? These are genuine questions which could be asked at any level. If the teacher cannot answer, why *should* the student accept everything that hinges on the Law of Inertia?

Dr. Gage: Well, let me put it another way. I recently glanced a little bit at a book that you probably know of better than I do, *The Structure of Scientific Revolutions*.

Dr. Hanson: Kuhn's.

Dr. Gage: I think he says that most scientists are really just devoting their careers to mopping-up operations. The paradigms get set by a Newton or an Einstein or a Mendel or whoever, and the rest of the people in that discipline just clean up after him for a long time. I think what you are saying is that every Tom, Dick, and Harry has a right to try to be a Mendel or a Newton or an Einstein and ask the fundamental questions. I think I am inclined to say that most of us are doomed to be mopper-uppers.

Dr. Hanson: I am certainly saying that everyone has the *right* to ask them. There isn't any legislation from Tom Kuhn or anyone else about this. Incidentally, about his book, what does Tom mean by "a paradigm"? He doesn't make it clear. After four hundred pages Tom says that sooner or later they are the kinds of things which, if upset, will result in a scientific revolution. Okay, so now we have another term here. Now, "What is a revolution in science?" Answer: That's the kind of thing that happens after you get a *paradigm upset*. It looks as if this is a big wheel going around in small circles. So you say: "Well, look here, I can remark the following three important events, each one of which is usually recorded in history books as a scientific revolution in some important sense. But there was no paradigm upset in any of these cases." Then Tom tells us, "They weren't really revolutions, despite what the historians say." Then you add: "Look, here is a cluster of paradigms; the organization, the entire discipline at this particular time, the group of chaps— *all* cleave to this paradigm set. And there has been a most serious challenging of such paradigms amongst practitioners of the sciences. But lo—nothing that one would call a 'scientific' revolution has resulted." Tom says, "Not really paradigms then." You see, this gets like saying, "Why does opium put one to sleep? Because of its soporific properties—and what's a soporific property? It's what opium has got such that it puts you to sleep when you take it." Well, really! This thesis goes around and around. Kuhn starts out with an *informative* historical thesis— a contingent, factual thesis—to the effect that when you find a revolution in science you should look for an upset in some paradigm and vice versa. Now this actually conveys something, and is informative in that it makes good sense to suppose his claim to be false, but *in fact* it happens to be true. Or it happens to be true 98 per cent of the time. But Tom is so impressed with the fully general thesis that when chaps begin to bring up possible counter-instances Kuhn kicks them into the general pattern by definition. So he ends up by transforming what was originally an informative historical claim into a specifically Kuhnian defini- tion. It couldn't be false, and if it couldn't be false in these terms then it could not really be both true and informative.

Thus for Tom Kuhn the only level on which one can effect a scientific revolution is to challenge the super capital-lettered- purple-inked paradigms about which Tom has so much to say. He says it all in a highly illuminating and in a very informative way; but the kinds of questions that I have been posing here with re- spect to classical physics can be posed equally well in quite nar- row and special disciplines like the history of science. If you get a man who uses templates for setting out transistor circuits— for *pouring* the things instead of having to solder wires—he might use the technique gratefully. Yet he might have many questions concerning why it is that when the stuff is put on in liquid form it has other effects later on when dried. Or he can ask "simple" questions about radio-set circuitry in general; but it's the *nature* of the question and the nature of the *attitude* he adopts toward them that strikes me as being so important.

I fly an airplane, a fifteen-year-old Navy fighter which needs lots and lots of attention. I can always remark the repair shops where they have the mechanic I would want to do my work *by the nature of his questions*. The chap who gives it a lick and a rub on the outside, but doesn't check the magneto falloff, the fuel pressure, or the tank filters—such a man I am not quite so interested in as in he who takes any little imperfection to be a possible sign of something that might in the long run cause mischief.

The average physicist who goes to graduate school today and develops a concern with problems that involve weak interaction at high energies—he gets into formal problems over "renormalization," "ghost states," etc.; the class of physicists divides at that juncture. Some will feel profound nagging perplexities about using techniques over which mathematicians would get sick. Others say, "Look, we are grinding out the right numbers in predictions, let's not look for any trouble. So long as we keep quiet and get the correct magnitudes we are doing what we are supposed to be doing." Now it's this division which requires our attention. The chaps who ask the nagging questions are not necessarily getting any more or any better numbers. They are (in a sense) holding back the seminars and discussion groups from grinding out finer determinations and setting up new experiments. But in the long run the nagging problems that the "worriers" raise might be the critical ones. There is no given moment in a man's scientific development when he is for the first time qualified to ask questions like this. I think he is entitled to ask these questions right at the beginning; indeed, if he does not, he does not really understand what is being ladled into his head.

DR. SCHWAB: Indeed it would be nice if teaching were a narrative of inquiry in which the profound and the small questions are exhibited in their relations to one another.

DR. HANSON: Well, this is actually done. Eric Rogers of Princeton has written a book, *Physics for the Inquiring Mind*. This is for senior high school students and for freshmen in college. There is no compromise here. This is not a cheap popularization. It is a serious work, but it is written with a specific focus on the kinds of questions that I have been calling your attention to here. Now you might very well point out that no student in Rogers' courses will, from that alone, become a hot candidate for I.B.M. employment. True! But such a fellow might be better off in the long run. He might even end up teaching at Princeton. Worse things have happened to Ph.D.'s.

DR. GAGE: In the chemistry lab the high school student is asked to, say, do an experiment in which he is supposed to get the atomic weight of carbon. He knows very well it's supposed to be 12 but he's sloppy and it comes out to be 12.01, so on Thursday he might say, "I am going to challenge the whole structure of the theory underlying atomic weight," and chases off in that direction. Then on Monday he comes back to the lab and he gets an inexact figure for the molecular weight of water. When is a student supposed to know that he should take certain things for granted and not rock the boat, and when is he supposed to start rocking the boat? If he rocks the boat every time he gets an inexact answer he'll—well, he won't get past the first lab assignment.

DR. HANSON: What one must do is develop judgment and discrimination in this sort of thing, as with anything else; and the earlier one starts, the better. You know perfectly well that learning the difference between chemical atomic mass and physical atomic mass constituted a profound discovery which was made—when in the hell was it made?

DR. GAGE: Oxygen in 1820.

DR. HANSON: No, much later. (After the discovery of oxygen's *isotopes*.)

DR. GAGE: I agree with you if the judgment that most students come to is that 99 per cent of the things that they are asked to do in laboratories or learn out of books they had better well take for granted and only after they have won their spurs and are in graduate school or working on a dissertation can they start rocking boats. But most students—and I think I was an average student—maybe that's why I was an average student—but most of us learn to receive or take for granted, to accept what is in the books. This judgment is something we do learn. That's why we are able to go ahead and take courses one after the other.

DR. SCHWAB: At the dissertation level the professors are still asking them not to rock the boat, so naturally the guy who gets 12.1 instead of 12 never discovers isotopes.

DR. BEREITER: I think that this might be clarified a little by pointing out that there is a difference between taking for granted that somebody else's empirical results might be a little better than the ones you have gotten and knowing what other things you might take for granted and what ones not. I would also like to add a little empirical finding here. We did some experiments using some artificial sciences. Graduate students in physical science were taught their sciences and given some data to work on. They were carefully told at the outset that they should not assume that any physical laws that they believed in necessarily held in this imaginary universe. Invariably the next question they would ask would be, "Could we assume that mathematical laws hold here?" Now it was staggering to think that they would feel that you could suspend mathematics hypothetically the same way that you could suspend facts. Then after we assured them that mathematics still works here they would be constantly wrestling with the question, "What can we assume and what can't we?" Now there was vast ambiguity here. We used some terms that were familiar to them such as "charged," and I remember an electrical engineer who looked me straight in the eye and said, "Can we assume that unlike charges attract and like charges repel?" I said, "I can't tell you that." So they looked at each other and arrived at the conclusion that unless you assumed this everything collapsed. So they decided they would assume that this held. Although it's a matter of empirical fact, it was mathematical to them. We did the same experiment using bright high school students. None of them had the slightest bit of trouble with any of this and the outcome was that they were much more successful.

DR. HANSON: Well, if I may follow this up with Professor Gage's question (it wasn't really a question, it was a torpedo). Obviously a man doesn't show his originality by working out his own logarithm tables. There are some things that you just take up because you must learn to: one must learn how to operate with the slide rule, how to use a retort, how to use the several balances, etc. You have to know how to make appropriate inferences, how to use the most fitting language. This is the ground floor of any discipline, and any student who would rather be asking the "philosophical" questions I've been discussing here *instead* of learning his ABC's, he is not the kind of chap I am talking about. And I'm not concerned with the bright brat who is forever bent on badgering the busy teacher.

I am saying that if a student, in addition to doing his homework, is *also* asking these more fundamental questions, then everything should be done to encourage him. Now I mentioned to someone here that a close friend of mine started his university life as one of my students at Cambridge University; and I don't know how he will finish—but he certainly used to worry me. I've never encountered such an aggressive, nasty, mean student. Actually he was quite serious, but he was quite mean, too! He made my life miserable—until I discovered that he behaved even worse in his physics courses. I noticed one thing leading to another and asked a senior Nobel physics prize recipient, "How do you get along with John now?" He said, "Oh, he is the bain of my existence. I have never met a man like that." Well, to make a long story short, Newton is supposed to have received 16 "alphas" in his Part Three Mathematical Tripos exam; my friend, John, got 18 "alphas"! He's really a pretty electric sort of guy. I don't know what one is to say about him. Certainly his complete mastery of algorithms was at least comparable to that of all the other chaps around him. The only way that I can distinguish him from the others is to note that, in addition, he was always probing beneath the algebra, asking, "Why this?" "Why that?"

Just one final twist of a quarter-turn. Here's the kind of thing one finds in some of Newton's recently published notes and papers: he makes two statements (in adjacent paragraphs) which are really pregnant. No person in Newton's time called attention to this. He granted Kepler's law of $1/r^2$ as giving the falloff in the intensity of radiation from a light source. Thus if I have a given point source of light at radius 1 from us, and if then we move that light out to radius 2, it will only appear 1/4 as bright. If I move it out to radius 3 it will appear only 1/9 as bright, etc.

In the next paragraph Newton then calls attention to what we now call "the cosmological principle"; the actual population of the stellar warehouse goes up as r^2 if one supposes that in each spherical spatial shell enclosing us the stars are distributed homogeneously and relatively equally. Then the number of stars 2 radii away will be 4 times as great as they had been at radius 1; and at 3 radii away there will be 9 times as many stars—so the fact that each one of them appears but 1/9 as bright as they would have seemed at radius 1 is, in effect, compensated for and cancelled out altogether. In short, it follows that from each spherical shell, from each new distance, there is a positive increment of light radiation, *such that at midnight the sky should be blindingly bright*. Now these two correlations—r^2 for the stellar population increase, and $1/r^2$ for the radiation falloff—these are well accepted facts. Any student in high school could go through these with no trouble. But if a kid puts these two together and makes of them what Clairveaux and Olbers made of them—he has gone beyond the normal requirement of his homework. Any student might notice this particular correlation; by easy steps it leads to Olbers' Paradox, The Red Shift, and lots of other things in modern cosmology. Fully to explain how it is that despite these two correlations being true it is nonetheless not bright at midnight—that's the kind of question that has marked the great illuminations in the history of ideas. Such queries are quite compatible with learning one's homework; but the teacher who is *so* concerned with getting the homework across that he suppresses questions like this is stifling the attitude toward physical inquiry that constitutes the real excitement of physics. More, he is failing fully to make clear the very material he *does* want to teach—for even to manage the formulae properly requires some "natural philosophy."

ADJOURNMENT

CHAPTER VI

THE STRUCTURE OF KNOWLEDGE IN THE SOCIAL SCIENCES

WM. OLIVER MARTIN

The term "social sciences" is usually said to include such subjects as sociology, social psychology, anthropology, history, political science, economics, etc., and hence is a group-category referring to various kinds of knowledge concerned with human beings in social relations. There is also the term "social studies" which, in ordinary use, has a slightly different meaning, for it is essentially a curriculum-category, and as such it often includes even subjects like geography. We shall be concerned only with the former term, since our problem has to do with the structure of knowledge, not curriculum structure.

In addition to the "social sciences" is there something that can be called "social science" which has a definite subject matter and method such as, for example, physical science? The answer must be negative, for certainly the subject matter and method of history and (say) social psychology are not the same. The latter is an experimental science, the former is not. One can take a connotational approach, defining carefully "social science," and then rule out any kind of knowledge that does not have the defining characteristics. The danger here is that of arbitrariness, that of "game-playing." One can do it, but the critic may simply say: "Of course you can define social science that way, and I would grant that everything else you say logically follows. However, it just so happens that I don't agree with your stipulating definition." This approach cuts off discussion, for, just as in solitaire, only one person can play the game.

Let us, then, take an experiential and denotative approach and examine the knowledge structure present in those kinds of knowledge called "the social sciences." How does someone in the social sciences reason? What is the nature of the evidence to which appeal is made? What knowledge of a nonsocial science kind is presupposed? Can there be different kinds of presuppositions? What is the relation of the philosophical disciplines to the social sciences? All of these questions have to do with the structure of knowledge in the social sciences. This problem is something quite different from, and should never be confused with, the problem of methodology in any specific social science.

This paper will be divided into two parts, the first part being critical and negative. Using a "case study" approach, we shall take a sample of reasoning by a social scientist—in this case, a historian—and through analysis show the many confusions that can occur if one is not clear about the order of knowledge. The second part will be positive and constructive, briefly outlining the structure of knowledge in the social sciences.

A worker in a field of knowledge should know the nature and limitations of that field of knowledge, what it is and what it is not. If he does not know what it is not, he cannot clearly know what it is, for all determination is negation. If he does not know clearly what it is, then he may be confused about what is and what is not relevant evidence in the support of a thesis. If there is a confusion as to relevant evidence, then the worker may make false or impossible claims as to what a kind of knowledge can "prove" or "demonstrate." From the standpoint of education the practical effects of such confusion can be very unfortunate, especially in curriculum construction.

AN ANALYSIS OF AN ARTICLE BY A HISTORIAN, BEING CONCERNED WITH THE PROBLEM OF WHAT "HISTORY" DOES OR DOES NOT "PROVE."

The example chosen for analysis is typical only of a kind of confused thinking in the social sciences. Needless to say, it would be both false and unfair to take it as typical of all such thinking. The article in question is to be found in a well known magazine, and the author, whom we will call "Professor X," is one of the best known historians in the United States. Since the problem we are concerned with, and the purpose of the analysis, is completely impersonal, neither the author nor the article is identified. We could have used some other article as typical, written by someone else. Hence, it is best to avoid all complications that might arise psychologically because of one's knowledge of the author.

Most of the article in question is composed of historical facts about the Soviet tyranny and other similar tyrannies that have existed in the past. A group of historical facts are presented and the conclusion drawn that the Soviet Union must fall. This process is repeated to the end of the article. What proves that the Soviet Union must fall, we are told, is "history." The strong modality, "must fall," is constantly used. It is "inevitable," it is "impossible" for the Soviet Union to survive. It is not merely the case that the Soviet Union "in fact" will fall or "may fall." The strong conclusion is drawn, and called a "proof," by means of such phrases as "history states," "history proves," "history demonstrates." Hence the fall of the Soviet Union is absolutely predictable.

Upon what kind of evidence is such a "proof" based? We are told that the proof comes from "plain historical facts and established historical principles." Let us examine the reasoning involved. What are these "historical principles"?

The evidence appealed to is the fact that the Soviet Union is a tyranny. Of course this proposition alone cannot be sufficient evidence to prove that the Soviet Union must fall. The suppressed premise is: "tyrannies must fall." The conclusion is on the cover page and the suppressed premise is the title of the article. Part of the evidence, then, that is appealed to is this suppressed premise. The reasoning may be expressed as follows:

    1.   Tyrannies must fall.

(A)2.   The Soviet state is a tyranny.

3. The Soviet Union must fall.

The conclusion is not merely a prediction of a particular historical event of the future. It is said that the Soviet Union *must* fall, not merely *will* fall, or *may* fall. This conclusion follows not merely from the fact that the Soviet Union is a tyranny, but from the stronger assertion of the major premise. The latter, however, is certainly not "history." When we turn to the minor premise we find that not only is it not sufficient to prove the conclusion, but that it is not even a proposition *of* history. It is an evaluation of certain historical facts in terms of some standard of values and disvalues. The Soviet Union and its acts are *appraised*. Of course, if the two premises are true, then the conclusion is true. But neither premise is an historical proposition, a proposition *of* history. Where, then, is the history, the historical evidence that proves that tyrannies must fall, and finally that the Soviet Union must fall?

Throughout the article Professor X does give evidence for the fact that the fall of tyrannies has happened in the past. This proposition is historical, and the evidence is historical. But the historical fact that the fall of all tyrannies has happened in the past does not itself prove that the fall of tyrannies must happen again. The proof is only established if the truth of another suppressed premise is granted, to wit, that what has happened must happen again.

The reason now is as follows:

4. Whatever has happened in the past must happen again.

(B)5. The fall of tyrannies has happened in the past.

6. The fall of tyrannies must happen again.

While the minor premise is an historical proposition and is based upon historical evidence, the conclusion follows essentially from the principle stated in the major premise. It is a case of reasoning in which a principle is applied to a fact and then a conclusion is drawn. The major premise states the "reason why." It is a metaphysical proposition that states the philosophy of fatalism, or expresses a cyclic interpretation of history. The so-called proof is accomplished neither by historical facts nor by historical principles. The proof involves a philosophical position that applies the metaphysical category of necessity to certain spatio-temporal happenings, thus enabling one to state an absolute, and not a probable, prediction of a certain event.[1]

It is not our problem here to consider either the truth of the conclusion or that of the metaphysical premise. We merely wish to point out through this analysis that Professor X's historical facts do not prove his conclusions, and that the unanalyzed preconception that is necessary, if his conclusion is to hold, is a metaphysical premise—and an extremely questionable one at that. The statement that historical facts and principles prove his conclusion is not merely false, but is also the statement of an impossibility. Such a statement arises not only from a confusion of types of knowledge, but also from an unawareness of the logic of proof and the nature of different kinds of evidence.

Let us return to the reasoning (A). We have seen that what allowed the conclusion, made possible the implication, was the nature of tyranny, the "middle term." What must be understood, then, in order to predict the fall of the Soviet Union is the nature of tyrannies. Now "tyranny" is a value predicate used in the appraisal of historical acts. It cannot be equated with the acts themselves. The distinction here is similar to that which is made beween killing and murdering. An act of killing may or may not be an act of murder. The act of killing is not the judge of itself; rather it is to be judged. If the act was morally unjustified, then it was murder. Otherwise not. What is of importance to recognize here is that the evidence that would prove an act to be one of killing is not the same kind of evidence as is necessary to prove the goodness or badness—in other words the morality—of the act.

And so it is in the case of tyranny. That a state has committed a certain act is an historical fact. Whether it is a tyrannical act or not is a matter to be judged. Regardless of the answer

[1] Some positivistic philosophers would use the term "meta-language" instead of "metaphysics," but this does not bear on the *fact* that distinctions in types of statements must be made.

given, certain truths about values are presupposed and applied to the case. It is these truths about values that determine in part the truth or falsity of the evaluation. The act of the state, the historical fact, is what stands under moral judgment. It is this kind of evidence that demonstrates or proves the act to be tyrannical, and not something called "history" at all.

If we are to understand the nature of "tyranny," which is a moral and philosophical problem, in order to understand why the Soviet Union must fall, the question arises as to what there is about the nature of "tyranny" that would lead to such a conclusion.

We are told that tyrannies must fall because they are incompatible with human freedom. Professor X quotes Jan Smuts, " 'The denial of free human rights must in the long run lead to a cataclysm.' Why? Because the passionate desire of men to exercise their faculties freely is a basic trait that cannot permanently be repressed."

The reasoning is as follows:
7. Whatever is, in the long run, incompatible with human freedom must fall.
(C)8. All tyrannical states are incompatible with human freedom.
9. All tyrannical states must fall.

We now understand the kind of evidence that is necessary to draw the conclusion, which is also the proposition that is the title of the article. Statement (7), however, presupposes certain metaphysical propositions concerned with the relation of human nature to the reality which accounts for it. It is the "middle term," the nature of human freedom, that allows the conclusion to be drawn.

Statement (8) is a deduction from the nature of human freedom, and must be accounted for. To do so one would have to come to grips with the moral problem of the state as an institution and discover the criteria by which it could be determined that such-and-such acts under certain conditions and for certain purposes are incompatible with human freedom. It will suffice at present merely to indicate the structure of the reasoning involved:

10. Whatever is characterized by such-and-such acts under certain conditions and for certain purposes is incompatible with human freedom.

(D) 11. A tyrannical state is characterized by such-and-such acts. . . .

12. A tyrannical state is incompatible with human freedom.

Taking the three pieces of reasoning (A), (C), and (D), by beginning with (D) and going through (C), we may reach the conclusion of (A), which is the title of the article. It is this that Professor X wishes to prove. But in (A), (C), and (D) there are no historical propositions. The proof does not come at all from so-called historical principles, but from ethical principles. Such principles are stated in a few sentences in the article. The rest of the article, for the most part, is made up of statements of historical facts which are interesting and undoubtedly true. But so far from proving that tyrannies must fall, there is merely an illustration of a moral thesis.

We still have to account for the proposition that the Soviet Union must fall. Saying that tyrannies must fall is not the same as saying that the Soviet state must fall. For the latter proposition it so happens that history is relevant as *partial* evidence. This may be seen by setting up three chains of reason, making use of the propositions with which we are already acquainted:

13. Whatever is characterized by such-and-such acts under certain conditions and for certain purposes is incompatible with human freedom.

(E) 14. The Soviet state is characterized by such-and-such acts. . . .

15. The Soviet state is incompatible with human freedom.

Now if we may assume that any state that is intrinsically incompatible with human freedom is a tyrannical state, we have the following:

16. Any state that is incompatible with human freedom is a tyrannical state.

(F) 17. The Soviet state is incompatible with human freedom.
18. The Soviet state is a tyrannical state.

Now we can finally return to (A):

1. Tyrannies must fall.
(A) 2. The Soviet state is a tyranny.
3. The Soviet state must fall.

The truth of statement (13) would have to be based upon a philosophical analysis of the nature of human freedom. Statement (14) is based upon historical evidence. Statement (15) is an appraisal, an evaluation. Statement (16) is derivative from the definition of tyranny. Statement (17) is the same as (15). Statement (18) is a further evaluation mediated by the logical predicate of statement (15).

Now we have seen that "history" does not at all prove the title of the article, that tyrannies must fall. In the proof of the more specific proposition, that the Soviet state must fall, we have seen that historical evidence only proves one out of many of the propositions necessary for the demonstration. The condensed argument is this, that the Soviet state must fall in the future because it is in fact of such a nature that it contradicts the moral nature of man. Now history is relevant in the following way in the prediction of this specific future historical event. If a judgment about the future of a state is to be made in terms of its relative morality or immorality, of course one's prediction might be wrong because of a "misapplication" of principles. The "historical," hence, does enter constitutively into the proof. But "history" is only part of the evidence. And if principles are more important than facts, the historical part is not the most important part of the evidence. The most important part is concerned with ethical and philosophical principles.

At the beginning of the article, Professor X says, "We base our confidence in a coming Russian revolution on plain historical facts and established historical principles." What is the verdict of this logical analysis? The so-called historical principles do not exist. The principles turn out to be moral and philosophical, only a few sentences in the whole article—and interestingly enough some of these sentences are quotations. In one instance it is the case of quoting someone who quotes someone else.

In the first part of the analysis another alternative was considered, culminating in reasoning (B). In this case the principle is not concerned with the moral nature of man. But neither is it a historical principle. Rather it is a metaphysical principle *about* the historical process. A proposition *of* history is not the same as a proposition *about* history. "History" and the "philosophy of history" are two different subjects requiring different kinds of evidence and different methods.

THE STRUCTURE OF KNOWLEDGE IN THE SOCIAL SCIENCES

We have just seen something of the ambiguity lurking in the phrase, "history proves. . . ." One could also inquire as to what it means to say that social psychology or economics or sociology "proves" or "demonstrates" this or that about juvenile delinquency, population problems, taxation, alcoholism, public opinion in a democracy, etc. That they certainly do, there is no doubt. But it would be begging the question to analyze at present each of the social sciences denoted by the term "social science." Shall we include psychology as well as social psychology; and if so, why not psychiatry? Furthermore, some of these names have come into being historically for departmental, and hence institutional, purposes and not because they stand for a distinct kind of knowledge.

The real, as contrasted with conventional, distinctions among social sciences may be discovered by finding out what kind of proposition is sought for, e.g., singular propositions, or generalizations, or appraisals. In this manner we can discover whether a given science is positive and autonomous, or is a hybrid, synthetic science created by bringing two or more kinds of knowledge together. Also, in this manner we can understand the actual structure of knowledge in the social sciences, which structure has noetic being as independent of all human interests as does the atomic structure of a molecule.

As positive, any experimental science, physical or social, seeks true generalizations. The term positive refers to the relative autonomy of a science in relation to ontological considerations—metaphysical and/or theological. The scientific method is that instrument by which a scientist seeks true rather than false generalizations. A generalization is to be contrasted with a singular proposition, and it states something that is, is probably, or may be the case. The "something" may be qualified by "some," "for the most part," or "all." In any positive science propositions that are singular or are generalizations refer to phenomena, not to the ontological (either the metaphysical or the theological). The singular proposition, "John Jones does not like to wear neckties" can be a proposition of positive science, but not the proposition, "John Jones is a God-created being."

When a "social study" is concerned primarily with seeking true singular propositions, reconstructing the past, then the subject of history as positive is defined.

A kind of knowledge is to be understood in terms of the following four elements: the kind of proposition that is sought; the method used to seek it; the nature of the evidence to which appeal is made; and, finally, the relation of the kind of knowledge (or the type of proposition sought) to other kinds of knowledge (other kinds of propositions) by way of "presuppositions." With these criteria in mind, let us consider the meanings of "social sciences."

History as Positive

Since the aim of the historian qua historian is to reconstruct the uniqueness of the past, the historian seeks true singular propositions. We shall call the singular propositions "historical propositions." The name is justified, for although we usually think of historical propositions in terms of such examples as "Caesar crossed the Rubicon at T_1," "here is a coin struck by Vespasian," "this is a college account book dated 1752," nevertheless we must also remember that all the data in the notebook of any research scientist is also concerned with what has happened, and is expressed in the form of singular propositions.

There are certain canons of historiography which constitute what is called the "historical method." This method is not the same as the "scientific method" when reference is to the method used in such sciences as physics, chemistry, or social psychology. The latter are experimental sciences; history is not experimental, although it is experiential. The evidence to which appeal is made in historical research is the same kind of proposition, i.e., singular propositions, as that which is sought. However, the evidence is mediated through generalizations which are, in turn, constituted by singular propositions. For example, propositions of chemistry, relative to the nature of carbon, may enter constitutively as evidence in determining approximately the date of an ancient manuscript. Yet, those same general propositions of chemistry are constituted, so far as evidence is concerned, by *classes* of singular propositions.

In historical research generalizations are constitutive as evidence to the singular propositions that are sought, whereas in an experimental social science such as, say, social psychology, singular propositions are constitutive as evidence to generalizations which are sought. It is to be observed that it is not the function of the historian qua historian to establish the truth of the generalizations which he may use in historical research.

By way of presupposition, historical knowledge will imply certain philosophical disciplines, logic or the theory of knowledge, and metaphysics. Logic, other than formal, is concerned with the different methodologies which vary according to subject matter. When the historian uses the notion of "causation," he is using a metaphysical category. However, logic and metaphysics are not constitutive as evidence in historical research. Rather, their function is a regulative one. As regulative these disciplines delimit what can be true historically, but they do not determine what is true. Through methodology relevant evidence is sifted out from irrelevant evidence, and there is a process by means of which one is more likely led to true rather than false historical propositions. It is by means of logic and metaphysics that we know that Copernicus could not have influenced the thinking of Pythagoras. But the converse is possible. Whether or not it is actual is a historical, not a metaphysical, problem.

It should be remarked at this point that a certain kind of objection is completely irrelevant to this analysis. Let us suppose that someone says that there is no such thing as metaphysics, and hence. . . . Now there are those who prefer to speak of "sentences" or "statements" instead of "propositions," or of "meta-history" or "meta-science" instead of "metaphysics," and of "function" instead of "cause." One may do so. But the essential thesis is not changed. The problem is a philosophical one; it is not a historical problem. It still remains the case that certain philosophical propositions ("statements" or "sentences") are presupposed in a regulative fashion in historical research. When the historian, as a man, considers his methodology, or the problem of "causation" in history, then he is functioning, for better or worse, as a philosopher and not as a historian qua historian. Philosophy does not help to determine *what* is true historically, but it does delimit the realm of possible historical truth. History, then, as positive, is relatively autonomous. It is independent of philosophical categories and propositions in a constitutive, but not in a regulative, sense.

History as Nonpositive: The Philosophy of History

No one seems satisfied with defining history merely as a positive kind of knowledge. Ranke's notion of history and of historical knowledge is not sufficient. The answer to "what happened" is, of course, "this happened" and "that happened." But the historian is also interested in the "why" as well as the "that." Hence, it has been said that the historian makes generalizations about the historical process, but in addition he will not only appraise various historical events but also attempt to discover some meaning in the whole flow of events. Do both of these interests generate different kinds of knowledge, over and above history as positive? There is reason to believe the answer must be affirmative as to the latter, but negative as to the former.

It is true that the historian may state propositions of the form "All *A* is *B*" or "Most *A* is *B*." For example, he may be interested in the revolutions that have occurred from the beginning of human history as known, and he may state general propositions that he believes are descriptive of their common elements. But these are not generalizations of the kind that are sought for by the positive sciences. In the first place, historical "generalizations" are limited to what is already known. In contrast, the generalization sought for in the positive sciences, and which is a hypothesis, theory, or law, must, if it is to be fruitful and of worth, intentionally refer to events other than those of which consituted the data which gave rise to the hypothesis. Another way of saying this is that the data which confirms or disconfirms a generalization in a positive science must always be other than the data out of which the generalization was constructed. Second, in contrast to the generalization of a positive science, the "generalization" made by a historian is in reality only a shorthand statement for summing up a group of historical propositions. For example, instead of saying that "revolution *A* has characteristic *Q*," "revolution *B* has characteristic *Q*," and so on, the historian may say that "all revolutions have characteristic *Q*." This kind of generalization is of the kind a person might make when, instead of saying, "this book is bound," "that book is bound," and so on, for each and every book on a certain shelf in his study, he says instead that "all books on the shelf are bound." The historian must already have his history before he makes his "generalizations," which are really only summations. There is, then, literally, no science of history.

The matter is somewhat different when we consider the philosophy of history. When history is appraised or interpreted, it is also transcended, i.e., it is not self-interpretative. Some kind of knowledge, philosophical and/or theological, is brought to bear upon historical knowledge. This means that the "philosophy of history" is a hybrid kind of knowledge, synthetic and non-autonomous. In any condensed argument in which the conclusion is a proposition of the kind of knowledge that may be called "philosophy of history" it will be found that one premise is a proposition of history as positive (*what* is interpreted) and the other premise is ontological (i.e., a philosophical and/or theological proposition, *that in terms of which* interpretation is made). The evidence to which appeal is made, then, in the philosophy of history is always of two kinds, the ontological and the facts of history. Hence, it follows also that any disagreement as to the truth of any proposition of the philosophy of history must be a disagreement either on the ontological level or on the purely factual level of history.[2]

Whereas in history as positive, philosophy has only a regulative function, and does not determine what propositions in history are true, in the philosophy of history "philosophy" (and possibly theology) enters constitutively into that kind of knowledge. In short, any proposition in the philosophy of history is partially determined, so far as its truth is concerned, by ontological truth. If it be said that no truth-claim can be made at all for any ontological proposition, then the philosophy of history ceases to be a kind of knowledge and is reduced to an ideology which has only a functional being relative to the promotion of some group-interest.

Social Science as Positive

That propositions in the form of generalizations are what the social scientist seeks, and hence constitute their "findings," may be discovered by reading the reports or books authored by social scientists. To illustrate, let us turn to a book on *Theory and Problems of Social Psychology* (D. Krech, and R. S. Crutchfield,

[2] It may be said that there is still another kind of problem which may give rise to disagreements, namely, that of the relation of ontological categories to the categories of history as positive. This is true. But this is simply another kind of philosophical problem, whether it is dealt with in terms of the "analogy of knowledge" of classical realism, or it is handled in terms of "metaphors" and "models."

1948). We find such propositions as these: "The dynamics of moral behavior result from properties of the immediate psychological field (p. 33)"; "The frustration of goal achievement and the failure of tension reduction may lead to a variety of adaptive or maladaptive behaviors (p. 50)"; "All people in all cultures behave according to the same set of basic principles of dynamics (p. 47)."

What constitutes the evidence for a generalization? The evidence may come from other generalizations, but ultimately the data is in the form of singular propositions, e.g., of the form "This person, under the circumstances *a, b, d, d, e,* acted in this way." Singular propositions, in reference to the object or objects intended, are descriptive of uniqueness rather than generality. The evidence is always a class of singular propositions, for no single proposition alone is sufficient as evidence for a generalization.

The method of social science is essentially the same as that which characterizes any positive science, although the mode and manner of its use will vary somewhat according to the limitations imposed by the nature of the objects studied. In any social science there are at least two unique kinds of limitations. In the first place, the kind of object studied is also the kind doing the studying. Planets do not study the behavior of planets, nor electrons the behavior of electrons. But human beings study the behavior of human beings. In the second place, in using the scientific method the object studied must of necessity be considered an "it." In the case of nonhuman behavior this procedure requires no abstraction or reduction of the object from an "I" or "that" to an "it." The object is nothing but an "it." However, in any positive social science such an abstraction and reduction must be made. Such a procedure is quite legitimate only if consciously made and recognized. Otherwise there is the danger of falling into what Whitehead calls the fallacy of "misplaced concreteness," for an epistemological abstraction is substituted for, and confused with, real existential human beings. If, on the other hand, the reduction is deliberately and consciously made, i.e., existence is identified wholly with the product of abstraction, then it is done on "philosophical grounds," on postulates that constitute the essence of naturalism or materialism. But all of this lies outside of a positive social science and should be so recognized. If it is not so recognized, then the consequence is a question-begging argument. Social science as positive is used as evidence to "prove" the ontological postulates which have already, in an a priori fashion, absolutized positive social science. Social science as positive is science. Positiv*ism* occurs when positive science is absolutized. However, the absolutizing is always in the form of a proposition *about* social science; it cannot be a proposition *of* social science.

The relation of ontological propositions (metaphysical or theological) to positive social science is the same as that to any positive science, i.e., they have only a regulative function, delimiting what is possibly true, but not determining, in any manner whatsoever, what is true. For example, if a social psychologist says, "The frustration of goal achievement and the failure of tension reduction may lead to a variety of adaptive or maladaptive behaviors," then whether or not the proposition is true or false is to be determined wholly by the procedures of the scientific method. No ontological discipline (metaphysical or theological) can be used either to prove or disprove, to confirm or disconfirm, a proposition of positive science. As regulative, ontology, either through logic, epistemology, or metaphysics, does delimit what can possibly be true, and also establishes what is *relevant* as evidence.

Social Science as Normative

Values enter into the social sciences as normative in two ways, as appraisals of existing situations or as policies that are programs of action. An appraisal is of the form "this is good or bad." A policy is a program of action not only recommending something that ought or not to be done, but also presupposing that it is possible to say that one program can be better or worse than another.

With respect to a policy, an appraisal or evaluation in social science is always a conclusion of a condensed argument in which one premise is a factual statement of the consequences of the policy. The other premise is a proposition stating a standard or norm in terms of which the policy is judged, the judgment being expressed by the conclusion. Using the generic terms "good" and "bad," the general form of the argument may be stated in this manner: "this policy is good. Why? Because it leads to consequences *a, b, c,* and whatever produces such consequences is good." Any given specific argument is, of course, very complex. It may take half of a book to establish one premise. However, the importance of understanding the general form is this, that if in a conclusion one is applying a value predicate, then it is seen that of necessity there must be a proposition stating the nature of the value and another proposition stating what it is that is to be evaluated.

Let us suppose a committee of social scientists advocates a policy or a program of action to come to grips with the problem of narcotic addiction in the United States. What is presupposed? A policy cannot be intelligently and responsibly recommended unless there has first been a study of the situation. This study of the factual state of affairs, independent of all norms, is the function of social science as positive. Second, a condemnation (appraisal) of the given situation is presupposed, otherwise there would be no reason to advocate a particular policy. Finally, there is presupposed one or more propositions on the level of ethical principles or standards. A policy is always on the level of means, and there can only be a moral means if there are certain ethical principles which are not themselves statements of policy. For example, to state that health is a value, that it is not the most important value, but that it is necessary in order to experience some higher values—such propositions are presupposed in the formation of policy action, but are not themselves propositions stating policy action.

The purpose of social science as normative is practical action. As a practical science it is nonautonomous, a hybrid science which, from the standpoint of the structure of knowledge, relates philosophy with social science as positive. But the function of relating or applying norms is not the same thing as establishing them. The latter is strictly an ethical problem, and ethics is a philosophical discipline. When a person functions as a (normative) social scientist he will of necessity assume certain ethical propositions, whether he knows it or not. As a man he may become interested in what he is assuming, in the kind of knowledge which is ethics. When he does so, for better or worse, he becomes a philosopher.

It is to be observed that the understanding of the structure of knowledge in normative social science is quite independent of what is proved normatively or ethically. The structure of the reasoning is the same regardless of the philosophical foundation of the norms—whether they derive from naturalism, materialism, theism, idealism, etc. Even if one were to take the position that there is no ethical knowledge, that "true" and "false" have nothing to do with expressions of norms, that thesis itself is a philosophical one, and has to be defended on that level. It may be a presupposition of a social science, but the thesis itself is not a proposition *of* social science.

Since normative social science is nonautonomous, any disagreement on a conclusion will be found to be a disagreement either on the level of philosophy or of social science positive, or of both. In short, any disagreement in the normative social sciences, other than on the purely factual level of social science as positive, is philosophical, and hence rationally should be discussed on that level. If this is not understood, that a philosophical (ethical) proposition partially constitutes the evidence that establishes a conclusion in normative social science, then the inverse will be believed, that the conclusion helps to "prove" or "demonstrate" the truth of the philosophical proposition. At its best this procedure is begging the question or arguing in a circle. What is most debatable is not allowed to be debated. At its worst the procedure reduces normative social sciences to noncognitive patterns of idea-manipulations. The reduction is to that of mere ideology, in which for "truth" is substituted "usefulness," and the latter is determined by the efficiency with which certain group interests are satisfied. Instead of human interests being judged ethically, the interests become the standard of judgment. There is no normative, only instrumental, reasoning. Such a reduction would, of course, qualify (say) the Nazis as excellent social scientists.

SUMMATION

Social Science as Positive

a.   The singular propositions descriptive of uniqueness, and which the historian seeks, are constitutive as evidence to the generalizations which are sought for by the experimental social scientist. And conversely. The difference in the kind of proposition sought accounts for the differences in methodology, e.g., history is an experiential, but not an experimental, subject.

b.   Any positive science, physical or biological, may be constitutive as evidence to the social sciences.

c.   Philosophical disciplines are regulative of, but not constitutive of, social science as positive. That is, the former delimit what is possibly true, but do not determine what is actually true, in any social science.

Social Science as Normative

The propositions of various philosophical disciplines are constitutive as evidence to propositions of normative social science. Instead of history as positive, there is the philosophy of history. The social sciences become the various moral sciences.

Some Implications for Education

To be intellectually sophisticated, and not naive, is at minimum to be aware of one's presuppositions. There is no (philosophically) presuppositionless science. If there is no philosophical truth independent of history and the other social sciences as positive, then there can be no normative social science at all. But neither could there be any positive science, for positive science and normative science are correlative terms. The one has meaning only in terms of the other.

If positive science is absolutized, then it ceases to be a science. It becomes a philosophy. But even this is inexact, since the absolutizing eliminates philosophical truth. Hence, instead of philosophy, there is anti-philosophy. The social sciences (and "studies") are reduced to ideological weapons lacking any truth-function—which is identical with saying that such "sciences" are "true" to the degree that they "work" in satisfying the various social and political interests to which they are instrumental.

DISCUSSION OF DR. MARTIN'S PAPER

DR. PHIL SMITH: You say that the historian looks at the data and then draws generalizations. I take it that these are inductive inferences or summaries. But does he not also look at data and then make creative abductive inferences, that is, generalizations that account for or explain what he has observed? Isn't this what converts data to history?

DR. MARTIN: No, I do not mean that. Let us suppose that you are comparing and relating the French Revolution, Russian Revolution, and the English, etc., and you are pointing out similarities and differences. You can do this, but you can only do it because you have already got your history. In other words, in doing this you don't create some more history.

DR. PHIL SMITH: But you create a way of looking and use this on more data than was used initially.

DR. MARTIN: In the sense that it may be a condition for further research, I think you are right. In other words, you may get ideas and say, "Well, look now, we haven't explored this. I'll bet there's a lot of stuff, a lot of manuscripts, etc." Yes, I think you are correct, but then this would be the condition for further research work, that's all.

DR. KRUG: I find myself in disagreement with your definition of what history is.

DR. MARTIN: You mean history *as positive?*

DR. KRUG: Yes, but history is not an assembly of facts as, it seems to me, you have suggested in your paper. When you talk about history, I would suggest, Professor Martin, that you are talking about bad pedestrian history. Good history is not concerned with the accumulation of facts because its generalizations are far from being only summations of the available data. Well, let me give some examples. First, when Namier, for instance, created a veritable revolution in English historiography by his research. He followed an intuition that all the previous suggestions that the Elizabethan and then later the Parliament of George II were dominated by people who believed in freedom and reform.

Namier proved by monumental research of contemporary record that this hypothesis was not true. He suggested that it was the self-interest of the M.P.'s and the general rise of the gentry that governed the actions of the members of Parliament. Namier's hunch had proven to be correct and his work gave rise to a whole new school of research in English history.

Now, would you suggest that such a generalization is merely a summation from known facts? You have given a definition of what a generalization in history is. According to this definition, a generalization in history is a summary of facts and data gathered by the historian. That was not true in the case of Namier. He didn't have all of his "facts" before he formulated his generalization, and I am sure that it was not true in the case of Beard when he wrote his *Economic Interpretation of the Constitution*. A generalization in history is often a hunch, an intuition quite similar to a revelation of Newton or Einstein. This is just the opposite of the summation—all the facts are there for all historians to see, except that Beard and Namier have seen the same facts differently. Take Turner's frontier theory. Would you suggest that this is a summation of facts? Turner's spectacular historical insight had little, if anything, to do with a summation of facts. It was a brilliant exposition of a new understanding of the unique nature of American institutions. What I am suggesting, Professor Martin, is that your definition of an historical generalization is the result of a misunderstanding of what history is and of how a good historian goes about his work. Because of lack of time you did not read to us the pages in your paper dealing with the case study. It seems to me that the paper stands or falls with this case study. If, in this case study you have cited, Professor X is correct in his reasoning, then your conclusions must be wrong. Now I submit that your analysis of the article written by Professor X raises many questions. I think that this was a splendid article written by a competent historian who I think made his point exactly, logically, according to the rules of good historical research. Early in your paper you discuss the first premise of the author: the Soviet Union must fall. You question Professor X's assumption that since tyrannies have fallen in the past that the Soviet Union would also have to fall. As a matter of fact, that is a very valid assumption. You then suggest that Professor X falsely reasoned that "whatever has happened in the past must happen again." Professor X has never said it. He has never intimated that. I suggest that this is a distortion of what he has written. What he did say was that we have ample historical evidence to prove that any tyrannical government that suppressed freedom has eventually fallen. That's what he said. Not that whatever has happened in the past must happen again.

You continue somewhat later again reconstructing the thinking of Professor X. You suggest that he reasoned: "Whatever in the long run is incompatible with human freedom must fall." Professor X has never said it. He never intimated it. What he did say was that whenever in history an attempt was made by a state to deny the basic rights to the citizens, such a state has eventually failed because all tyrannical states are incompatible with human freedom. Since the reconstruction of the basic reasoning of Professor X is wrong, obviously the conclusions drawn from this reasoning are also faulty. The case study was supposed to prove a point that this renowned historian has used false logic. It seems to me that the point was not proven. I suggest that the difficulty lies in the assumption of the author of the paper that all history is pedestrian history which never lives beyond the lifetime of the man who writes it. But the fact is that a Trevelyan, a Toynbee, or a Parkman represents a different kind of history.

And the other point that you made as a kind of consequence of this case is that what is wrong about Professor X is that he says, "We base our confidence in a coming Russian revolution on plain historical facts and established historical principles." You suggest that "the so-called historical principles do not exist. The principles turn out to be moral and philosophical, only a few sentences in the whole article—and interestingly enough some of these sentences are quotations." Are you suggesting that moral philosophical data and conclusions and evaluations do not belong to history? Because if this is so, then Gibbon's *Decline and Fall of the Roman Empire* was a bad book because it does deal with moral and philosophical-metaphysical judgments. The same thing is true of Francis Parkman's *Oregon Trail;* the same is true of Macaulay's *Essays.* These books abound in moral judgments and philosophical insights. Is it not the job of the historian to try to understand the motives of the people? Historians will have to write why Truman decided to drop atomic bombs on Hiroshima and Nagasaki. This involves a moral, ethical judgment similar to those which historians have been making for generations. It seems to me, therefore, that our main difficulty is a different approach to and a different understanding of what history is.

DR. MARTIN: I think perhaps the difficulty is in understanding what I am trying to do, because I don't find myself disagreeing with you except on your conclusions. I simply made a distinction in the way the word history is used. Sometimes the word history is used to refer to history as positive, sometimes to the philosophy of history. I didn't say that "history" was merely history as positive, which you call pedestrian; I would say that if that is all that history is, you are quite correct. So I would agree with you. My whole point was that history can never be merely that.

DR. KRUG: History can never be what?

DR. MARTIN: Merely positive. In order to have the "philosophy of history" you have to have the history that you are philosophizing about. History cannot be merely history as positive. I would be the first one to agree. However, it is very important to understand that the evidence for the one is not identical with that for the other. But the point is, I think, that there is a great danger in denying this. Historians may commit this error because they haven't come to grips with the problem of the order of knowledge which demands that you understand what history is and what it isn't. I think that they constantly switch from history as positive to the philosophy of history. I think Toynbee does this. Now, when you do this it isn't clear what evidence you are appealing to. What I tried to do was to clarify the distinction. History as positive is autonomous; it is independent of philosophy insofar as evidence is concerned. This was my point. Consider the proposition "Caesar crossed the Rubicon." (Of course that is an incomplete proposition. You'd have to say a place P_1 and a time T_1, obviously, because he doesn't cross it "generally.") Now the ontological doesn't enter into that. The research historian seeks such facts as that Robespierre walked out of a certain building. He crossed a certain street, not streets in general, and not buildings in general. He walked across to a cafe, not cafes in general, and talked with a certain man, not men in general. Now in this sense there is nothing wrong with the pedestrian work that the historian does when he does this kind of work. As a matter of fact I would say that unless the historian does this he can't go any farther; so, this is peculiarly the work of the historian. Now from there on as an historian, if he wishes to speak, say, of the philosophy of history—fine. If you want to call that "history," it's all right; but I do think that you ought to make the distinction. Why? Because when you are making a proposition which is the conclusion of an argument, and it's a proposition in the philosophy of history, then the evidence to which you appeal is not the same as that in history as positive. That's the only point that I am making. So I happen to agree with you, you see, and I think you have made a good point, but I still think that you have to recognize distinctions. Oftentimes where there is a disagreement it isn't on the history as positive; rather it's on the philosophy which is presupposed in interpreting history as positive. Now if this is a point of disagreement, then you have got to tackle the problem on philosophical grounds. You can't use the word history to cover up the problem.

DR. KRUG: Would you say, Professor Martin, that the biography of Jefferson or Lincoln is a philosophy of history, or history?

DR. MARTIN: Well, I'd have to see. I can't answer in the abstract. I'd have to take the book and have you show me a given proposition. There are many nonhistorical propositions in any history book.

Dr. Krug: Thomas' biography of Lincoln?

Dr. Martin: Well, I'd have to see a copy.

You may have various kinds of propositions. Now when I mentioned generalizations I tried to show how they fit into history. My whole point was this and only this, that the historian used generalizations, but the generalizations that the historian used he doesn't seek as a historian, as a positive historian. Generalizations are instrumental to his getting historical truth, so I do not deny the notion of generalization. I was trying to say that a generalization in physical science is one thing, in history another. And you don't equate them because they have different functions. That was my only point. Now the third point, about morals that belong to history, etc. They are not, obviously, in history as positive, but if what you mean is the philosophy of history, since you are in a sense appraising history, then the historian is using as evidence for his conclusion, in a way of presupposition, certain propositions which he may or may not be willing to defend. But if they were to be defended in terms of evidence, then it would be a philosophical, not an historical, problem.

Dr. Bereiter: I am trying to relate a point here back to what Phil Smith brought up. I will accept the distinction between history and philosophy of history. But then you claim that any generalizations that purport to go beyond the data are already used in deriving a generalization. This takes you out of history as positive. This I can't accept because in all sorts of disciplines people are deriving generalizations from data that are already there when they started. This is commonplace in anthropology. Astronomy has used this approach to the best of my knowledge. Psychologists do it all the time. It seems there are two bases on which you can defend generalizations of this kind. One is by deriving, as you said, the generalization from only a part of the data. Psychologists will do this deliberately. They will deliberately take a sample of two hundred people and say, "I am going to look at only this hundred and devise some general statement about them, then test it on the other hundred and call it cross validation." This is a very acceptable technique, but another way of doing it makes it admissable to do this even if you look at all of the data, and that's the case where you assume that the degrees of freedom are so large that you couldn't fortuitously happen upon a generalization which would fit all of them. Now if you test a thousand people and find something that is really true of all of them, it is hard for somebody to argue that the next thousand wouldn't show this same property. It may well be that in history events relative to a generalization are not numerous enough that you can use this the second way, so maybe you will have to use the partition of your data most of the time.

DR. MARTIN: I will agree with you that generalization is *sought* in physics, let us say, whereas it's *instrumental* in history. This was the whole point.

DR. HANSON: Here is kind of an olive branch for you both, or a fig leaf, or something. Both of you agree that respectable history is a lot more than chronicle. Where the difficulty comes up is partly terminological; consider again the *Decline and Fall of the Roman Empire*. One of its great theses was that the seeds of the decay of the Roman Empire were planted during the Golden Age the Antonines. Now this is an important contribution of Gibbon *as* an historian. He is not functioning here as a philosopher of history. Remarks typical of the philosophy of history would be such things as this: "What is the nature of historical causation?" Or what about Hempel's thesis back in 1942? He tried to give an analysis of the nature of explanation in history. There ensued a great controversy as to whether prediction in history and explanation in history were really symmetrical, as he claimed they were. This was a genuine philosophical controversy. Gardinner's book on *The Nature of Historical Explanation*, Dray's work *Explanation in History*—these are what I would call "philosophy of history." One can specify what would be philosophical statements about the technique of historical inquiry.

The question between the two of you really comes down to this: whether every statement by an historian—statements which are not simply chronicle and not simply a registration of the data

—is really a statement of the philosophical kind. I think that you, Professor Krug, are denying this and you, Professor Martin, are asserting this.

DR. MARTIN: All that I was saying was this, and it seems rather evident. How can you use philosophical presuppositions to draw conclusions as to the meaning of history without making any presupposition as to philosophy? That's all I was saying. In other words, if you have a conclusion stating something about the meaning of history, you are appraising. Usually this is what you are doing. Somewhere in your premises you are going to have to have a philosophical statement.

DR. HANSON: Gibbon doesn't—I read this remarkable work, believe it or not, at the University of Chicago (when I had plenty of time)—it doesn't seem to me that Gibbon is telling us *about* history. He is giving an historical account of the decline and fall of the Roman Empire. What he is doing *as* history is not itself a matter of historical inquiry but of methodological inquiry. And here is the issue: every exercise in the philosophy of history is meta-historical, it's talk *about* history; and to the extent that an historian goes beyond chronicle it looks as if you, Professor Martin, are obliged to say that he is doing meta-history. And Krug wants to deny this, rightly.

DR. MARTIN: Using the term that way I know what you mean. Yes, I would agree with you.

DR. BEREITER: My difficulty is this: I don't see why history has to be restricted to matters of singular fact any more than any other experimental positive science. That is, the same situation that applies to history applies to other nonexperimental natural sciences. For example, geology or astronomy or archaeology are not restricted to statements of singular fact. How is history any different from these other sciences?

DR. MARTIN: You see I have already admitted that. I think in written history you sometimes mean by history just what happened. At still other times you don't mean "what happened," or even history as written, but rather just what is known, the information about these historical events. The third meaning of history is your written history, which of course is always a selection. You don't just put down everything. Now the point is that I will agree with you that you use generalizations of history all the time. What I tried to do was to show the difference between history as positive and what you call positive science in the sense of physics or chemistry. In history the generalization has a different function and it is for that reason that your methodology in history is different from that in the physical sciences. That's the reason, for example, why the historian doesn't experiment like, say, the physicist does. He may go down to the third sub-basement of the London museum and pore over manuscripts or something of this kind. What I am trying to do is to point out that in a written history, of course, you find generalizations, you find singular propositions, you find all kinds of propositions. What I was trying to do was show the different functional relationships of propositions to each other in order to explain the different kinds of knowledge.

DR. SCHWAB: Concerning the argument which Mark Krug developed, let us grant that there has been a syntax which established a reasonably warrantable chronicle. At this point, the historian must choose a substantive structure, a conception which asserts the character of the stuff he is dealing with: history is a tale of heroes, or the unfolding of a developing ideal, or the consequence of psychological laws, or what-have-you.

DR. MARTIN: That is my third meaning of history.

DR. SCHWAB: That's right. Consequently, I find genuinely a serious and useful contribution here, since you distinguished the peculiar syntax of history that establishes the warrantable chronicle. Then you proceed to talk about the superimposition, on such a body of data, of a conceptual substantive structure when you say historians attempt to discover some meaning in the flow of events. It is out of the attempt to discover some particular meaning that the facts are selected, then interpreted.

DR. MARTIN: I will agree with you.

DR. SCHWAB: And all I am saying is I don't find a fruitful opposition to you. If we notice what questions you were asking and if you had happened to label your question or I labeled mine . . . .

DR. KRUG: I believe you are a peacemaker. I would like to ask you, Professor Martin, what was wrong with the argument of Professor X?

DR. MARTIN: Well, simply this . . . .

DR. AUSUBEL: The wrong, illogical thinking on the part of the historian. What was wrong with his thinking?

DR. MARTIN: I have already shown what was wrong. If you disagree, then somewhere in these nine pages of analysis you would have to show that I said something false. I may call attention to the fact that the author confuses modalities. This is something that occurs in many social sciences. There is a difference between *is* and *must*. He can't get a *must* in his conclusion without having something up there in the premises that allows him to get it. Secondly, the so-called historical principles he appeals to are really statements about the ethical nature of man and freedom. He is really appealing to certain things about the nature of man. Now I happen to agree with him when he makes that appeal, because I think that you have to. My only point is that when he makes the appeal the truth of that proposition isn't a historical principle, it's an ethical principle. That's all my point is. I am not denying that this is what you have to do. I am just simply saying it isn't history that proves his conclusion, but rather he's applying a certain ethical principle to historical events in drawing this conclusion. But this isn't what he says. He says it is merely history; but really it isn't the history that "proves"—it's the history in combination with certain ethical principles which he is applying to history. I am not denying that this is what you have to do, regardless of whether or not you may agree with him that the Soviet Union must fall. You are going to have to put in a premise somewhere along the line—something that goes beyond history. That's all.

DR. AUSUBEL: I think that your entire rationale for distinguishing between problems in history and problems in other sciences hinges on the fact that you are conceiving of generalizations in history as serving solely an instrumental function in relation to the eliciting of singular fact. I would maintain, however, that generalizations in history are important or valuable in their own right apart from any other instrumental use. In this sense generalizations in history would be no different than generalizations in any other field.

DR. MARTIN: But if you say they are no different, it just seems to me it isn't the function of the researcher in history (as positive, for that's what we are talking about) to make generalizations in history. He isn't doing the same thing as, say, the physicist or chemist. It just seems to me factually that this is not the case.

DR. AUSUBEL: Well, I will quarrel with the original premise that the only function of history is to establish matters of singular fact. I don't think that this is the main business of history at all.

DR. MARTIN: I should imagine that's precisely its function. Somebody has to do it. I thought it would be the historian. I don't know who does it if the historian doesn't.

DR. AUSUBEL: I agree.

DR. SCHWAB: Why not accept the distinctions that Martin chooses in order to talk his stuff?

DR. HANSON: Now *don't* be a referee! There's a general discussion going on here. One way of probing the point further is just to raise such a question. I think that was Ausubel's point as to whether or not one can really play the chronicle game and come out with more data than would appear to a camera or computer—in the utter absence of any historian's "organizational" hypotheses. That's the issue. It isn't a question of talking different languages; it's the question of assessing the data.

DR. MARTIN: I am going to insist upon what you are saying. I am trying to point out that in history as positive, in comparison with physical science as positive, your generalizations versus singular propositions have different functions, that's all.

DR. AUSUBEL: Are you suggesting that history as positive is not history at all? It isn't worthy to be written?

DR. MARTIN: I would grant you that if you stopped . . . .

DR. AUSUBEL: The only history to be written is to be written like Professor X has written.

DR. MARTIN: You see I would agree with you. The same thing is true in social science. For example, suppose we study the slums in Chicago. You have a nice fat report here and you just file it away. Now we know something about the slums in Chicago. I should imagine that the only reason that you make the study is that you want to eliminate the slums. If you are going to remedy a situation, you want to find out what it is. So, now you go ahead. You are presupposing certain things, namely, that the slums are bad, which of course brings up a whole series of evaluations. So in normal social science you are presupposing the evaluations in a sense in which you are not when you are merely describing the slum situation in Chicago.

DR. PHIL SMITH: But aren't there generalizations constituted which are not merely summary statements?

DR. MARTIN: Yes, yes, but instead of being what the historian seeks, as the physicists are seeking, they become instrumental to the construction of uniqueness. In other words, they have a different function in history than in a physical science, but you always have them.

DR. BEREITER: I think what we need to settle some of this argument is a three-part division rather than the two-part one that you propose. Initially there's the business of getting the facts in order to establish what happened. Then there's the business of making scientific generalizations from these facts. There is then the using of these generalizations in normative problems, policy decisions, and value judgments. This could all be said of any line of inquiry. The only thing that seems to set history apart particularly is the first step. It is a much more difficult and complex one than you have in most other sciences and thus occupies a good bit more time. At the second level, the making of generalizations, this could be history as positive or it could be something else as positive: Sigmund Freud, for instance, could use historical facts to support a psychological generalization just as the historian can use historical facts in support of a historical generalization. Then anyone may use these generalizations to argue about slum clearance or whatever. If you accept this three-part division, then I don't see that anybody disagrees with anybody here.

DR. ARNSTINE: I think I want to amend Dr. Bereiter's steps, and this amendment is another way of getting at your conception of history. I should think that the first step would be an awareness that there is some section of the universe about which information is wanted, and to go around looking for facts is already to have made a value judgment, a commitment that something is important and that therefore there is no such thing as data collection without having made judgments of value. Consequently, the talk about history as a mere chronicle is not to talk about the work of people at all, because people do history and people make judgments before they gather any facts.

DR. MARTIN: Yes. When you use value judgment in that sense it has a regulative function. It is not constituting evidence. For example, I should imagine, as you say, that in any subject you never just collect the facts. The physicists don't go around getting bumped by sensations. In a sense, and Whitehead has pointed this out very forcefully, everything you do is under the criterion of importance. But notice how "importance" functions. You may put it in the form of a value judgment and select out the realm that you are to study, or the facts that you are going after. But in this case it isn't constitutive as evidence of what is fact or what is not.

ADJOURNMENT

CHAPTER VII

SOME PSYCHOLOGICAL ASPECTS
OF THE STRUCTURE OF
KNOWLEDGE

DAVID P. AUSUBEL

INTRODUCTION

In the light of Professor Schwab's opening remarks yesterday, I suppose that I am guilty of considerable temerity in even venturing to appear at this symposium to discuss some psychological aspects of the structure of knowledge. You will recall that the second sentence of his paper read as follows: "We have had more than enough scrutiny, discussion, and debate about the learning process, thanks to the popularity of psychological investigations." And now, in the face of this sober pronouncement, I propose to add another hour's worth of psychological discussion to the existing sickening surfeit.

Strangely enough, I agree for the most part with Professor Schwab's appraisal. I would put it somewhat differently, however. Instead of saying that we have had more than enough scrutiny and discussion of the learning process, I would say that insofar as the learning of subject-matter knowledge is concerned, we have more than enough wild and naive extrapolation of evidence and theory from rote, motor, animal, short-term, and stimulus-response learning. I still cling to the opinion that psychological processes are implicated in the individual acquisition of a body of knowledge and that it is important for teachers and curriculum-builders to understand the nature of these processes. The task that lies ahead, then, demands *not* that we dismiss the relevance of learning processes for the activities involved in transmitting and acquiring subject-matter knowledge, but rather that we formulate and test theories of learning that are relevant for the kinds of meaningful ideational learning that take place in school and similar learning environments.

The major portion of this symposium is rightly concerned with various problems associated with the logical structure of knowledge in general and with the logical structure of knowledge in particular subject-matter fields. It should not be forgotten, however, that in addition to organized bodies of knowledge that represent the collective recorded wisdom of recognized scholars in particular fields of inquiry, there are corresponding psychological structures of knowledge as represented by the organization of internalized ideas and information in the minds of individual students of varying degrees of both cognitive maturity and subject-matter sophistication in these same disciplines. I am making a distinction, in other words, between the formal organization of the subject-matter content of a given discipline, as set forth in authoritative statements in generally accepted textbooks and monographs, on the one hand, and the organized, internalized representation of this knowledge in the memory structures of particular individuals, especially students, on the other.

This paper will be devoted to these latter psychological aspects of the structure of knowledge. After a preliminary general inquiry into the relationship between the logical and the psychological structure of knowledge, I propose to suggest some principles of accretion, organization, and retention that apply to the psychological structure of knowledge, to examine some variables influencing these processes, and to discuss some pedagogic implications arising from these various psychological considerations.

RELATIONSHIP BETWEEN THE LOGICAL AND THE PSYCHOLOGICAL STRUCTURE OF KNOWLEDGE

In some ways the logical and psychological structures of knowledge are quite similar, and in some ways they are very different. These similarities and differences can be demonstrated most conveniently, in my opinion, by comparing the two structures of knowledge with respect to four of their principal attributes: (a) meaning, (b) process of organization, (c) arrangement of component elements, and (d) cognitive maturity of content.

Meaning

Corresponding to the distinction between the logical and the psychological structure of knowledge is an equally important distinction between logical and psychological meaning. Actual phenomenological meaning, I submit, is an idiosyncratic psychological experience. Subject-matter content can at best have logical or potential meaning. Potential meaning becomes converted into actual meaning when a *particular* individual, employing a meaningful learning set, incorporates a potentially meaningful proposition or unit of information within his cognitive structure.

Subject-matter material possesses logical or potential meaning if it consists of possible and nonarbitrary relationships that are relatable on a nonarbitrary, substantive basis to a hypothetical human cognitive structure exhibiting, in general, the necessary ideational background and cognitive maturity. This criterion of logical meaning applies primarily to the attributes of the learning material itself. If the material manifests the characteristics of nonarbitrariness, lucidity, and plausibility, then it is by definition also relatable to the aforementioned hypothetical cognitive structure. Obviously excluded, therefore, from the domain of logical meaning is the vast majority of the almost infinite number of possible relationships between concepts that can be formulated on the basis of purely random pairings. This does not mean that all propositions with logical meaning are necessarily valid or even logically correct. The questions of substantive and logical validity are issues that simply do not enter into the determination of logical meaning. Propositions based on unvalidated premises or on faulty logic may conceivably abound in logical or potential meaning.

It is nonarbitrary subsumability of logically meaningful propositions within a *particular* cognitive structure that creates the possibility of transforming logical into psychological meaning. Hence the emergence of psychological meaning depends not only on the learner's possession of the requisite intellectual capacities and ideational background, but also on his *particular* ideational content. When an individual learns logically meaningful propositions, therefore, he does not learn their logical meaning but the meaning they have for him. Psychological meaning is always an idiosyncratic phenomenon. The idiosyncratic nature of psychological meaning, however, does not rule out the possibility of social or shared meanings. The various individual meanings possessed by members of a given culture are ordinarily sufficiently similar to permit interpersonal communication and understanding. This intracultural homogeneity of shared meanings reflects both the same logical meaning inherent in potentially meaningful propositions and the interindividual commonality of ideational background.

Process of Organization

The logical and psychological structures of knowledge obviously differ in terms of the kinds of processes that enter into their organization. From a process standpoint the laws applying to the psychological organization of knowledge are the laws of meaningful learning and retention, whereas the laws governing the logical organization of knowledge are derived from the logic of classification. Nevertheless these two sets of process laws overlap to the extent that the meaningful learning of new ideas conforms to principles of logical classification insofar as it may be described as a process of subsumption under those relevant existing ideas in cognitive structure which exhibit a higher order of generality and inclusiveness. Thus not only do both kinds of organizational processes rely on the logic of classification, but they also employ the same principle of structuring knowledge in terms of unifying elements which manifest the greatest generality, inclusiveness, and explanatory power, and which are capable of relating and integrating the widest possible array of subject matter.

The difference between the two kinds of organizational processes stems from two facts: (a) that the psychological structure of knowledge is subject throughout its development to systematic decrement resulting from the gradual loss of the identity and availability of subsumed materials as their distinctive import is assimilated by the more general meaning of their more inclusive and established subsumers; and (b) that both the learning of new ideas and their memorial resistance to the aforementioned decremental processes are largely a function of such properties of existing cognitive structure as the availability of relevant subsumers, the stability and clarity of these subsumers, and their discriminability from the new learning material. These two limiting conditions obviously do not apply to the logical structure of knowledge.

The psychological, unlike the logical structure of knowledge, therefore, is in a very real sense both an organized residue of inclusive subsumers and those elements of related subsumed materials that have managed to resist the process of memorial reduction or assimilation, plus the residual products of forgetting, namely, the original subsuming ideas which have completely assimilated their subsumed materials.

Arrangement of Component Elements

It is also reasonable to assume that the psychological and logical structures of knowledge differ with respect to the sequential placement, ordering, and arrangement of component elements. The kinds of processes involved in the psychological organization of knowledge, i.e., in meaningful learning and retention, imply a hierarchical type of structure which is progressively differentiated in terms of degree of generality and inclusiveness. This is the kind of structure which obviously results when new learning materials are subsumed under relevant, more inclusive concepts in existing cognitive structure. The logical structure of knowledge, on the other hand, although using general and inclusive ideas as organizing elements, strives for topical relatedness and homogeneity rather than progressive differentiation in the sequential arrangement of subject matter. Psychologically, however, this kind of structure is not approached until the terminal stages of subject-matter sophistication. Only after an individual develops mature cognitive capacities and acquires an expert, specialized knowledge of a subject does his psychological structure of knowledge in that discipline correspond (although in somewhat less systematized form) to the logical structure of knowledge in the same discipline; in any case he can at this stage easily reorganize this psychological structure in terms of the topically most homogeneous and systematic ordering of relationships between component facts, concepts, and propositions. This degree of parallelism between the logical and the psychological structure of knowledge does not exist during earlier stages of intellectual development and subject-matter sophistication.

It is apparent from the previous discussion that the logical structure of a subject is necessarily dependent on and a product of human cognitive processes. Only human beings who possess mature cognitive capacities and whose psychological structure of knowledge in a given discipline is highly sophisticated can structure this field of knowledge in a logically satisfactory fashion.[1] It is evident therefore that the following degree of interdependence prevails between the logical and the psychological structure of knowledge: on the one hand, the psychological structure of knowledge is a derivative of subject-matter content abstracted

[1] This does not necessarily imply, of course, that the logical validity of a particular organization of subject-matter relationships is dependent on human ability to appreciate these relationships or to execute logical operations.

from the logical structure of knowledge, and psychological meaning is an idiosyncratic elaboration of logical meaning; on the other hand, the logical structure of knowledge is a topically systematized reorganization of the psychological structure of knowledge as it exists in mature scholars in a particular discipline.

Cognitive Maturity of Content

Just as level of subject-matter sophistication determines the sequential arrangement of the psychological structure of knowledge, general level of cognitive maturity, particularly along the concrete-abstract dimension of intellectual functioning, determines the cognitive maturity of the content contained in this structure. The logical structure of subject matter, on the other hand, does not manifest any developmental variability in cognitive maturity of content. Whereas the level of abstraction, generality, explicitness, and precision characteristic of the logical structure of subject-matter content is invariably and necessarily high, being the product of sophisticated scholars, the same high level of maturity in these cognitive attributes of content is found in the psychological structure of knowledge only when the individual is in the terminal stages of intellectual development.

During the elementary school period, for example, when the child is in the stage of concrete logical operations (10), he is dependent upon current or recently prior concrete-empirical experience for the understanding or manipulation of relationships between abstractions or ideas about ideas. When such experience is not available he finds abstract propositions unrelatable to cognitive structure and hence devoid of meaning. This dependence upon concrete-empirical props self-evidently limits his ability meaningfully to grasp and manipulate relationships between abstractions, since he can only acquire those understandings and perform those logical operations which do not go beyond the concrete and particularized representation of ideas implicit in his use of props. Thus where complex abstract concepts and propositions are involved, he is largely restricted to a concrete or intuitive level of cognitive functioning, a level that

227

falls far short of the clarity, precision, explicitness, and generality associated with the more advanced stage of intellectual development.

Beginning in the junior high school period, however, children become increasingly less dependent upon the availability of concrete-empirical experience in meaningfully relating complex abstract propositions to cognitive structure. Eventually, after sufficient gradual change in this direction, a qualitatively new capacity emerges: the intellectually mature individual becomes capable of understanding and manipulating relationships between abstractions without any reference whatsoever to concrete, empirical reality. Instead of reasoning directly from a particular set of data, he uses indirect, second-order abstractions for structuring the data; instead of merely grouping data into classes or arranging them serially in terms of a given variable, he deals with all possible or hypothetical relations between ideas. He can now transcend the previously achieved level of intuitive thought and understanding, and formulate general laws relating general categories of variables that are divorced from the concrete-empirical data at hand. His concepts and generalizations, therefore, tend more to be second-order constructs derived from relationships between previously established abstractions already one step removed from the data itself.

Relative level of abstraction of subject-matter content becomes an important pedagogic consideration in determining the order in which pupils should be introduced to the different scientific disciplines. On strictly logical grounds one might argue that the various disciplines should be introduced in the order of their relative phenomenological complexity, i.e., that the phenomenologically more fundamental and simple laws of physics and chemistry should be mastered before the phenomenologically more complex and variable data of biology are studied. Psychologically, however, the logically simple laws of physics and chemistry are more abstract and difficult than the logically complex laws of biology which are both more descriptive in nature and closer to everyday, concrete experience.

THE PSYCHOLOGICAL ACCRETION AND ORGANIZATION OF KNOWLEDGE

The principle of subsumption, in my opinion, provides a key to understanding the processes underlying the psychological accretion and organization of knowledge. The human nervous system as a data processing and storing mechanism is so constructed that new ideas and information can be meaningfully learned and retained only to the extent that more inclusive and appropriately relevant concepts are already available in cognitive structure to serve a subsuming role or to provide ideational anchorage. Thus subsumption accounts for accretion to the psychological structure of knowledge by determining the acquisition of new meanings, their retention or resistance to assimilation, and the forgetting process itself; and over a period of time the nature and outcome of this accretion process, i.e., the cumulative residue of what is meaningfully learned, retained, and forgotten, determines how knowledge is psychologically organized. The subsumption process, therefore, also ultimately explains why an individual's organization of the content of a particular subject-matter discipline in his own mind consists of a hierarchical structure in which the most inclusive concepts occupy a position at the apex of the structure and subsume progressively less inclusive and more highly differentiated subconcepts and factual data.

Learning

Meaningful reception learning occurs as potentially meaningful material enters the cognitive field and interacts with and is appropriately subsumed under a relevant and more inclusive conceptual system. The very fact that such material is subsumable in nonarbitrary, substantive fashion accounts for its potential meaningfulness and makes possible the emergence of phenomenological meaning. If it were not subsumable it would form discrete and relatively isolated traces.

The initial effects of subsumption, therefore, may be described as facilitation of both learning and retention. Only orienting, relational, and cataloguing operations are involved at first. These preliminary operations are obviously essential for meaningful learning and retention, since the hierarchical incorporation of new material into existing cognitve structure is both the basis for the emergence of new meaning and must also necessarily conform to the prevailing principle of cognitive organization. Furthermore, subsumption of the traces of the learning task by an established ideational system provides anchorage for the new material, and thus constitutes the most orderly, efficient, and stable way of retaining it for future availability. Hence, for a variable period of time, the recently catalogued subconcepts and informational data can be dissociated from their subsuming concepts and are reproducible as individually identifiable entities.

Retention and Forgetting

Although the stability of meaningful material is initially enhanced by anchorage to relevant conceptual foci in the learner's cognitive structure, such material is gradually subjected to the erosive influence of the reductionist trend in cognitive organization. Because it is more economical and less burdensome to retain a single inclusive concept than to remember a large number of more specific items, the import of the latter tends to be incorporated by the generalized meaning of the former. When the second or obliterative stage of subsumption begins, the specific items become progressively less dissociable as entities in their own right until they are no longer available and are said to be forgotten. Thus the same subsumability that is necessary for meaningful reception learning somewhat paradoxically provides the basis for later forgetting.

This process of memorial reduction to the least common denominator capable of representing cumulative prior experience is very similar to the reduction process characterizing concept formation. A single abstract concept is more manipulable for cognitive purposes than the dozen diverse instances from which its commonality is abstracted; and similarly, the memorial residue of ideational experience is also more functional for future learning and problem-solving occasions when stripped of its tangential modifiers, particularized connotations, and less clear and discriminable implications. Hence, barring repetition or some other special reason (e.g., primacy, uniqueness, enhanced discriminability, or the availability of a specially relevant and stable subsumer) for the perpetuation of dissociability, specific items of meaningful experience that are supportive of or correlative to an established conceptual entity tend gradually to undergo obliterative subsumption.

Unfortunately, however, the advantages of obliterative subsumption are gained at the expense of losing the differentiated body of detailed propositions and specific information that constitute the flesh if not the skeleton of any body of knowledge. The main problem of acquiring a firm grasp of any academic discipline, therefore, is counteracting the inevitable process of obliterative subsumption that characterizes all meaningful learning.

Learning versus *Retention*

In reception learning the distinctive attribute of both learning and retention is a change in the availability of the meanings derived from the subsumed learning material. Learning refers to the process of acquiring meanings from the potential meanings presented in the learning material and of making them more available. It represents an increment in the availability of new meanings, i.e., the situation that prevails when they emerge or are first established, or when their dissociability strength is increased by repetition or by conditions increasing discriminability. Retention, on the other hand, refers to the process of maintaining the availability of a replica of the acquired new meanings. Thus forgetting represents a decrement in availability, i.e., the situation that prevails between the establishment of a meaning and its reproduction, or between two presentations of the learning material. Retention, therefore, is largely a later temporal phase and diminished aspect of the same phenomenon or functional capacity involved in learning itself. Later availability is always at least in part a function of initial availability.

Derivative versus Correlative Subsumption

It is important to distinguish between two basically different kinds of subsumption that occur in the course of meaningful learning and retention. *Derivative* subsumption takes place when the learning material constitutes a specific example of an established concept in cognitive structure, or is supportive or illustrative of a previously learned general proposition. In either case the material to be learned is directly and self-evidently derivable from or implicit in an already established and more inclusive concept or proposition in cognitive structure. Under these circumstances the meaning of the derivative material emerges quickly and effortlessly, and unless greatly overlearned tends to undergo obliterative subsumption very rapidly. If such data are needed, however, they can easily be synthesized or reconstructed by appropriately manipulating specific elements of past and present experience so that they exemplify the desired concept or proposition.

More typically, however, new subject matter is learned by a process of *correlative* subsumption. The new learning material in this case is an extension, elaboration, or qualification of previously learned propositions. It is incorporated by and interacts with relevant and more inclusive subsumers in cognitive structure, but its meaning is not implicit in and cannot be represented by these latter subsumers. Nevertheless, in the interests of economy of cognitive organization and of reducing the burden of memory, the same trend toward obliterative subsumption occurs. But in this instance the consequences of obliterative subsumption are not as innocuous as in the case of derivative subsumption. When correlative propositions lose their identifiability and can no longer be dissociated from their subsumers, a genuine loss of knowledge occurs. The subsumers cannot adequately represent the meaning of the propositions in question, and hence the availability of the subsumers in memory does not make possible a reconstruction of the forgotten material.

The problem of acquiring a body of knowledge, therefore, is largely concerned with counteracting the trend toward obliterative subsumption in retaining correlative materials. Bruner's exclusive emphasis on "generic learning" or acquiring "generic coding systems" (5, 6, 7) as a means of facilitating school learning is unrealistic because it focuses on derivative aspects of subsumption which are atypical both of the subsumption process in general and of most instances of incorporating new subject matter. It is true, as he asserts, that most specific content aspects of subject matter can be forgotten with impunity as long as they are derivable or can be reconstructed when needed from those generic concepts or formulae which are worth remembering. But the analogous forgetting of correlative content results in a loss of knowledge that cannot be regenerated from residual generic concepts. The conceptualizing trend in memorial reduction (i.e., obliterative subsumption), which is functional or at the very worst innocuous in the case of derivative material, constitutes the principal difficulty in acquiring a body of knowledge in the more typical context of learning correlative propositions. Hence the problem of meaningful learning and retention cannot ordinarily be solved by incorporating "a representation of the criterial characteristics of [a] situation, [or] a contentless depiction of the ideal case" (7), and then ignoring the loss of specific content that occurs. The main purpose of learning generic concepts and propositions is not so much to make possible the reconstruction of forgotten derivative instances as to provide stable anchorage for correlative material; and it is the inhibition of the rate of obliterative subsumption in relation to this material that is the major problem confronting teachers in transmitting subject-matter content.

FACTORS INFLUENCING MEANINGFUL LEARNING AND RETENTION

It follows from the very nature of accretion to the psychological structure of knowledge through the subsumption process that existing cognitive structure—an individual's organization, stability, and clarity of knowledge in a particular subject-matter field at any given time—is the major factor influencing the learning and retention of meaningful new material in this same field. Since potentially meaningful material is always learned in relation to an existing background of relevant concepts, principles, and information, which provide a framework for its reception and make possible the emergence of new meanings, it is evident that the stability, clarity, and organizational properties of this background crucially affect both the accuracy and the clarity of these emerging new meanings and their immediate and long-term retrievability. If cognitive structure is stable, clear, and suitably organized, accurate and unambiguous meanings emerge and tend to retain their dissociability strength or availability. If, on the other hand, cognitive structure is unstable, ambiguous, disorganized, or chaotically organized, it tends to inhibit meaningful learning and retention. Hence it is largely by strengthening relevant aspects of cognitive structure that new learning and retention can be facilitated. Thus it is a commoplace that the details of a given discipline are learned as rapidly as they can be fitted into a contextual framework consisting of a stable and appropriate body of general concepts and principles. When we deliberately attempt to influence cognitive structure so as to maximize meaningful learning and retention we come to the heart of the educative process.

In my opinion, the most significant advances that have occurred in recent years in the teaching of such subjects as mathematics, chemistry, physics, and biology have been predicated on the assumption that efficient learning and functional retention of ideas and information are largely dependent upon the adequacy of cognitive structure. And inasmuch as existing cognitive structure reflects the outcome of all previous subsumption processes, it in turn can be influenced substantively by the inclusiveness and integrative properties of the particular unifying and explanatory principles used in a given discipline, and programmatically by methods of presenting, arranging, and ordering learning materials and practice trials.

Cognitive Structure and Transfer

I have just hypothesized that past experience influences or has positive or negative effects on new meaningful learning and retention by virtue of its impact on relevant properties of cognitive structure. If this is true, all meaningful learning necessarily involves transfer because it is impossible to conceive of any instance of such learning that is not affected in some way by existing cognitive structure; and this learning experience, in turn, results in new transfer by modifying cognitive structure. In meaningful learning, therefore, cognitive structure is always a relevant and crucial variable, even if it is not deliberately influenced or manipulated so as to ascertain its effect on new learning —as for example, in those short-term learning situations where just a single unit of material is learned and transfer to new learning units is not measured. A single practice trial both reflects the influence of existing cognitive structure and induces modification of that structure.

Much more saliently than in laboratory types of learning situations, school learning requires the incorporation of new concepts and information into an existing and established cognitive framework with particular organizational properties. The transfer paradigm still applies here, and transfer still refers to the impact of prior experience upon current learning. But prior experience in this case is conceptualized as a cumulatively acquired, hierarchically organized, and established body of knowledge which is organically relatable to the new learning task, rather than a recently experienced constellation of stimulus-response connections influencing the learning of another discrete set of such connections. Furthermore, the relevant aspects of past experience in this type of transfer paradigm are such organizational properties of the learner's subject-matter knowledge as clarity, stability, generalizability, inclusiveness, cohesiveness, and discriminability—not degree of similarity between stimuli and responses in the two learning tasks; and recent prior experience is not regarded as influencing current learning by interacting *directly* with the stimulus-response components of the new learning task, but only insofar as it modifies significant relevant attributes of cognitive structure.

Because training and criterion tasks in laboratory studies of transfer have usually been separate and discrete, we have tended to think in terms of how prior task *A* influences performance on criterion task *B*. If performance has been facilitated, in comparison with that of a control group which had not been exposed to task *A*, we say that positive transfer has occurred. Actually, however, in typical classroom situations, *A* and *B* are not discrete but continuous. *A* is a preparatory stage of *B* and a precursive aspect of the same learning process; *B* is not learned discretely but in relation to *A*. Hence in school learning we deal not so much with transfer in the literal sense of the term as with the influence of prior knowledge on new learning in a continuous sequential context. This latter learning context also typically involves correlative subsumption. Hence, as pointed out above, the relevant transfer effect with which we are usually concerned is not the ability to reconstruct forgotten details from generic principles or to recognize new phenomena as specific variants of these principles, but rather enhanced ability to learn and *retain* the more detailed correlative material.

Moreover, unlike the kind of transfer Bruner calls nonspecific (7), the kind of transfer just described is not restricted to those instances in which "a general idea . . . can be used as a basis for recognizing subsequent problems as special cases of the ideas originally mastered." Actually, the principal effect of existing cognitive structure on new cognitive performance is on the learning and retention of newly presented materials where potential meanings are given—not on the solution of problems requiring the application and reorganization of cognitive structure to new ends. Thus a transfer situation exists whenever existing cognitive structure influences new cognitive functioning, irrespective of whether it is in regard to reception learning or problem-solving.

Principal Cognitive Structure Variables

The learner's acquisition of a clear, stable, and organized body of knowledge constitutes more than just the major long-term objective of classroom learning activity or the principal *dependent* variable (or criterion) to be used in evaluating the impact of all factors impinging on learning and retention. Cognitive structure is *also* in its own right the most significant *independent* variable influencing the learner's capacity for acquiring more new knowledge in the same field. The importance of cognitive structure variables, however, has been generally underestimated in the past because preoccupation with noncognitive, rote, and motor kinds of learning has tended to focus attention on such situational and intrapersonal factors as practice, drive, incentive, and reinforcement variables. But in searching for knowledge about the processes underlying meaningful reception learning and retention, it is not enough to stress the importance of relevant antecedent experience that is represented in existing cognitive structure. Before fruitful experimentation can be attempted it is necessary to specify and conceptualize those properties (variables) of cognitive structure that influence new learning and retention.

In the more general and long-term sense, cognitive structure variables refer to significant organizational properties of the learner's *total* knowledge in a given subject-matter field and their influence on his future academic performance in the same area of knowledge. In the more specific and short-term sense, cognitive structure variables refer to the organizational properties of just the *immediately* or proximately relevant concepts within a particular subject-matter field and their effects on the learning and retention of small units of related subject matter.

One important variable affecting the incorporability of new meaningful material is the availability in cognitive organization of relevant subsuming concepts at an appropriate level of inclusiveness to provide optimal anchorage. The appropriate level of inclusiveness may be defined as that level which is as proximate as possible to the degree of conceptualization of the learning task—considered, of course, in relation to the existing degree of differentiation of the subject as a whole in the learner's cognitive background. Thus, the more unfamiliar the learning task, i.e., the more undifferentiated the learner's background of relevant concepts, the more inclusive or highly generalized the subsuming concepts must be in order to be proximate.

What happens if an appropriate relevant subsumer is not available in cognitive structure when new potentially meaningful material is presented to a learner? If some existing though not entirely relevant and appropriate concept cannot be utilized for subsuming purposes, the only alternative is rote learning. More typically, however, some tangentially relevant subsumer is pressed into service. This type of subsumer obviously cannot provide very adequate or efficient anchorage, thereby giving rise to unclear, unstable, and ambiguous meanings with little longevity. The same outcome may also result when appropriate relevant subsumers *are* available, if their relevance is not recognized. For both reasons, therefore, in meaningful learning situations, it is preferable to introduce suitable organizers whose relevance is made explicit rather than to rely on the spontaneous availability of appropriate subsumers.

A second important factor presumably affecting the retention of a potentially meaningful learning task is the extent to which it is discriminable from the established conceptual systems that subsume it. A reasonable assumption here, borne out by preliminary investigation, is that if the new concepts are not originally salient and clearly discriminable from established subsuming foci, they can be adequately represented by the latter for memorial purposes, and would not persist as dissociable entities in their own right. In other words, only discriminable categorical variants of more inclusive concepts have long-term retention value.

Lastly, the learning and longevity of new meaningful material in memory are a function of the stability and clarity of its subsumers. Ambiguous and unstable subsumers not only provide weak anchorage for related new materials, but also cannot be easily discriminated from them.

IMPLICATIONS FOR TEACHING

What are some of the pedagogic implications both of the foregoing model of the psychological structure of knowledge and of the factors that influence its accretion and organization? The major implication for teaching perhaps is that control over the accuracy, clarity, longevity in memory, and transferability of a given body of knowledge can be most effectively exercised by attempting to influence the crucial variables of cognitive structure. This can be done both substantively and programatically: (a) by using for organizational and integrative purposes those unifying concepts and propositions in a given discipline that have the widest explanatory power, inclusiveness, generalizability, and relatability to the subject-matter content of that discipline; and (b) by employing suitable programatic principles of ordering the sequence of subject matter, constructing its internal logic and organization, and arranging practice trials.

The principal strategy advocated in this paper for deliberately manipulating cognitive structure so as to enhance proactive facilitation or minimize proactive inhibition involves the use of appropriately relevant and inclusive introductory materials (i.e., organizers) that are maximally clear and stable. These organizers are introduced in advance of the learning material itself, and are also presented at a higher level of abstraction, generality, and inclusiveness; and since the substantive content of a given organizer or series of organizers is selected on the basis of their appropriateness for explaining, integrating, and interrelating the material they precede, this strategy simultaneously satisfies the substantive as well as the programing criteria specified above for enhancing the organizational strength of cognitive structure. Summaries and overviews, on the other hand, are ordinarily presented at the same level of abstraction, generality, and inclusiveness as the learning material itself. They simply emphasize the salient points of the material by omitting less important information, and largely achieve their result by repetition.

The function of the organizer is to provide ideational scaffolding for the stable incorporation and retention of the more detailed and differentiated material that follows in the learning passage, as well as to increase discriminability between the latter and related interfering concepts in cognitive structure. In the case of completely unfamiliar material, an "expository" organizer is used to provide relevant proximate subsumers. These subsumers primarily furnish ideational anchorage in terms that are already familiar to the learner. In the case of relatively familiar material, a "comparative" organizer is used both to integrate new concepts with basically similar concepts in cognitive structure, as well as to increase discriminability between new and existing ideas which are essentially different but confusable.

Progressive Differentiation of Learning Tasks

When subject matter is programed in accordance with the principle of progressive differentiation, the most general and inclusive ideas of the discipline are presented first and are then progressively differentiated in terms of detail and specificity. This order of presentation presumably corresponds to the postulated way in which knowledge is represented, organized, and stored in the human nervous system, and recognizes that new ideas and information can be meaningfully learned and retained only to the extent that more inclusive and appropriately relevant concepts are already available in cognitive structure to play a subsuming role or to furnish ideational anchorage.

But even though this principle seems rather self-evident, it is rarely followed in actual teaching procedures or in the organization of most textbooks. The more typical practice is to segregate topically homogeneous materials into separate chapters, and to present them throughout at an undifferentiated level of conceptualization in accordance with a logical outline of subject-matter organization. This practice, of course, although logically sound is psychologically incongruous with the postulated process whereby meaningful learning occurs, i.e., with the mechanism of accretion through a process of progressive differentiation of an undifferentiated field. Thus, in most instances, students are required to learn the details of new and unfamiliar disciplines before they have acquired an adequate body of relevant subsumers at an appropriate level of inclusiveness.

As a result of this latter practice, students and teachers are coerced into treating meaningful materials as if they were rote in character, and consequently experience unnecessary difficulty and little success in both learning and retention. The teaching of mathematics and science, for example, still relies heavily on rote learning of formulas and procedural steps, on recognition of stereotyped "type problems," and on mechanical manipulation of symbols. In the absence of clear and stable concepts which can serve as anchoring points and organizing foci for the incorporation of new potentially meaningful material, students have little choice but rotely to memorize learning tasks for examination purposes.

Progressive differentiation in the programing of subject matter is accomplished by using a hierarchical series of organizers (in descending order of inclusiveness), each organizer preceding its corresponding unit of detailed, differentiated material. In this way not only is an appropriately relevant and inclusive subsumer made available to provide ideational scaffolding for each component unit of differentiated subject matter, but the various units in relation to each other are also progressively differentiated, i.e., organized in descending order of inclusiveness. The initial organizers, therefore, furnish anchorage at a global level before the learner is confronted with *any* of the new material. Hence, for example, a generalized model of class relationships is first provided as a general subsumer for *all* new classes, subclasses, and species before more limited subsumers are provided for the particular subclasses or species they encompass.

Thus when undergraduates are first exposed to organizers presenting relevant and appropriately inclusive subsuming principles they are better able to learn and retain completely unfamiliar ideational material (1). Differential analysis in another similar study showed that the facilitating effect of organizers occurs only for those individuals who have relatively poor verbal ability, and who therefore tend spontaneously to structure such material less effectively (3). The greater retention by pro-Southern than by pro-Northern students of a controversial passage presenting the Southern point of view on the Civil War can also be explained in terms of the relative availability of appropriate subsuming ideas (9). The pro-Northern students lack relevant subsumers to which the pro-Southern passage can be functionally related. The material therefore cannot be clearly and securely anchored to cognitive structure, concepts with existing meanings, and is consequently ambiguous and subject to rapid forgetting. The pro-Southern students, on the other hand, possess relevant subsuming concepts; hence the material can be readily anchored to cognitive structure and is less ambiguous and subject to forgetting.

In sequential school learning, knowledge of earlier appearing material in the sequence plays much the same role as an organizer in relation to later appearing material in the sequence: it constitutes relevant ideational scaffolding and hence a crucial limiting condition for learning the latter material. One of the principal advantages of programed instruction is its careful sequential arrangement and gradation of difficulty which insure that each attained increment in learning serves as an appropriate foundation and anchoring post for the learning and retention of subsequent items in the ordered sequence.

Consolidation

By insisting on consolidation or mastery of ongoing lessons before new material is introduced, we make sure of continued readiness and success in sequentially organized learning. This kind of learning presupposes, of course, that the preceding step is always clear, stable, and well organized. If it is not, the learning of all subsequent steps is jeopardized. Hence new material in the sequence should never be introduced until all previous steps are thoroughly mastered. This principle also applies to those kinds of intra-task learning in which each component task (as well as entire bodies of subject matter) tends to be compound in content and to manifest an internal organization of its own.

Abundant experimental research (e.g., 8, 11) has confirmed the proposition that prior learnings are not transferable to new learning tasks until they are first overlearned. Overlearning, in turn, requires an adequate number of adequately spaced repetitions and reviews, sufficient intra-task repetitiveness prior to intra- and inter-task diversification, and opportunity for differential practice of the more difficult components of a task. Frequent testing and provision of feedback, especially with test items demanding fine discrimination among alternatives varying in degree of correctness, also enhances consolidation by confirming, clarifying, and correcting previous learnings.

The stability and clarity of existing cognitive structure are important both for the depth of anchorage they provide for related new learning tasks as well as for their effects on the discriminability of these new tasks. The discriminability of new learning material is in large measure a function of the clarity and stability of existing concepts in the learner's cognitive structure to which it is relatable. In learning an unfamiliar passage about Buddhism, for example, subjects with greater knowledge of Christianity make significantly higher scores on the Buddhism retention test than do subjects with less knowledge of Christianity (2, 4). This significantly positive relationship between Christianity and Buddhism scores holds up even when the effect of verbal ability is statistically controlled. When a parallelly organized passage about Zen Buddhism is introduced after the Buddhism passage, knowledge of Buddhism similarly facilitates the learning of Zen Buddhism when verbal ability is held constant (4). In more directly sequential tasks, where the learning of Part II materials presupposes understanding of Part I materials, the stability and clarity of the antecedent material crucially affects the learning and retention of the later-appearing material (3). Even in the learning of controversial ideas contrary to prevailing belief (e.g., the learning by Illinois students of the Southern point of view about the Civil War), the more knowledgeable students, namely, those who know more about the Civil War period, are better able to learn and remember the "other side" arguments (9), presumably because they find them more discriminable from established ideas than do less knowledgeable subjects. Thus, much of the effect of overlearning—both on retaining a given unit of material and on learning related new material—is probably a reflection of enhanced discriminability, which can be accomplished by increasing the clarity and stability of either the learning material itself or of its subsumers.

Perhaps the most important feature of automated instruction insofar as the facilitation of meaningful learning and retention is concerned is not the incentive and drive-reducing effects of immediate feedback, but the extent to which such instruction influences learning by enhancing the stability and clarity of cognitive structure. By deferring the introduction of new material until prior material in the learning sequence is consolidated, it maximizes the effect of stability of cognitive structure on new learning; and by supplying immediate feedback, it rules out and corrects alternative wrong meanings, misinterpretations, ambiguities, and misconceptions before they have an opportunity to impair the clarity of cognitive structure and thereby inhibit the learning of new material.

Integrative Reconciliation

The principle of integrative reconciliation in programing instructional material can be best described as antithetical in spirit and approach to the ubiquitous practice among textbook writers of compartmentalizing and segregating particular ideas or topics within their respective chapters or subchapters. Implicit in this latter practice is the assumption (perhaps logically valid, but certainly psychologically untenable) that pedagogic considerations are adequately served if overlapping topics are handled in self-contained fashion, so that each topic is presented in only *one* of the several possible places where treatment is relevant and warranted, i.e., the assumption that all necessary cross-referencing of related ideas can be satisfactorily performed, and customarily is, by students. Hence little serious effort is made explicitly to explore relationships between these ideas, to point out significant similarities and differences, and to reconcile real or apparent inconsistencies. Some of the undesirable consequences of this approach are that multiple terms are used to represent concepts which are intrinsically equivalent except for contextual reference, thereby generating incalculable cognitive strain and confusion, as well as encouraging rote learning; that artificial barriers are erected between related topics, obscuring important common features, and thus rendering impossible the acquisition of insights dependent upon recognition of these commonalities; that adequate use is not made of relevant, previously learned ideas as a basis for subsuming and incorporating related new information; and that since significant differences between apparently similar concepts are not made clear and explicit, these concepts are often perceived and retained as identical.

The principle of integrative reconciliation also applies when subject matter is organized along parallel lines, that is, when related materials are presented in serial fashion but there is no *intrinsic* sequential dependence from one topic to the next. Unlike the case in sequentially organized subject matter, successive learning tasks are inherently independent of each other in the sense that understanding of Part II material does not presuppose understanding of Part I material. Each set of material is logically self-contained and can be adequately learned by itself without any reference to the other; order of presentation is therefore immaterial. This situation, for example, prevails in presenting alternative theoretical positions in ethics, religion, and epistemology; opposing theories of biological evolution; and different systems of learning and personality theory.

Nevertheless, although successive learning tasks of parallelly organized material are not intrinsically dependent on each other, much cognitive interaction obviously occurs between them. Earlier learned elements of a parallel sequence serve an orienting and subsuming role in relation to later-presented elements. The latter are comprehended and interpreted in terms of existing understandings and paradigms provided by analogous, familiar, previously learned, and already established concepts in cognitive structure. Hence for learning of the unfamiliar new ideas to take place, they must be adequately discriminable from the established familiar ideas; otherwise the new meanings are so permeated with ambiguities, misconceptions, and confusions as to be partially or completely nonexistent in their own right. If, for example, the learner cannot discriminate between new idea A^1 and old idea A, A^1 does not really exist for him, it is phenomenologically the same as A. Furthermore, even if the learner can discriminate between A and A^1 at the moment of learning, unless the discrimination is sharp and free from ambiguity and confusion, there will be a tendency over time for A^1 to be remembered as A as the two ideas interact during the retention interval.

In some instances of meaningful learning and retention, the principal difficulty is not one of discriminability but of apparent contradiction between established ideas in cognitive structure and new propositions in the learning material. Under these conditions the learner may dismiss the new propositions as invalid, may try to compartmentalize them as isolated entities apart from previously learned knowledge, or may attempt integrative reconciliation under a more inclusive subsumer. Compartmentalization, of course, may be considered a common defense against forgetting. By arbitrarily isolating concepts and information, one prevents interaction with and obliterative subsumption by relevant concepts in cognitive structure. This is a modified variety of rote learning in which new learning material is allowed to interact with only certain of several potential subsumers. Through overlearning, relatively stable subsumption may be achieved, but the fabric of knowledge as a whole is unintegrated and full of internal contradictions.

Organizers may also be expressly designed to further the principle of integrative reconciliation. They do this by explicitly pointing out in what ways previously learned, related concepts in cognitive structure are either basically similar to or essentially different from new ideas in the learning task. Hence, on the one hand, organizers explicitly draw upon and mobilize all available concepts in cognitive structure that are relevant for and can play a subsuming role in relation to the new learning material. This maneuver effects great economy of learning effort, avoids the isolation of essentially similar concepts in separate, noncommunicable compartments, and discourages the confusing proliferation of multiple terms to represent ostensibly different but essentially equivalent ideas. On the other hand, organizers increase the discriminability of genuine differences between the new learning materials and analogous but often conflicting ideas in the learner's cognitive structure. Comparative organizers, for example, have been successfully used in facilitating the meaningful learning and retention of an unfamiliar passage dealing with Buddhism (2, 4), and of a controversial passage presenting the Southern point of view about the Civil War (9).

Internal Logic of Learning Material

The internal logic of the learning task is obviously relevant for meaningful learning and retention outcomes since the existence of logical or potential meaning within the material (i.e., its relatability to a hypothetical human cognitive structure with the necessary background knowledge) is a prerequisite for the emergence of psychological (phenomenological) meaning. Logical meaning, as previously pointed out, is a function of the plausibility, lucidity, and nonarbitrariness of the material rather than of its logical or substantive validity. Hence "internal logic" is used somewhat idiosyncratically here to designate those properties of the material that enhance these latter criteria of logical meaning.

At least four aspects of the internal logic of material affect the extent to which it is endowed with potential meaning: (a) adequacy of definition and diction (i.e., precise, consistent, and unambiguous use of terms; definition of all new terms prior to use; and the use of the simplest and least technical language that is compatible with conveying precise meanings); (b) the use of concrete-empirical data and of relevant analogies when developmentally warranted or otherwise helpful in the acquisition, clarification, or dramatization of meanings; (c) encouragement of an active, critical, reflective, and analytic approach on the part of the learner by requiring him to reformulate the material in terms of his own vocabulary, experiential background, and structure of ideas; and (d) explicit delineation of the distinctive logic and philosophy of each subject-matter discipline (i.e., its implicit epistemological assumptions; general problems of causality, categorization, inquiry, and measurement that are specific to the discipline; and the distinctive strategy of learning how to learn the particular subject matter of the discipline).

As Professor Phenix has so succinctly expressed it, "it is difficult to imagine how any effective learning could take place without regard for the inherent patterns of what is to be learned." Yet he was careful to point out that "attention to the structure of knowledge in the disciplines is certainly not a *sufficient* condition for learning to occur. Aptitude, maturation, and motivation are other important factors in learning." In this paper I have also stressed the importance of such cognitive structure variables as the availability of relevant subsumers, the stability and clarity of these subsumers, and their discriminability from the learning material. Finally, I have tried to show how these variables can be most advantageously manipulated for purposes of facilitating meaningful learning and retention by following the principles of progressive differentiation and integrative reconciliation in programing learning materials; by emphasizing sequential organization and prior consolidation of subject-matter content; by using advance organizers; and by employing for organizational and integrative purposes those unifying concepts and propositions in a given discipline that have the widest explanatory power, generalizability, and relatability to the subject-matter content of that discipline.

REFERENCES

1. Ausubel, D. P. "The Use of Advance Organizers in the Learning and Retention of Meaningful Verbal Material," *Journal of Educational Psychology*, LI (1960), 267–72.
2. Ausubel, D. P., and Fitzgerald, D. "The Role of Discriminability in Meaningful Verbal Learning and Retention," *Journal of Educational Psychology*, LII (1961), 266–74.
3. Ausubel, D. P., and Fitzgerald, D. "Organizer, General Background, and Antecedent Learning Conditions in Sequential Verbal Learning," *Journal of Educational Psychology*, LIII (1962), 243–49.
4. Ausubel, D. P., and Yousef, M. "The Role of Discriminability in Meaningful Parallel Learning," *Journal of Educational Psychology*, in press.
5. Bruner, J. S. Going beyond the information given. In *Contemporary approaches to cognition*. Cambridge, Mass.: Harvard Univ. Press, 1957.
6. Bruner, J. S. "Learning and Thinking," *Harvard Educational Review*, XXIX (1959), 84–92.
7. Bruner, J. S. *The process of education*. Cambridge, Mass.: Harvard Univ. Press, 1960.
8. Duncan, C. P. "Transfer after Training with Single versus Multiple Tasks," *Journal of Experimental Psychology*, LV (1959), 63–72.
9. Fitzgerald, D., and Ausubel, D. P. "Cognitive versus Affective Factors in the Learning and Retention of Controversial Material," *Journal of Educational Psychology*, LIV (1963), 73–84.
10. Inhelder, Barbel, & Piaget, J. *The growth of logical thinking from childhood to adolescence*. New York: Basic Books, 1958.
11. Morrisett, L., and Hovland, C. I. "A Comparison of Three Varieties of Training in Human Problem Solving," *Journal of Experimental Psychology*, LVIII (1959), 52–55.

DISCUSSION OF DR. AUSUBEL'S PAPER

DR. SCHWAB: Dr. Ausubel, it seems to me that you have proved that learning is impossible. You say, "New ideas and information can be meaningfully learned and retained only to the extent that more inclusive and appropriately relevant concepts are already available in cognitive structure to serve a subsuming role." In brief, then, there could be no first learning on the part of the child unless there is either some original born-in organizers or some other modes of learning than subsumptive learning. Would you mind speaking to that?

DR. AUSUBEL: I would agree that the "original" learning does not occur as the product of a subsumptive process. That is, it takes a long period of time until some stable subsumers are brought into existence; and prior to that time I'd say that the meaningfulness of the learning that occurs is somewhat subject to doubt. In any case, this "original" learning is not comparable to meaningful verbal learning.

This is somewhat of a chicken-and-egg type of question, however, which can never be finally resolved because there must always be a first bit of meaningful background in relation to which new meaning can be developed. How then do we develop this meaningful background to begin with without the prior existence of some meaningful propositions? Well, I don't see further profit in pursuing that chicken-and-egg type of question. All I can say is that, over a period of time, from the original conceptual confusion that exists, some relatively clear concepts are developed through a process of abstraction, generalization, and differentiation, and that these concepts in turn then serve as a basis for meaningful learning.

DR. SCHWAB: Well, I suggest that the question is possibly fruitful. I suggest the possibility that there is another kind of learning which not only occurs once as original learning but can under appropriate classroom or other circumstances be evoked time and again, a kind of learning which I shall call fresh learning or new learning. It is precisely the contrary of subsumptive learning in that you do make a fresh start, and you make a fresh start using a primitive beginning, not previous knowledge but a capacity on the part of human beings.

I submit, further, that the available capacities are not limited to the capacity for physical experience. There is reason to believe, for example, that many children find it easy to learn symbol systems and their manipulation *before* they are able to extract much meaningful understanding of events taking place around them.

DR. AUSUBEL: What you call "built-in ability to learn symbol systems" is simply descriptive of the fact that children are able to form certain concepts and to represent or symbolize these concepts by means of conventional symbol systems which exist in our culture. So what you call learning *de novo* really isn't learning *new symbols de novo* at all. It consists of attaching the conventional symbols of the culture to concepts which have been laboriously built up, abstracted, and generalized through a great deal of previous concrete experience.

DR. SCHWAB: I miscommunicated. I am talking about teaching kids to add, subtract, multiply, and divide by using decimals where they can't count *things* over three or four. They are not attaching the symbol manipulation to experience of things, nor even to knowledge of numbers beyond, say, three or four, although the decimal system involves nine and the primary system, of course, involves greater numbers.

DR. AUSUBEL: I wonder what these operations are—whether they have any meaning or are just rote operations.

DR. SCHWAB: Well, it may be rote.

DR. AUSUBEL: If that is the case, then this is not the kind of learning I am talking about.

DR. BEREITER: Whether it is rote or not, it could serve as a subsumer for later learning. It seems to be something you have to accept to some point that something learned rotely can nevertheless serve as a subsumer.

DR. AUSUBEL: I'd say "no" to that, because something which is learned rotely does not have any clear mental content as its reference point in cognitive structure. It is merely an arbitrary association, which, by definition, doesn't have any meaning, and hence can't be the product of subsumption.

DR. SCHWAB: But if you say that rote learning is not meaningful and there are not original in-born learnings, aren't you really stuck with an argument that no learning is possible?

DR. BEREITER: What Dr. Schwab is talking about is learning rules by rote rather than learning content by rote. I think you are right that a bunch of facts learned by rote could never subsume anything, though they might later be subsumed. But you could learn formal structures rotely which then could have content of various sorts attached to them.

DR. MARTIN: I'd like to raise a question about something that you said earlier. Now it may be merely a matter of clarification. I am not sure. You say, "When an individual learns logically meaningful propositions, therefore he does not learn their logical meaning but the meaning they have for him." Now in one sense I think I understand what you mean. You are distinguishing between the objective and the subjective. In one sense your paper stresses something that the other papers do not stress. A lot of us have been stressing the objective structures but you are talking about the mode by which we get these—*this* knowledge, etc. So granted that your point is that the mode by which the individual learns is an individual matter, it is also true that *what* he knows is not. If so, I understand what you mean. If you don't mean that, it seems to me that you would lapse into very dangerous subjectivism. When the individual learns logical, meaningful propositions, then he does not learn logical meaning. Now this would be a straight contradiction unless what you mean is that in the order of temporal priority anything that has a logical meaning must first go through the individual learning processes. Is that what you mean?

DR. AUSUBEL: Yes, this is what I mean.

DR. MARTIN: Yes. Otherwise it would be a direct contradiction.

DR. AUSUBEL: Concepts exist in the world as stimulus realities.

This is what I mean by "logical meaning." When these logical meanings are incorporated into the individual's idiosyncratic cognitive structure, they then acquire psychological meaning, which is his own subjective meaning.

DR. PHIL SMITH: I would like to know more about this. As you see it, when new material is not logically implicit in the subsumers that already exist—when this kind of new material is learned—is it ever the case that the subsumers are reconstructed and changed in such a way that the new material becomes logically implicit in them?

DR. AUSUBEL: I think that sometimes in order to incorporate certain kinds of new material into cognitive structure, one has to reorganize established subsumers, because they are not adequate for the task. I think that the best example of this would occur in the case of new ideas that apparently contradict existing propositions in cognitive structure, but could be subsumed under a more inclusive principle. When this step is required, what one is essentially doing is formulating a new subsumer which is broad enough to encompass two subprepositions which originally seem incompatible with each other.

DR. PHIL SMITH: I was wondering how, as teachers, we can facilitate this kind of reconstruction. I think an emphasis on the reconstruction of subsumers would be a better way of getting at the problem. You have pointed out that material that is not implicit in the subsumers is undifferentiated for the learner. He can't simply reconstruct or rebuild it when he needs it. Do you understand what I am saying? I am not saying it very well.

DR. AUSUBEL: Yes, I get the point.

DR. BEREITER: What I have to say takes us out of your discussion somewhat, but I think it is important because of the approach that has been taken to the structure of knowledge so far in the symposium. You apparently treat aptitude and ability as given. You say it is relevant to how readily a person will learn meaningful material, how readily he can transfer this learning to newer learning; and presumably it would govern how well he could use the learning in making discoveries and in practical applications. Nonetheless, the ability, though relevant, is just taken as given. Couldn't we at least entertain the thought that ability itself is a product of the learning that goes on?

This might force us to a different kind of pedagogy from the kind you arrive at if you simply look at the building of cognitive structure. For one thing, certain of the abilities that are needed for adding to cognitive structure and for using it might be best gained by a disorganized kind of learning—one which makes greater demands on the person's cross-referencing tendencies, his ability to change subsumers rather than have them handed to him in advance—things of this kind. I am talking about something you probably don't like, the development of thinking ability and creative ability.

DR. AUSUBEL: I have two responses to that. First, I do not regard ability as a given. I am not that much of an hereditarian; I regard as given only certain genic limitations on acquiring cognitive capacities. Typically the acquisition of these capacities is influenced by the character of one's cognitive experience.

With respect to the second consideration, I would say that I am also interested in developing thinking and creative abilities, and I would maintain that this concern with developing the thinking abilities constitutes a primary objective of education in its own right, quite apart from any contribution it makes to the acquisition of subject-matter disciplines. Both objectives have to be fostered by the school, and each calls for the employment of different strategies. In promoting one of these objectives, one will supply the learner with the most relevant and proximate subsumers; in promoting the other objective, the learner will be left more on his own to develop these subsumers independently. In the latter instance, one will not stress the optimal presentation of potential meanings to the learner, but rather the acquisition of meanings that he himself has to discover from problem situations. These two kinds of learning are not antithetical or mutually exclusive. Each supplements the other in most classroom learning tasks. Both have to be stressed by the school.

DR. BEREITER: I don't think that there is anything in your

paper where you said they are actually antithetical. But you have defined disciplines in such a way as virtually to exclude the disorganized kind of learning. In these meetings we have seen disciplines defined in various ways. They have been defined in terms of "chaps," in terms of ongoing activities, in terms of rules, etc. It seems to me that you are defining disciplines in terms of books, as the classic works which memorialize the structure of discipline in the way that it would be remembered in a super-memory or by subsumption that was not obtained at the price of obliteration. You have given us what seems like a perfectly reasonable way of setting up a psychology of learning for inculcating disciplines when the discipline is defined as what exists in a good textbook. This emphasis I object to somewhat. I am not saying that you can't define disciplines this way or that this is not one of the important ingredients in existence.

DR. AUSUBEL: I deny that I am defining a discipline in the sense that it constitutes what is contained in textbooks. I think I am defining discipline more broadly to include not only what is in textbooks but also what is contained in the current thinking of the best informed people in the field. A lot of this thinking is still not sufficiently clarified to be represented in textbooks; and even if it were, there would naturally be a time lag. I just referred to textbook study as the most convenient and rapid way of ascertaining the scope and content of a discipline. I did not mean to imply that a standard textbook is coextensive with the discipline.

DR. SCHWAB: Let's agree that you are not talking about books, but I would join Dr. Bereiter in saying you seem to be putting the emphasis on learning as a kind of transmission of a body of stuff, whether it be in the book or in the voice of the teacher or structured by the teacher according to a proposition in an experiment or an experience in an ideal textbook.

DR. AUSUBEL: That's right.

DR. SCHWAB: So that it becomes, nevertheless, a kind of slave's learning. That is, the king is the man with the stuff to be taught. Learning is a docile submission. It seems there is another kind of learning which is important, so that your list should read: noncognitive, rote, motor, subsumptive, and *inquiring* learning. And this last also needs some attention. Again, I am not objecting to what you are saying but harping on its incompleteness.

Dr. Ausubel: Well, again I would say that the fact that I haven't explicitly alluded to other kinds of learning doesn't necessarily mean that I deny their existence or importance. In this paper I have simply placed major emphasis on the most important kind of learning involved in acquiring subject-matter knowledge, namely, reception learning. But as I have said before, a very important aspect of school learning also consists of learning ideas and meanings that one has to work out for oneself. This is not only important in learning how to think but is also part of learning the subject matter of a discipline. But psychologically speaking, these are two entirely different kinds of learning. My paper only considers the nature of reception learning. I would have to write another paper to deal adequately with discovery learning. There is nothing in my present paper which implies that I subscribe to one kind of learning as against another.

Dr. Schwab: No, I am not saying that you are asserting the nonexistence of other learnings, but that it is lost in your treatment. For instance, I submit that your apparatus of organizer and subsumer would not have the importance they have here if you were talking about inquiry learning too.

Chairman B. Smith: I am not sure that he would have to yield to you in order to go along with you on inquiry, but Professor Arnstine wishes to speak.

Dr. Arnstine: I have a difficulty that I wish you would straighten out for me. I am trying to imagine what a model of the mind would look like on the basis of this discussion. I have a notion of the cognitive structure in which assertions are stored, or from which assertions are retrieved. Then there is another place that you have called intellectual capacity. Now this seems to be some kind of operating mechanism that puts new things over into this cognitive structure. My question will relate to that, but first I want to check whether or not this is correct, whether the intellectual capacity is in the cognitive structure, or whether it is conceived as a distinct function or a distinct entity?

DR. AUSUBEL: Intellectual capacities refer to individual differences in ability to perform particular cognitive functions or operations. By virtue of exercising these abilities one builds a cognitive structure. Without these abilities one could not incorporate potentially meaningful material into a cognitive structure.

DR. ARNSTINE: If this is the case, it is not a cognitive structure itself which reaches out and latches on to new material, but rather the intellectual abilities operate to put new material into the cognitive structure.

DR. AUSUBEL: I think you will really find that cognitive structure is not a thing or a person that reaches out, and neither are there abilities that have tentacles and reach out. Cognitive abilities are capacities of an intellectual nature which make it possible either to comprehend potentially meaningful material or to solve problems that eventuate in meanings that can be internalized within cognitive structure.

DR. ARNSTINE: Could you give me any help on what it is that gets this whole business going? That is, if I am presented with a new piece of material which may or may not relate to some subsumer that I have, why should I pick up on it at all? My question relates to making it more clear. In your paper you said, "Existing cognitive structure is the major factor influencing the learning and retention of meaningful material," and later you repeat that cognitive structure is also in its own right the most significant independent variable influencing the learner's capacity, etc. I am possessed of certain cognitive structures that relate to certain fields of knowledge with which I am familiar, yet I am constantly having the experience of being exposed to new information within these fields. It passes through me. It doesn't stop and reside in my cognitive structure, and so I think it is relevant in teaching and learning to ask how it is that the capacities operate and put new presentations into the cognitive structure so they stay there and are truthful.

DR. AUSUBEL: First, as I mentioned in the paper, there must be a meaningful learning set, that is, a set to relate this potentially meaningful material to cognitive structure in a nonarbitrary, substantive fashion. Even if the material is potentially meaningful, if one does not intend to relate this material to one's cognitive structure in this fashion then what emerges is simple, a sequence of randomly connected words that have no meaning. Thus one must first start out with a meaningful learning set; and if, in addition, one has appropriate subsumers in one's cognitive structure that are clear and stable, these will provide anchorage for the potentially meaningful new material to which one has been exposed. If these two conditions exist, new meanings should be incorporated into your cognitive structure and should remain available for a certain length of time.

DR. ARNSTINE: Now you haven't mentioned the intention of the learner very much in the paper. You have mentioned several points, for example, the importance of the cognitive structure for the acquisition of new learning material. Could you give us any clarification or any order of importance? Does the learner's intention count for as much as his existing cognitive structure? Is it more important or less important, or to what extent are they to be taken account of in a teaching situation?

DR. AUSUBEL: I think it would be pointless to arrange a hierarchy of importance here. I said very explicitly in the paper that for meaningful learning to occur there are two prerequisites. First, a meaningful learning set or intention on the part of the learner, and, second, the exposure to potentially meaningful material that is relatable to the learner's cognitive structure on a nonarbitrary, substantive basis. These are the two pre-conditions for meaningful learning to occur. I think it is rather pointless to weigh these in terms of relative importance.

CHAIRMAN B. SMITH: Professor Schwab, may I ask if you would clarify your point a bit more? I am interested in the point that you were making a moment ago when I cut you off. If subsumptive learning occurs, then I don't see what the issue is that you are raising.

SOME PSYCHOLOGICAL ASPECTS OF THE STRUCTURE OF KNOWLEDGE

DR. SCHWAB: My point was that in inquiry there might be another species of learning, which for the moment I am calling inquiry learning, which does not take place by a process merely of subsumption but by a more or less simultaneous dual process of developing a subsumer and using it.

CHAIRMAN B. SMITH: But subsumption does take place in this process.

DR. SCHWAB: But in a new sense, because you see in a sense that I understand. . . .

CHAIRMAN B. SMITH: With a new subsumer.

DR. SCHWAB: A new subsumer developed by the learner so that we have to think about the possibility of a species of learning which is not dependent on past learning in quite the fashion that Dr. Ausubel is describing. I will cite one example. I will pose to undergraduates a statement that is novel to them. I will watch the very processes that Dr. Ausubel describes take place in the students, that is, by feedback. They will say, "Oh, you mean that is . . . ," trying to push it into one subsumer. And I will slap it down and say that I don't mean that at all. Someone else will try another, relating the new thing to a second, a third, and a tenth familiar object, until finally it becomes desperately clear to the student that somehow I am asking them to take hold of a brand new starting point which I am not permitting them to subsume and they do grasp it—not all of them but a good many. It will then actually constitute the creation of a new subsumer coordinate with others, not under, therefore not hierarchical.

Let me describe what I think to be an example.

I begin a fourth-year undergraduate course by voicing a statement which I know from previous trial to be novel and strange in content. Immediately, the students engage in the process which Dr. Ausubel describes. One student will say, "Oh, you mean . . . ," thus voicing his effort to equate the strange statement to something already known, into a subsumer already in hand. I inform him that he is mistaken. Another student tests another subsumer, a third, a fourth, and so on. Finally it becomes clear to the students that I am inviting them to relinquish depend-

259

ence on all easily available subsumers and, instead, to develop a new subsumer which will embrace and give meaning to the novel statement. Some students, though by no means all, accept the invitation. They proceed to do just this—developing a new subsumer coordinate with rather than subordinate to conceptions already in hand. We have some evidence of what this is. By reasonably reliable techniques I shall not describe now, we find that when this experience has been successfully instigated, the experience itself is experienced as of a special and subjectively desirable quality. Months, even several years, after the event, the playback of tapes of the class discussion will evoke in those who had the experience a memory of acutely noted physical details— the temperature, odor, lighting, and sounds of the classroom at the moment of the experience. These students then tell us that these moments of well-remembered hyper-awareness were also moments in which they felt that a revolution in their whole habit of thinking had occurred. This is not a memory only of a subjective, emotional experience such as may be remembered from dreams, for these students also remember the verifiable *content* of the problem posed, and the solutions reached. The meaning of this testimony is, of course, anybody's guess.

DR. PHENIX: It seems to me that the paper really doesn't deal with the question of original learning versus later learning. The paper really deals with the question of whether learning efficiency is increased by some process of organizing what is to be learned. I also think that the paper might be clarified somewhat by getting back to your distinction between the subsumptive concept and the syntactical organizational structure. Syntactical structure would appear to be a kind of structuring or subsumption of syntactical concepts so as to learn methods of inquiry. Learning in the subsumption of substantive concepts would be the basis for textbook learning.

DR. SCHWAB: That was our thought and Bereiter's emphasis, too, when he talked about learning to learn and finding some rules so that you could do a job for yourself.

DR. PHENIX: But these are not excluded from this analysis.

DR. SCHWAB: I think that I agree. I am not attacking the

paper. I am suggesting that its content implies the existence of another kind of learning which is not developed.

DR. PHENIX: I see both kinds of learning here. I see learning both as the presentation of subsumers and as the invention of new organizing principles.

DR. SCHWAB: I just didn't find the page in which that last exists. I found organized exhibit for the student, I found the subsumers already in the student, but nowhere did I see anything about the development of subsumers or organizers by the student.

DR. AUSUBEL: Well, it will take me time to find it, but I am sure I did mention the fact that there are instances where there is really no problem in discriminating between a new idea and an existing idea in cognitive structure but rather a problem of apparent incompatibility between two ideas which require the learner to construct a more inclusive subsumer. I think this covers just the point you have been raising and accounts for the kind of cognitive activity which you say I have completely ignored.

DR. SCHWAB: I urge you to push your analysis further. You say, "A second important factor presumably affecting the retention of a potentially meaningful learning task is the extent to which it is discriminable from the established conceptual systems that subsume it."

DR. AUSUBEL: I don't think it really is replaced. What is happening, I think, is that you are developing a new subsumer, and this new subsumer is serving as a focus for the incorporation of the new knowledge.

DR. SCHWAB: I agree, but will you give me the referent of new—is it the learner or the teacher?

DR. AUSUBEL: It's the learner.

DR. SCHWAB: Okay, fine, that makes all the difference.

DR. BURNETT: I know there are lots of types of inquiries pending. But would you say, in connection with Professor Smith's earlier remark, that perhaps you don't have to give up the subsumptive theory in order to explain inquiry? That is, should most approaches to inquiry training be handled on the subsumptive theory?

DR. AUSUBEL: Discovery learning is an entirely different kind

261

of learning than reception learning. It itself is not a manifestation of subsumption, but its product undergoes subsumption. In reception learning the substance of what one has to learn (i.e., the new idea) is presented or given. It calls for no autonomous discovery on the part of the learner, no reorganization of existing ideas in cognitive structure to meet the demands of a problem situation. But where the substance of what has to be learned, i.e., the new meaning, involves some independent manipulation on the learner's part we have an example of discovery learning. This discovery activity is a separate kind of learning that precedes the incorporation into cognitive structure of the idea that is discovered. Thus in inquiry there is first discovery learning, which is a distinct kind of process quite different from subsumption, and then a subsequent process of incorporating into cognitive structure the newly discovered ideas.

DR. BURNETT: From your point of view you could explain inquiry learning without involving subsumptive theory. Correct?

DR. AUSUBEL: Inquiry learning per se doesn't involve subsumptive theory. But if one just discovered and had no means of incorporating these newly discovered ideas into cognitive structure and of making them stick, then the whole point or a good part of the point of the discovery would be lost. Hence once the discovery phase of inquiry learning is complete, subsumptive theory *is* involved in the incorporative process.

CHAIRMAN B. SMITH: In closing, on behalf of the college I want to thank all of the people who participated, all the speakers and the participants around this table. And let me say, also, that I am very happy that we have had visitors from other states here. I hope you have enjoyed your stay and I hope this symposium has been profitable to you, as it has been to me. Let me say also that I appreciate the help of the local chapter of Phi Delta Kappa in making all the physical arrangements and taking care of the details and of the good help of the international organization in more ways than I can mention. I thank all of you both for myself and for the organizations cooperating and for the college.

ADJOURNMENT

CHAPTER VIII

KNOWLEDGE STRUCTURE AND THE CURRICULUM*

ARNO A. BELLACK

During the current period of curriculum reform, most of the debate hinges on an old and familiar question: "what shall the schools teach?" This is a perennial question, one that apparently every generation has to solve over again for itself in the light of changing conditions and changing needs. And it is a question that can be answered only by reference to one's view of the nature of knowledge, for by universal agreement knowledge is the stock-in-trade of the school. Few would deny that the fields of organized inquiry are significant aspects of our culture that the school is uniquely equipped to introduce to students.

But there is also general agreement that the school's responsibility extends beyond teaching the organized fields of learning and inquiry; the school must also serve a variety of ends and needs created by our society and our culture. At different times in the history of our schools widely different views have been held regarding the way in which knowledge should be organized and taught to meet these ends and needs. The traditionalists, for example, taught the time-honored subjects as anthologies of separate topics, with the hope that the bits and pieces of information would somehow or other turn out to be useful in the lives of their students. History became a recital of "one damned thing

*This paper was prepared after a transcript of the symposium was available to Dr. Bellack.

after another" (the phrase is Toynbee's), civics turned out to be a collection of miscellaneous information about government, and geography was nothing more than a catalogue of facts about places scattered over the globe.

Convinced that this kind of teaching would not prepare students to face the increasingly complex problems of their society, the progressive reformers of the 1930's and 1940's proposed a new curriculum—one centered on the personal and social problems of youth and drawing on the academic disciplines as they became relevant to the problems under study. The disciplines were viewed as reservoirs from which facts and ideas could be drawn as needed; emphasis was on the *practical* ordering of knowledge with reference to problems to be solved.

Contemporary efforts to redefine the role of knowledge in the curriculum place emphasis on the *logical* order inherent in knowledge itself, on the structure of concepts and principles of inquiry that characterize the various fields of learning. Whereas formerly factual and descriptive content was stressed, now the emphasis is on basic concepts and methods which scholars use as intellectual tools to analyze and order their data.

Several claims are made for teaching the fundamental structures of the disciplines, two of which are of central importance and are worth considering here. The first is that understanding of fundamental ideas is the main road to adequate transfer of training. Professor Bruner, who has been influential in introducing the concept of structure into educational discourse, observes that

knowledge is a model we construct to give meaning and structure to regularities in experience. The organizing ideas of any body of knowledge are inventions for rendering experience economical and connected. We invent concepts such as force in physics, the bond in chemistry, motives in psychology, style in literature as means to the end of comprehension. . . . The power of great organizing concepts is in large part that they permit us to understand and sometimes to predict or change the world in which we live. But their power lies also in the fact that ideas provide instruments for experience.

Therefore, he contends, "the structure of knowledge—it's connectedness and its derivations that make one idea follow another —is the proper emphasis in education."[1]

The second important claim for emphasis on structure is that by constantly re-examining material taught in the schools for its fundamental patterns of organization, the schools will be able to narrow the gap between "advanced" knowledge and "elementary" knowledge. Since scholars at the forefront of their disciplines are able to make the greatest contribution to the substantive reorganization of their fields, current curriculum projects place great emphasis on the participation of university researchers in continuing revision of the program of studies. Scholars in the various disciplines and their professional organizations have in recent years made proposals for revamping the curriculum in elementary and secondary schools—first in mathematics, physics, chemistry, and biology; then in English; and recently and belatedly in economics, geography, anthropology, and history.

The focus of attention in each of these projects is an individual discipline. Little or no attention is given to the relationships of the individual fields to each other or to the program of studies within which they must find their place. National committees in the fields of chemistry, physics, and biology have proceeded independently of each other. The projects in economics, geography, and anthropology are unrelated to one another or to the other social sciences. Only in mathematics has there been a disposition to view the field as a whole, but this is a reflection of developments within the discipline of mathematics at the highest levels of scholarship.

The situation developing in the elementary and secondary schools thus begins to reflect, at least to some degree, the state of affairs in the universities with respect to the development and organization of knowledge, which Professor John Randall has described in this way:

As reflected in the microcosm of the modern university, the world of knowledge has today become radically plural. It is a world of

[1] Jerome S. Bruner, *On Knowing* (Cambridge, Mass.: Harvard Univ. Press, 1962), p. 120.

many different knowledges, pursued in varied ways to diverse ends. These many inquiries are normally carried on with little thought for their relation to each other. The student of John Donne's poetry, the student of the structure of the atom—each gives little enough attention to what the others are doing, and none at all to any total picture of anything. Each has his own goals, his own methods, his own language for talking about what he is doing and what he has discovered. Each seems happiest when left to his own devices, glad indeed if he can keep others from treading on his toes. Each is convinced that what he himself is doing is worth while. But none has too much respect for the others, though he is willing enough to tolerate them. They have all little understanding of each other's pursuits—what they are trying to do, how they are doing it, and what they really mean when they talk about it.[2]

I emphasize this pluralism in the academic world not to deplore it but to call attention to the problem that it presents for those who are concerned with the organization of the curriculum as a whole. For the curriculum-builder is concerned not only with the structures of the individual disciplines, but also with the structure of the instructional program within which the fields of knowledge find their place. The problem can be very simply stated, if not easily solved: what general structure of the curriculum can be developed so that autonomy of the parts does not result in anarchy in the program as a whole?

In focusing attention on the broad range of disciplines which constitute contemporary knowledge and on the relationships of these fields to one another, the authors of the papers prepared for this symposium make a major contribution to the solution of this problem. "To identify the disciplines which constitute contemporary knowledge," writes Professor Schwab, "is to identify the various materials which constitute both the resources and obligations of education. To locate the relations of these disciplines to one another is to determine what may be joined together for purposes of instruction, what should be held apart, and in what sequence they may best be taught."

Several possible ways of categorizing knowledge for ped-

[2] John H. Randall, Jr., "The World to be Unified," in Lewis Leary, ed., *The Unity of Knowledge* (New York: Doubleday, 1955), p. 63.

agogical purposes are proposed in the papers included in this volume. The variety of viewpoints presented demonstrates clearly the diversity of available modes of classification. Professor Phenix, for example, identifies nine generic classes of knowledge grouped in six major categories which describe the range of cognitive functions of which a person is capable and hence suggest the essential components of a curriculum for general education: synnoetics, aesthetics, symbolics, empirics, ethics, and synoptics. In contrast, Professor Tykociner identifies twelve areas of knowledge grouped in five major categories according to the functions performed by the disciplines included in each category. The papers by Professors Broudy, Martin, and Hanson reflect the traditional organization of knowledge found in most college and university curricula: the natural sciences, mathematics, social sciences, and the humanities.

These three contemporary approaches do not exhaust the range of available modes of categorizing knowledge for pedagogical purposes. Numerous other formulations by other philosophers and educators might be cited.[3] Given this diversity and variety, what criteria shall the educator use in selecting a classification scheme to serve as the basis for organizing the curriculum? Professor Phenix suggests two criteria: *learning* and *use*. The teacher needs knowledge organized in such fashion that the most learning takes place in the least time. He also wants knowledge organized in such a way as to be as useful as possible to the learner in meeting the demands of life in nature and society.

These criteria are helpful in identifying classifications of knowledge that are relevant to pedagogical purposes, but they do not permit unequivocal judgment regarding the relative merits of contrasting approaches. On what basis then shall the curricu-

---

[3] See, for example, Ernest Cassirer, *An Essay on Man* (New York: Doubleday, 1953), Florian Znaniecki, *Cultural Sciences* (Urbana: Univ. of Illinois Press, 1952), Sidney Hook, *Education for Modern Man* (New York: Dial Press, 1946), James B. Conant, *Education in a Divided World* (Cambridge, Mass.: Harvard Univ. Press, 1948), A. D. C. Peterson, *Arts and Science Sides in the Sixth Form* (Oxford, Eng.: Dept. of Education, Oxford Univ., 1960).

lum-builder make his selection? In view of diversity and variety of available modes for organizing knowledge, Professor Schwab observes that "nothing could be more foolish than to suppose that the problems posed to us by this variety of doctrines is the problem of determining which one is 'right.' With very few exceptions, each of them is, in its own way, 'right.' What is important about each one is not so much the list of disciplines which it may provide, but rather: (a) the distinctions it uses to distinguish disciplines; and (b) the educational problems and issues which these distinctions raise to visibility."

Professor Schwab's comment suggests that what is needed, given the present state of affairs in curriculum theory, is inquiry into problems and issues. This paper will therefore focus attention on three questions that the educational theorist must deal with in developing curriculum proposals based on the contrasting modes for classifying knowledge. These questions do not exhaust the problems faced by the curriculum theorist, but they are representative of the issues which confront him.

HOW SHALL INSTRUCTION BE ORGANIZED WITHIN THE MAJOR CATEGORIES OF KNOWLEDGE IDENTIFIED IN THE VARIOUS CLASSIFICATION SCHEMES?

Categorizing knowledge in broad groupings of related disciplines on the basis of criteria relevant to the educational task is the essential first step in establishing a pattern of studies for general education. But once knowledge has been so classified, difficult instructional problems remain.

Each broad category of knowledge in the various classification schemes includes more than one discipline. For example, Professor Phenix includes the physical sciences, life sciences, psychology, and social sciences in the general class of knowledge labeled "empirics." Professor Tykociner groups together four areas of knowledge (exelignology, pronoetics, regulative sciences, disseminative sciences) in one broad category serving the functions of systematizing knowledge of the past, projecting future needs, and regulating activities. Professor Broudy includes among the "arts" the fields of music, literature, architecture, dance, and fine arts. The question arises, How shall the disciplines included in the same broad category be organized for instructional purposes? Should they be taught separately? Or is it feasible to integrate for purposes of instruction fields that are not integrated at the level of enquiry?

This basic problem has been of concern to philosophers and educators at least since the time of Plato, as Professor Schwab reminds us. Professors Phenix and Hanson discuss this question and express somewhat similar viewpoints. Professor Phenix contends that, "Although the materials of instruction should all be drawn from the disciplines, they need not always be organized into distinct courses according to disciplines. The generic classes provide the possible general patterns of course organization."

Professor Hanson, in discussing the physical sciences, maintains that "The departmental structures within physical science soon melt under the student's sizzling, searching questions—*if* he is encouraged to ask them. Quantum electrodynamics and classical optics emerge for him as two different attempts to comprehend the one subject matter, LIGHT. . . . In this way physical science is a conceptual mosaic reflecting the natural phenomena of our world first this way, then that way—sometimes with quite different objectives. . . . An architectonic of physical science, then, should never be more than loose guidelines for the guidance of syllabus drafters and textbook writers. But an architectonic ought never to crystallize into a set of *rigid* criteria for determining relevance or significance. Anyone who seeks to break down a wall rather than go through a door should be encouraged whenever possible. Physics today is a powerful instrument of mind and matter because of the irreverent wall-breakers of the seventeenth and twentieth centuries. A purported 'Structure of Physical Knowledge' can never be more than a pedagogically heuristic blueprint. When conceived of as more—as an hierarchical series of disciplines, trials and achievements—it must fail, even for the youngest students."

A curriculum proposal based on a set of broad categories of knowledge must eventually deal with the issue under discussion here. Regardless of the criteria or distinctions that are used to group the various disciplines into "families" of related fields for teaching purposes, the curriculum theorist is faced with the difficult task of developing a rationale for organizing instruction within these major groupings. To identify some of the problems involved in developing such a rationale, let us consider the social sciences—a broad field of study included in the program of general education in most elementary and secondary schools.

The social sciences (including such disciplines as economics, social psychology, political science, sociology, anthropology, geography, and possibly history) are all seeking explanations of the same phenomenon, man's social life. This common goal is what makes it reasonable to group them together as the *social* sciences. All of them have grown out of man's attempt to interpret, understand, and control the social environment. But each field formulates its own questions about this subject matter and develops its own system of concepts to guide its research. The economist is preoccupied with the concept of scarcity, the political scientist with the concepts of power and authority, the anthropologist with the notion of culture, and the sociologist with social functions and social systems. Each science is thus abstract, dealing with only certain facets of actual social relationships and institutions—facets that do not permit of physical separation but only of analytical separation.

Man's social life as it is actually lived is therefore far more complex than the limited image of it reflected in the concepts and generalizations of any one of the social disciplines. It follows then, as Professor Kingsley Davis has suggested, that "insofar as the prediction of actual events is concerned, the various social sciences are mutually interdependent, because only by combining their various points of view can anything approaching a complete anticipation of future occurrences be achieved."[4] Policies that are

---

[4] Kingsley Davis, *Human Society* (New York: Macmillan, 1948), p. 8.

proposed and actions that are taken to deal with problems in social affairs are of necessity interdisciplinary, for concrete social reality is not mirrored in the findings of any one discipline.

Now this is a matter of central importance to those whose job it is to plan and organize the social studies curriculum. To focus exclusive attention on certain aspects of the social world as seen through the eyes of one or two of the social sciences is to give students a myopic vision of man's social behavior and his institutions. To shape children's conceptions of the social world through exclusive emphasis on the language of the economist, for example, to the exclusion of the language of the sociologist, political scientist, anthropologist, and historian is to determine that they shall interpret human affairs principally in terms which the economist uses to view reality—in terms of supply, demand, scarcity, production, and consumption.

Students must be helped to see the limitations as well as the uses of a single discipline in interpreting events as they actually occur. And for anything approaching a comprehensive view of man's functioning in society, the specialized perspectives of all the social sciences are needed. Curriculum-builders in the social studies have the enormously difficult job of providing a place in their programs for all the social sciences, each of which contributes its distinctive perspective on human institutions and human behavior.

It is clear that such a program can be developed only on the basis of collaboration among the various social sciences. Such collaboration does not presuppose a "unified social science" as the basis for planning the elementary and secondary school curriculum. Quite the opposite is the case. For the social disciplines today are characterized by a plurality of methods and conceptual schemes developed by social scientists to deal with problems within their individual spheres. Instead of a unity of method or a single universe of discourse, we find a vast confederation of separate areas of study. Modes of thinking and analysis differ from field to field, and even from problem to problem within the same field. In time, a Bacon of the sciences that bear on the social and cultural behavior of man may emerge, but that time is not yet.

At the same time, in spite of increasing specialization and internal differentiation, there are interconnections among the social sciences that curriculum planning for the schools should take into account. For example, the various social sciences borrow rather handily from each other when it comes to both concepts and methods. Historians make use of concepts from all the other social sciences. Political scientists interested in political socialization get their methods from behavioral scientists and seem in many respects more closely related to sociologists and social psychologists than to fellow political scientists. Certain anthropologists have utilized the Freudian view of human development in analyzing patterns of various cultures. Geographers make extensive use of the perspectives of history and concepts developed by all the behavioral sciences.

Furthermore, we find not only interchange of concepts and methods but growing collaboration among specialists. For example, studies of the nature and function of "authority" are now undertaken jointly by political scientists and sociologists, and there have been recent studies conducted by economists in collaboration with anthropologists to determine whether certain theories hold for different types of economic systems. The convergence of social scientists upon the same problems has given rise to what Professor Robert Merton calls "interdisciplines," such as social biology, political sociology, and sociological history.

The picture that emerges from this cursory review of the current state of affairs in the social sciences is one of great diversity. Given this mosaic of disciplines and interdisciplines, each characterized by multiple conceptual schemes and methods, the curriculum-builder is faced with the problem of developing structures for teaching that relate the social sciences to each other in meaningful ways and avoid undue fragmentation of knowledge.

What has been said about the social sciences applies in principle to the natural sciences, mathematics, and the humanities. In all likelihood, different patterns of organization within these broad fields will be found to be appropriate for different levels of the school program. Dewey's notion of the "progressive organization of knowledge," long ignored by most of his interpreters, might serve as a guiding hypothesis in planning the sequence of the program through the elementary and secondary school years. In sum, scholars in the natural sciences, the social sciences, mathematics, and the humanities should now be invited to join in the search for new structures for teaching—structures that respect the integrity of the individual fields and at the same time help these fields find their place in a pattern of studies that provide a substantial measure of coherence and relatedness for the program as a whole.

HOW SHALL INSTRUCTION IN THE BROAD FIELDS OF KNOWLEDGE INCLUDED IN THE CURRICULUM BE RELATED TO HUMAN AFFAIRS?

That the schools ought to provide students with the means for intelligent action is not a new or controversial idea. As Professor Arthur Bestor, who scarcely qualifies as an advocate of education for life adjustment, reminds us, "The basic argument for the intellectual disciplines in education is not that they lift a man's spirit above the world, but that they equip his mind to enter the world and perform its tasks."[5] When, however, it comes to deciding what to teach and how to teach to accomplish this goal, we find marked differences of opinion.

These too are ancient questions, as Professor Schwab once again reminds us. For Plato, theoretical knowledge was the source of most effective practice. This view finds its modern counterpart in Professor Phenix's view that "The fruitfulness of the applied disciplines is in proportion to their consonance with the structures of knowledge as revealed in the pure cognitive disciplines. . . . The only really useful knowledge is that which conforms to the structures revealed in the cognitive disciplines,

[5] Arthur Bestor, *Educational Wastelands* (Urbana: Univ. of Illinois Press, 1953), p. 15.

where the growth of knowledge indicates that learning has effectively occurred." In contrast, Aristotle's view was that practice and theory each reigned supreme in its own bailiwick. Professor Schwab indentifies still other views concerning the relation between theory and practice; there is, for example, the pragmatic view that theory and practice, though distinctly different from one another, interpenetrate and interact in such a way that each is indispensable to the other.

These contrasting philosophical positions regarding the relation between theory and practice find their counterparts in contrasting approaches to curriculum organization. On the one hand, there are those who hold that "useful knowledge looks after itself"[6] and that the ability to relate what is learned in school to the world of human affairs comes as an inevitable by-product of the study of the organized disciplines. On the other hand, there are those who hold that problems in human affairs do not come neatly labeled "historical," "economic," or "political." They come rather as decisions to be made and force us to call upon all we know and make us wish we knew more. It was concern for broad cultural and moral questions that go beyond the boundaries of any one discipline that led the Progressive reformers to urge that students have the opportunity to deal with them in all their complexity. They proposed a new curriculum, one centered on the problems of youth and broad social issues and drawing on the academic disciplines as they become relevant to the problems under study. This idea became the hallmark of progressivism in curriculum building. It gained wide acceptance among educators and found expression in many influential statements of policy and opinion during the 1920's, 1930's, and 1940's. Attempted applications of this viewpoint were made in courses labeled core, common learnings, and the like.

Difficulties in this approach soon became apparent, not the least of which was the students' lack of firsthand acquaintance with the disciplines that were the source of the concepts and

[6] Bruner, *op. cit.*, p. 109.

ideas essential to structuring problems under study. Without adequate understanding of the various fields of knowledge, students had no way of knowing which fields were relevant to problems of concern to them. Indeed, without knowledge of the organized fields it was difficult for them to ask the kinds of questions about their problems that the various disciplines could help them answer.

Giving students an opportunity to grapple with broad social and cultural problems was basically a promising innovation. But at the same time, one is forced to recognize that problem-solving on such a broad base cannot be pursued successfully without growing understanding of the fields of knowledge on which the problem-solver must draw.

Recognizing then the value in systematic study of the fields of knowledge and the importance of developing competence in dealing with problems and issues that are broader than those of any one field, the question arises why opportunities for both types of activities should not be included in the program for all students. One might envision a general education program that would include basic instruction in the major fields of knowledge identified by the authors of the papers under discussion here, together with a coordinating seminar in which students deal with problems "in the round" and in which special effort is made to show the intimate relationships between the fields of study, as concepts from those fields are brought to bear on these problems. Such a seminar would also furnish excellent opportunities to help students become aware of the fundamental kinds of meanings involved in dealing with problematic situations and the necessity for making distinctions among them.[7]

Along similar lines, Professor Schwab, at the Disciplines Seminar convened by the Project on Instruction of the National Education Association, proposed a plan for elementary and secondary schools that would reconcile the demands of the disciplines and the needs of our culture and society by considering

[7] Association for Supervision and Curriculum Development. 1956 Yearbook, *What Shall the Schools Teach?* (Washington, D.C.: Author, 1956), Ch. IV.

the curriculum at each level of school as consisting of two parts: [8]

One part, to be called the nuclear curriculum, would contain materials from the disciplines, selected to fulfill those objectives of education which are determined primarily by the needs of the developing child and the aims imposed by our culture and society. Such materials would be taught, wherever possible, within the frame of the discipline from which they were taken. But where the exigencies of time, of learning competence, or other need required it, these materials would be freely removed from their theoretical or disciplinary context and put into the context of unquestioned principles designed for use.

The second, or cortical, component of the curriculum would be chosen by contrary and complementary principles. It would consist of materials chosen specifically because they are representative of the major disciplines. Such materials would display the more important conceptual frames of each discipline, its techniques of discovery and verification, and the variety of problems to which it addresses itself. Where alternatives existed, preferred materials would be those which also served present and recognized individual-social needs. But the criterion of representativeness of the discipline would be paramount.

HOW SHALL INSTRUCTION BE ORGANIZED TO TAKE INTO ACCOUNT BOTH THE LOGICAL ORDER OF DISCIPLINED KNOWLEDGE AND THE PSYCHOLOGICAL ORDER OF DEVELOPMENT OF THE COGNITIVE POWERS OF STUDENTS?

As Professor James McClellan has demonstrated, a great deal of confusion surrounds the distinctions between the "psychological" and the "logical" dimensions of educational theory. [9] Most educators would agree that the pedagogical order represented by teaching and learning is determined both by the logical order of disciplined knowledge and by the psychological order of the development of the cognitive powers of students. Few

[8] National Education Association, Project on Instruction, *The Scholars Look at the Schools* (Washington, D.C.: Author, 1962), pp. 51–52.
[9] James M. McClellan, "The Logical and the Psychological: An Untenable Dualism?" in B. O. Smith and R. H. Ennis, eds., *Language and Concepts in Education* (Chicago: Rand, 1961), pp. 144–60.

educational writers, however, have developed a theory of instruction that relates the logical and the psychological dimensions in systematic fashion. It is here that Professor Ausubel makes a major contribution. First of all, he makes a distinction between the "organized bodies of knowledge that represent the collective recorded wisdom of recognized scholars in particular fields of inquiry" and the "corresponding psychological structures of knowledge or represented by the organization of internalized ideas and information in the minds of individual students of varying degrees of both cognitive maturity and subject-matter sophistication in these same disciplines." He then goes on to present a model (reminiscent of the Herbartian view) of the psychological structure of knowledge and of the factors that influence its accretion and organization, based on the principle of *subsumption*.

This is not the place to argue the case for or against Ausubel's theory in relation to contrasting views represented by the work of Piaget, Bruner, and others. What is important for our purposes here is to take note of the fact that Professor Ausubel's closely reasoned theoretical view provides a framework for research and experimentation into instructional problems in which logical and psychological considerations are inextricably interwoven.

In current debates about what should be taught in the schools, the "conventional wisdom" long honored in pedagogical circles about the nature of knowledge and its role in the curriculum is being called into question. Special attention has been given in this reappraisal of the curriculum to the structural features of the individual disciplines included in the program of studies. This interest in the structure of the various fields of knowledge has in turn led educational theorists to raise questions about the structure of knowledge as a whole and to propose a variety of modes for classifying knowledge for teaching purposes. It is in this connection that the papers prepared for this symposium make a major contribution to current efforts to redesign the instructional program of the school.